Independent Television Over Fifty Years

INDEPENDENT TELEVISION OVER FIFTY YEARS

Edited by
Catherine Johnson
and Rob Turnock

Open University Press

Open University Press
McGraw-Hill Education
McGraw-Hill House
Shoppenhangers Road
Maidenhead
Berkshire
England
SL6 2QL

email: enquiries@openup.co.uk
world wide web@ www.openup.co.uk

and Two Penn Plaza, New York, NY 10121-2289, USA

First published 2005

A catalogue record of this book is available from the British Library.

ISBN- 10: 033521729 X (pb) 0335217303 (hb)
13: 9780335217298 (pb) 9780335217304 (hb)

Library of Congress Cataloging-in-Publication Data
CIP data applied for

Typeset by BookEns Ltd., Royston, Herts.
Printed in Great Britain by Bell & Bain Ltd, Glasgow.

The Publishers are grateful to the following for their assistance in providing images for the cover:

Steve Yates/TV-50
ITV
ITV Wales
South West Film and Television Archive
SMG TV
Moving Image Communications

CONTENTS

Part 3: Texts and intertexts

CONTRIBUTORS

Rod Allen is Head of the Department of Journalism at City University, London. Before entering academe he was a print journalist and editor of *Broadcast*. In 1978 he joined London Weekend Television (LWT) as a producer and subsequently became Controller of Development at LWT, and later head of international sales and co-production at Harlech Television (HTV). With Nod Miller he is co-editor of five volumes in the 'Current Debates in Broadcasting' series, and has contributed to books on broadcasting policy, new media technology and organizational behaviour.

Jonathan Bignell is Reader in Television and Film at the University of Reading, and Director of the Centre for Television Drama Studies. He is a series editor of Manchester University Press's 'Television' series, and author of (among other works) *Postmodern Media Culture* and *An Introduction to Television Studies*. He is the co-author of *Terry Nation*, editor of *Writing and Cinema* and co-editor of *British Television Drama: Past, Present and Future*. He currently leads an Arts and Humanities Research Board (AHRB) research project on 'Cultures of British Television Drama, 1960–82'.

John Ellis is Professor of Media Arts at Royal Holloway University of London. He is the author of *Seeing Things* and *Visible Fictions*. From 1982 to 1999 he was an independent television producer, running Large Door Productions. He made many deals with both Channel 4 and the BBC, but the closest he came to ITV was negotiating on the principle of independent access on behalf of the producers' association, The Producers Alliance for Cinema and Television (PACT).

Jackie Harrison is professor in the Department of Journalism Studies at the University of Sheffield. She is the author of *Terrestrial Television News in Britain*; co-author of *Violence on Television: Distribution, Form, Context and Themes* and *Violence on Television in Britain: An Analysis of Amount, Nature, Location and Origin of Violence in Programmes* and is a contributor to *Television Genres*. Her new book *News* is due to be published by Routledge in 2005.

Catherine Johnson is Lecturer in Television History and Theory at Royal Holloway, University of London. She has published on factual entertainment, US television drama, and early British television, in journals and in books such as *Small Screens, Big Ideas* and *The Contemporary Television Series*. Her new book *Telefantasy* was published by the British Film Institute (BFI) in 2005. Her current research examines the history and significance of branding in television.

Matt Hills is Lecturer in Media and Cultural Studies in the Cardiff School of Journalism, Media and Cultural Studies. He is the author of *Fan Cultures* and *The Pleasures of Horror*. He has recently contributed work on fandom to books such as *The Television Studies Reader* and *Teen TV*, and to journals such as *Mediactive*, *Social Semiotics* and *American Behavioral Scientist*.

Jamie Medhurst is Lecturer in Film and Television at the University of Wales, Aberystwyth. His teaching and research interests include broadcasting history, documentary film history and the relationship between television and national identity. He has published in the area of television history (with a particular focus on Wales and the Welsh language) and has contributed to *The Television History Book* and *Studying Television*.

Steve Neale is Professor of Film Studies in the School of English at Exeter University. He is a contributor to *Television Genres* and *The Historical Journal of Film, Television and Radio*. He is also the author of *Genre and Hollywood*, editor of *Genre and Contemporary Hollywood*, co-author of *Popular Film and Television Comedy* and co-editor of *Contemporary Hollywood Cinema*.

Rob Turnock is Lecturer in Media Theory at Bournemouth Media School, Bournemouth University. He has published on broadcasting history and on British and US television drama. He is author of *Interpreting Diana: Television Audiences and the Death of a Princess*.

Helen Wheatley is Lecturer in Film and Television Studies at the University of Warwick. Her research interests encompass television drama (particularly the Gothic and horror genres, drama for women, and questions of quality and creativity), television for women, 'lifestyle' television, factual entertainment, and natural history programming. Her book, *Gothic Television*, was published by Manchester University Press in 2005.

Sherryl Wilson is Lecturer in Media Theory at Bournemouth Media School, Bournemouth University. She is author of *Oprah, Celebrity and Formations of Self* and has written on *Six Feet Under*. Her current project is an exploration of the screen representation of older women and their life experiences.

ACKNOWLEDGEMENTS

The editors would like to thank the contributors to this book for producing interesting and challenging chapters, and Chris Cudmore and Hannah Cooper at Open University Press for their help and support throughout. Catherine Johnson would also like to thank her 'Television Histories' students at Royal Holloway who provided a stimulating context to explore many of the ideas in this book. Rob Turnock would like to acknowledge the Arts and Humanities Research Board for their funding of the research project 'Did ITV revolutionize British television?' which offered him a framework for thinking about the history of ITV. He would also like to acknowledge Bournemouth University for providing research leave to complete this book. Finally, the editors would like to thank the members of the Southern Broadcasting History Group (particularly its organizer Hugh Chignell) for providing a consistently lively and enjoyable space to talk about television history.

INTRODUCTION: APPROACHING THE HISTORIES OF ITV

Catherine Johnson and Rob Turnock

ITV has been a significant force in the British broadcasting landscape over its 50 year history since 1955. Its introduction broke the BBC's monopoly of broadcasting in Britain and introduced commercially funded public service broadcasting to Britain for the first time. The BBC and ITV went on to form a 'duopoly' in television broadcasting, which lasted for 27 years until the arrival of Channel 4 in 1982. Since the 1980s, the television marketplace has become increasingly competitive and fragmented with the expansion of terrestrial, cable, satellite and digital channels. In the run up to its fiftieth birthday on 22 September 2005, ITV's position within this industry became increasingly insecure. Once comprised of a consortium of individual, regional programme companies designed to compete with the London-centric and metropolitan bias of the BBC, in 2005 ITV had become increasingly consolidated, with ITV plc (the company with the largest share in the ITV network) operating as a major British media conglomerate. With the vast expansion in commercial broadcasting since the 1980s, and the current threat to public service as a foundational ethos of television's structure and content, ITV's future as a commercially funded public service broadcaster looks uncertain (see Johnson and Turnock, Chapter 1 in this volume). Yet ITV1 (as the ITV terrestrial channel is now known) remains in close competition with BBC1 for the highest rated broadcaster in the UK, and ITV as a whole has played a major part in Britain's cultural life. At this potentially pivotal moment in the history of ITV there is the need for a critical reassessment of this unique and significant British broadcasting institution.

Absent histories

With some heroic exceptions, however, ITV has often been marginalized or neglected in histories of broadcasting in Britain, especially in comparison with the BBC. There is an expansive 'official' history of ITV detailed in six volumes covering the pre-history of commercial television (from 1946) and the start of ITV in 1955 up to 1992.[1] Each of these volumes, sanctioned during writing by the regulator of the day, provides an important insight into the workings, pressures, debates and events that have shaped the organization and operation of ITV. Written by authors who were themselves involved in the running of ITV,[2] the scope of the volumes has something in common with the multi-volume history of the BBC written by Asa Briggs covering the period 1896 (*sic*) to 1974.[3] Overview histories of ITV have appeared in broader histories of British media, broadcasting and television, in particular Curran and Seaton (1997), Crisell (1997) and Hilmes (2003). ITV has also received some extended analysis in the examination of wider broadcasting policy and developments in works such as Darlow (2004) and Goodwin (1998) (see Bonner 1998 and 2003 for a detailed list). Its programming has also been explored and analysed in broader genre studies.[4] However, much of this work, while frequently attuned to and concerned with the specifics of ITV, has not taken ITV as a particular focus, rather exploring its programmes as part of a broader analysis of particular genres and forms of television programming more generally. Beyond these accounts, there has been little academic analysis of ITV as a *whole institution*. That is, an institution that commissions, produces and broadcasts television programmes and texts, and that is constituted by those programmes and texts in a given social and cultural context at a given historical moment.[5]

There are three main reasons why ITV has not received extended analysis of this kind, which arise because of the complex historical position that ITV holds as a commercial public service broadcaster with a regionally federated structure. The first is that whereas ITV has contributed to British public service broadcasting for 50 years, the BBC is widely regarded as the elder statesman and 'true' advocate of public service broadcasting. The BBC has traditionally been associated with Reithian paternalistic broadcasting values to 'inform, educate and entertain'. Although British broadcasting in 2005 is very different from broadcasting in the 1920s and 1930s, it is widely held that BBC television has inherited something of those values from early radio. Against the BBC's elder statesman ITV has perhaps been seen as less of a 'Cinderella' institution and more of an 'ugly sister'. The arrival of ITV in 1955, introducing commercial television to Britain and breaking the BBC's monopoly of broadcasting, is often and popularly seen as a moment of rupture. In this view the postwar consensus was shattered by commercial television whose introduction was characterized by controversy, acrimonious debate and anxiety (see Johnson and Turnock in this volume). Funded principally by advertising revenue, the new service provoked concern over brute commercial interest, fear of brash American consumerism, the erosion of traditional morals and values in broadcasting and a fragmentation of British society and culture. Yet ITV, under legislation and public regulation, was very much constituted as a public service broadcaster in the image of the BBC (Goldie 1977; Briggs 1995). Marking a degree of continuity with principles that had governed earlier developments in British broadcasting, the new ITV service's 'duopoly' with the BBC provided a mixed programme schedule with a balance of programming that informed, educated and entertained. Despite this, ITV's hybrid[6] position as a 'commercial public service broadcaster' has historically resulted in criticisms that see its value and ability as a public service broadcaster diluted or compromised by its financial basis in commerce.

This apparent conflict between ITV's public service remit and its commercial funding relates to a second reason why the study of ITV as a whole has been neglected. ITV has not been readily understood as a producer of 'quality' programming, instead being popularly associated with lowbrow quiz and gameshows, light entertainment and action-adventure series (see Hills in this volume). This is in contrast to the broader tendency to associate those programmes that have received 'serious' academic and critical attention with the BBC. This is apparent, for example, in studies of British television drama's 'golden age', generally understood to be the period between the mid-1960s and mid-1970s when television production in Britain was of a particularly high quality. In British television history, the 'golden age' is primarily associated with the single play, often produced within larger anthology series, most notably the BBC strands, *The Wednesday Play* and *Play for Today*. By contrast, other dramas of the period, such as the long-running action-adventure series primarily produced by ITV, tend to be excluded from analyses of the 'Golden Age', instead explored as products created for commercial export, and/or as indicative of a playful and irreverent pop culture. There emerges here something of a dichotomy between the value accorded to the (primarily BBC) single-authored play as public service television, and the (primarily ITV) popular long-running series as commercial television (despite being produced by a public service broadcaster). If a myth of a 'Golden Age' is to be believed, then it is the BBC that has provided 'quality' programming, and those ITV programmes that fit into the analysis of the 'Golden Age' (such as *Armchair Theatre*) are seen as exceptions rather than the rule.

Furthermore, the analysis of ITV's long-running drama series from the 1960s can have unfortunate and unintended consequences due to the frequent association of these programmes with 'cult' television. Hence 1960s ITV series such as *The Avengers, The Saint* and *The Prisoner* often emerge as valuable objects of study not because of their inherent value as cultural artefacts but rather because of their continued popular appeal to audiences today. There are, of course, technical issues here, which we will return to below, as these series remain current today in part because they were shot on 35 mm film. What is at stake here, however, is that the common association of these programmes with 'cult' television points to their extraordinariness, and suggests that they are of value because they stand out from their context of production, rather than because they are examples *of that* context of production (see Johnson 2005). As such, these programmes are of interest less because they are ITV products (and so can tell use something about ITV) but rather because they transcend their context of production. In addition, although there have been studies of, primarily, action-adventure series that are particularly mindful of their context of production (see, for example, Chapman 2002), such studies tend to be easier to publish because of the perceived fan audience for such books. On the other hand, however, analysis of ITV programmes that are more generally devalued (or forgotten) would be a less appealing proposition for a publisher without an apparent contemporary market. In academic publishing this becomes even more acute because the scholar needs to justify the value of his/her object of study. As such, the selection of programme forms for academic attention can unwittingly perpetuate, and even create, a value hierarchy in broadcasting history (see Ellis, this volume). Both the BBC and ITV have a long history of producing a wide range of programmes for mixed programme schedules. Both have produced light entertainment, game shows and comedies, and long-running popular series drama, as well as producing single plays, drama serials, news, current affairs and arts programming. Yet assessing the similarities and differences between this output in general terms, and hence to characterize ITV or BBC programming at any one time or over history, is a difficult, if not impossible, task. As a consequence, 'common-sense' notions of the differences between ITV and BBC tend to be perpetuated because they are difficult to challenge and because those programmes that deviate from such common-sense assumptions are assumed to be exceptional, rather than representative of the broadcaster's programming output overall. New archival developments, such as the *TV Times* database may help here as they provide the possibility to study scheduling, and to assess broad programming trends in generic terms.[7] However, such databases do not allow us to study the actual programmes and so cannot reveal differences in style, tone, address and narrative, which are so important in understanding the history of television programming.

The relative lack of access to archive material raises a third problem with any attempt to study ITV as a whole institution (see Ellis in this volume). As indicated above, there are limits to what programming there is available to view. Prior to the mid-1950s almost all programming was broadcast live and, even in the early 1960s, dramas such as *Z Cars* and *The Avengers* were initially transmitted live. By the end of the 1950s and the beginning of the 1960s film and videotape were increasingly being used. Yet the costs of using and storing film and videotape were high, and a lot of films were destroyed and tapes were wiped for reuse after programmes were broadcast. Ampex videotape, for example cost around

£100 a reel at the end of the 1950s (Goddard 1991), and the more a reel was used the more cost-effective it became. It was in this way that many programmes have been lost to future generations of scholars and viewers (Fiddy 2001). Prior to and during the 1960s and 1970s television was viewed as an ephemeral cultural form, and little value was placed on retaining programmes for posterity. In instances where programmes were kept it was because they were perceived as having reuse or resale value, or producers preselected programmes they believed of value. Programmes that are still available to view in archives, therefore, are often ones that were made on film for sale abroad, such as *The Avengers* and *The Prisoner*, or were made on film as part of a specific production (and potentially 'artistic') aesthetic, such as well-known works by Ken Loach and Peter Watkins. As a result, vast swathes of programming made to fill broadcast hours and the mixed programme schedule have been lost to future analysis, and have hitherto been neglected in hierarchies of popular memory or academic merit.

Furthermore, the archiving of ITV programmes has been hampered by the very factor which has made it a unique institution – its regional structure. Unlike the BBC which exists as a single broadcasting entity, the structure of ITV has meant that production has been regionally located (even if there has been a leaning toward London production and broadcast through a networking structure).[8] This has meant that what ITV programming exists has been spread out, and this problem has been exacerbated by companies losing their franchises and disposing of their collections or being bought up by other companies. As a consequence, many of the programmes that exist are those that were produced by the larger companies for transmission across the network, rather than the local programming produced for specific regions. Fortunately, some material is held at the National Film and Television Archive but this constitutes, effectively, only the tip of the programming iceberg. In relation to the BBC, this problem has been partly alleviated by the excellent written archive available in Caversham at the BBC Written Archive Centre. While no replacement for viewing programmes themselves, as Jason Jacobs (2000) has demonstrated it is possible from the scripts and notes in these files to construct some understanding of the style, content and form of television programmes for which there is no audiovisual record. A similar study of ITV has again been hampered by ITV's regional structure, which has lead to its paper archive being spread across a wide range of regional companies, many of which no longer exist. The fate of the paper records has been uneven. Some have fallen into the hands of the British Film Institute (such as the paper archive of Southern Television held in the Special Collections section of the BFI Library), whereas others are difficult to access as they form part of ongoing commercial enterprises (see MacDonald 1994 and 2001). The bodies that have historically regulated ITV, the ITA, IBA and ITC, kept an excellent library of books and records but this has now been discontinued with the advent of Ofcom, and has been passed to the British Film Institute. Although providing less information about programme production, this archive does offer an important and valuable resource from the regulatory perspective. Since 1993, the ITV Network Centre has kept an archive of papers. Issues of commercial confidentiality aside, the availability and fate of this archive at the time of writing is uncertain.

Although some company records do exist, and although the material held formerly at the ITC library is an invaluable resource for research, what has made ITV a particularly difficult and impractical institution to study is the sheer scale and complexity of the relationships between the regulators, the programme companies and the programmes that make up ITV. Furthermore, over the history of ITV these relationships have undergone significant change, and analysis of ITV has often been a matter of trying to hit a moving target. Between 1955 and 2005 ITV has operated under four different regulatory bodies, the Independent Television Authority (ITA), the Independent Broadcasting Authority (IBA), the Independent Television Commission (ITC) and the Office of Communications (Ofcom), and has comprised 28 companies. In this 50-year period ITV has broadcast an enormous number of programmes of different kinds, forms, genres, formats, which John Ellis (in this volume) estimates would take 35 years to watch in full.

Furthermore, the very question of what constitutes ITV has shifted over its 50-year history. Once a single channel with regional variations made up of programmes produced primarily by the ITV franchise companies, ITV has become complex in other ways. Since the rise of the independent sector in the 1980s and the requirement in the Broadcasting Act 1990 for ITV and the BBC to take 25 per cent of their programmes from independent producers, the production base of ITV has shifted. Furthermore, with the gradual relaxation of ownership rules, ITV companies have diversified into a wide range of other industries, and ITV itself has become increasingly consolidated, and in 2005 the 15 regional franchises are owned by four companies. In addition, technological changes have transformed the landscape of television broadcasting. The history of ITV is intertwined with the history of Channel 4 and satellite/cable/digital, and ITV has expanded into digital television platforms (unsuccessfully in the case of ONdigital) and digital services, ITV2, ITV3 and the ITV News Channel – although analysis of these channels and their programming is beyond the scope of this volume. Meanwhile, the Internet has also become increasingly important for an understanding of contemporary broadcasting (see Hills in this volume). Furthermore, the history of ITV is often transnational, and demands an understanding of broadcasting beyond national contexts. All these elements further complicate an already diverse and slippery object of study. Yet, despite these historical shifts, ITV remains discursively located in relation to its historical status as a commercially funded and regionally constituted public service broadcaster, and the current debates about the future of ITV resonate with concerns about the loss of its public service requirements and its regional structure within a new (and increasingly digital) media environment (see Johnson and Turnock in this volume).

ITV Cultures: writing the histories of ITV

This edited collection seeks to address the relative neglect of ITV in British broadcasting history, and to address the problems that have hitherto been a barrier to analysis and understanding. It will do this primarily by acknowledging that the history of ITV has indeed been complex, multifaceted and often contradictory. Although unable to offer anything like a definitive account of ITV's history, or even any sense of a single 'ITV culture', this book aims to establish commercial television as a legitimate object of future enquiry, and to open up a range of perspectives with which to tackle ITV's histories, institutions and programming. It argues that the features that have made it difficult to study ITV, its relationship to public service broadcasting, discourses surrounding populism and 'quality', and its pluralistic regional structure, are exactly what make ITV stand out as a unique institution. In particular it will take these three 'problem areas' as its central, unifying approach to offering alternative ITV histories. Like ITV itself, this volume will be pluralistic, drawing from a range of perspectives from television and media studies. Indeed, while this book acknowledges the impossibility of providing a comprehensive history of ITV, it equally proposes that the edited collection form, which enables a number of approaches, voices and perspectives, is perhaps best suited to the study of such a complex and hybridous object as ITV.

Yet in the construction of any edited collection, choices have to be made – choices that can have profound effects for the future analysis of ITV. In the first instance, the book has been envisaged as exploring the tensions between three areas that are key to understanding the specificity of ITV as a broadcaster:

- public service broadcasting versus commercial imperatives;
- 'popular' programming versus 'quality' programming;
- regional television versus national television.

In much the same way that ITV was devised as providing programme balance, this volume too has had to consider how to provide historical balance and equal weighting across a range of regional and national institutions, across a range of programme genres and forms, and across ITV's history. This proved a difficult enterprise as different combinations tended to weight chapters together in terms of genre, especially drama, or in terms of programme companies (especially Granada or London-based companies). The volume has tried to provide an even spread of coverage of subject matter, with attention given to programme forms often overlooked, and (rightly or wrongly) associated with ITV, and institutional situations that have arisen out of regional and historical factors specific to ITV. As a result, some important institutional and programme areas that have already received extended attention elsewhere have been omitted. These specifically include analysis of ITV soap operas, current affairs, documentary drama, and studies of major franchises such as Granada. There is also much within the history of ITV that has hitherto been neglected, and that does not receive detailed attention in this book, such as light entertainment, children's television, religious programming, magazine shows, celebrity, analysis of the smaller regional companies, and of issues such as censorship, advertising and the role of the unions, to name but a few. This is not in any way to devalue discussion of these areas, and analysis of these programme forms, companies and issues are an important part of any understanding of ITV's multiple histories. Our selection has been shaped in part by current trends within television and media studies and, as such, the omissions in this book are *as* important as the chapters themselves for indicating future areas for research. Despite the inevitable omissions that a volume of limited size entails, the contents of this book are intended to establish a framework for understanding ITV as a *whole institution*, and to set out an agenda for future research. These issues will be explored further in the conclusion.

The arrangement of the book is as follows. The first section, 'Histories', offers a critical introduction to the histories of ITV, and a critical reflection on the writing of those histories. The first chapter, by Catherine Johnson and Rob Turnock, offers an overview of ITV's institutional and regulatory history, examining the development of ITV from the first debates leading up to the Television Act 1954 to the uncertain position that ITV faces in 2005 in a highly competitive marketplace. In sketching this history, it focuses in particular on the shifting negotiation of ITV's position as a commercial public service broadcaster, and a regionally structured national broadcaster, in order to draw out, in broad terms, the ways in which the discourses surrounding the organization and regulation of ITV have changed over its history. The next chapter, by John Ellis, provides an accompaniment to this by examining the issues of writing the history of ITV programming. It sets out to offer an overview of what a canon of ITV programmes might look like, introducing the reader to some of the iconic programmes that have been transmitted by ITV. At the same time, however, the chapter also problematizes the notion of any simple canon. It examines the factors that influence canon formation to show that a reduction of ITV to its programmes, which may then become a criterion for dichotomous valuation (such as high quality/populist or good/bad), is a hazardous enterprise. The final chapter in this section by Jonathan Bignell examines the historiography of ITV's early history focusing on accounts of the role of the television mogul Lew Grade. Not only does the chapter examine Grade's early influence in ITV, but it also explores the tensions between popularity and quality, Britishness and Americanness that circulate around accounts of Grade's role, arguing that, as such, Grade stands as an iconic symbol of ITV in many historical accounts of British broadcasting.

The next section is 'Institutions', which examines the tensions between the commercial and public service, regional and national (and international) demands on ITV, focusing specifically on issues of production, and the institutions and institutional structures of ITV. This starts with a chapter by Steve Neale analysing the commercial imperatives that underpinned the production of the early ITV action-oriented series *The Adventures of Robin Hood* (1955–59). Neale demonstrates that *Robin Hood* (and a number of other ITV action series of the period) can be understood as 'runaway' productions. He argues that such transnational production practices were important in enabling the ITV franchises to develop as commercially viable companies, in terms of audience ratings and advertising revenue in Britain, and in terms of sales abroad. The second chapter, by Jamie Medhurst, also complicates an understanding of ITV as a 'British' broadcaster. Medhurst explores the troubled history of ITV company Wales (West and North) Television (Teledu Cymru), which ran between 1962 and 1964 and was the only ITV regional franchise ever to fold. Whereas Steve Neale examines transnational production, Jamie Medhurst looks at nationalism and the irreconcilable tensions that WWN faced in trying to operate a commercial service with ardent public service aspirations characterized by programming in the Welsh language. In the following chapter Rod Allen examines, from an industry perspective, the problems and possibilities of providing public service broadcasting in a commercial environment through an exploration of the production practices at London Weekend Television (LWT) in the late 1970s and 1980s. The chapter argues that at this time, the regulation of ITV and the networking structures created an environment within which LWT could produce a range of prestige and valued public service programmes without undermining their commercial viability. He goes on to look at the way programme finance under John Birt (later to be Director General of the BBC) was radically altered to change the way that programmes were commissioned, exchanged and sold in ITV (and ultimately changed the way the BBC operated). The final chapter in this section, by Jackie Harrison, gives a critical overview history of Independent Television News (ITN) from its start in 1955 to its precarious position in 2005 as part of ITV plc. The chapter will examine how ITN has had a problematic existence at ITV, caught between the constraints of commerce, public service broadcasting and professional journalism. In doing so, Harrison's history of ITN offers a microcosm of the overall history of ITV, which has moved from being relatively protected from the vagaries of the market to having to function in an increasingly competitive broadcasting landscape.

The next section, 'Texts and Intertexts', explores programme forms particularly associated with ITV and the discourses and metadiscourses that surround them – often drawing on notions of value. The first chapter in this section is Helen Wheatley's analysis of the costume, studio drama *Upstairs Downstairs*, which was a popular and successful series in the 1970s. The chapter explores the ways in which such studio drama has often been ignored in academic debates on grounds of both aesthetic and gendered discourses and offers a critical re-evaluation of *Upstairs Downstairs* as an historically and aesthetically significant British television drama. In the following chapter Sherryl Wilson examines the confessional daytime talkshow *Trisha*, a staple of the ITV morning schedules from 1998 until 2004. The chapter examines how such programmes constitute a form of public service broadcasting in their interplay between the public and the private, and their exploration of issues of class and gender, despite being derided for being commercial, exploitative and 'trashy'. The final chapter is Matt Hill's analysis of discourses surrounding the fandom of the popular ITV quiz show *Who Wants to be a Millionaire?*. This chapter examines the way in which quiz shows have been disregarded as a form of legitimate culture and the way that this has impacted on the study of the people who watch and follow them. In so doing, the chapter also explores the way in which the populism of ITV programming has been derided in hierarchies of quality, and offers a theorization of a 'popular aesthetics' to enable a more complex analysis of commercial cultures.

In the conclusions, the editors draw together the overarching themes that emerge throughout the book, and posit an agenda for future research into the history of ITV and British broadcasting more generally. Following this is an 'Historical Timeline' of the key Acts of Parliament and institutional/regulatory changes effecting ITV over its 50-year history, which should serve as a chronological overview and a point of reference.

Ultimately, the aim of this book is to provoke debate and interest in the history and historiography of ITV, and to prompt future research that will re-examine neglected areas of ITV's history, explore ITV's institutions and programmes and re-evaluate the significance of ITV to the overall history of British broadcasting. Our intention is that ITV should be placed more firmly on the agenda of research into the past, present and future of British broadcasting.

Bibliography

Bonner, P. (with Aston, L.) (1998) *Independent Television in Britain, Volume 5, ITV and IBA, 1981–92: The Old Relationship Changes*. London: Macmillan.

Bonner, P. (with Aston, L.) (2003) *Independent Television in Britain, Volume 6, New Developments in Independent Television, 1981–92: Channel 4, TV-am, Cable and Satellite*. London: Palgrave Macmillan.

Briggs, A. (1995) *The History of Broadcasting in the United Kingdom, Volume 5, Competition*. Oxford: Oxford University Press.

Chapman, J. (2002) *Saints and Avengers: British Adventure Series of the 1960s*. London: I.B. Tauris.

Corner, J. (1996) *The Art of Record*. Manchester: Manchester University Press.

Crisell, A. (1997) *An Introductory History of British Broadcasting*. London: Routledge.

Curran, J. and Seaton, J. (1997) *Power Without Responsibility: The Press and Broadcasting in Britain*. London: Routledge.

Darlow, M. (2004) *Independents Struggle: The Programme Makers Who Took on the TV Establishment*. London: Quartet Books.

Dyer, R., Geraghty, C., Jordan, M. *et al.* (eds) (1981) *Coronation Street*. London: British Film Institute.

Fiddy, D. (2001) *Missing Believed Wiped: Searching for the Lost Treasures of British Television*. London: British Film Institute.

Goddard, P. (1991) *Hancock's Half Hour*: a watershed in British television comedy, in J. Corner (ed.) *Popular Television in Britain: Studies in Cultural History*. London: British Film Institute.

Goldie, G.W. (1977) *Facing the Nation: Television and Politics 1936–76*. London: Bodley Head.

Goodwin, P. (1998) *Television under the Tories: Broadcasting Policy 1979–1997*. London: British Film Institute.

Hilmes, M. (ed.) (2003) *The Television History Book*. London: British Film Institute.

Hobson, D. (1982) *Crossroads: The Drama of a Soap Opera*. London: Methuen.

Jacobs, J. (2000) *The Intimate Screen: Early British Television Drama*. Oxford: Oxford University Press.

Johnson, C. (2005) *Telefantasy*. London: British Film Institute.

MacDonald, B. (1994) *Broadcasting in the United Kingdom: A Guide to Information Sources*, 2nd revised edition. London: Mansell.

MacDonald, B. (2001) Independent television from ITV to channel 3: franchises, licences and programmes, 1955–2000, in J. Ballantyne (ed.) *The Researcher's Guide: Film, Television, Radio and Related Documentation Collections in the UK*, 6th edition. London: British Universities Film and Video Council.

Miller, T. (1997) *The Avengers*. London: British Film Institute.
Osgerby, B. and Gough-Yates, A. (2001) *Action TV: Tough Guys, Smooth Operators and Foxy Chicks*. London: Routledge.
Potter, J. (1989) *Independent Television in Britain: Volume 3, Politics and Control, 1968–80*. London: Macmillan.
Potter, J. (1990) *Independent Television in Britain: Volume 4, Companies and Programmes, 1968–80*. London: Macmillan.
Sendall, B. (1982) *Independent Television in Britain: Volume 1, Origin and Foundation, 1946–62*. London: Macmillan.
Sendall, B. (1983) *Independent Television in Britain: Volume 2, Expansion and Change, 1958–68*. London: Macmillan.
Turnock, R. (forthcoming) *Television and Consumer Culture: Britain and the Transformation of Modernity*. London: I.B.Tauris.
Wegg-Prosser, V. (2002) *This Week* in 1956: the introduction of current affairs on ITV, in J. Thumim (ed.) *Small Screens, Big Ideas: Television in the 1950s*. London: I.B. Tauris.

Notes

1 Bernard Sendall (1982; 1983), Jeremy Potter (1989; 1990), and Paul Bonner with Lesley Aston (1998; 2003).
2 Sendall was deputy director-general of the ITA and IBA, Potter was managing director of Independent Television Publications and director of corporate affairs at London Weekend Television, and Bonner worked at ITV as director of the programming secretariat, then as a director at ITV Network Centre. Bonner was assisted by Lesley Aston who worked as a press officer at the IBA and ITC.
3 The subsequent history of the BBC is currently being undertaken by Jean Seaton at Westminster University.
4 Examples include soap operas (Dyer *et al.* 1981; Hobson 1982), action-adventure series (Miller 1997; Osgerby and Gough-Yates 2001; Chapman 2002), and current affairs (Corner 1996; Wegg-Prosser 2002).
5 One example, however, is John Ellis's AHRB-funded project 'Did ITV revolutionise British television?' (see Turnock forthcoming).
6 Jackie Harrison describes ITN as a 'hybrid organization' in this volume and develops an argument that can be applied to ITV as a whole.
7 As part of an AHRB-funded project at Bournemouth University, the listings magazine *TV Times* (from 1955 to 1985) has been digitized and the data entered into a searchable database.
8 See Johnson and Turnock (this volume), and Sendall (1982).

PART 1

HISTORIES

1 FROM START-UP TO CONSOLIDATION: INSTITUTIONS, REGIONS AND REGULATION OVER THE HISTORY OF ITV

Catherine Johnson and Rob Turnock

Introduction

The regulatory and institutional history of ITV is complicated not simply by the length of time covered (1955–2005) but also by the complex structure of the ITV franchise and the array of bodies involved in its regulation. To tell this history in one chapter is perhaps an impossible task. Yet an attempt to construct an overview of this history is important, primarily in order to understand in broad terms how both ITV and British broadcasting have shifted over the past 50 years. While such a diachronic approach to ITV's history will inevitably remove some of the complexity and detail evidenced in some of the focused studies found elsewhere in this book, it should provide an invaluable tool in understanding historical change over time. In attempting to construct this history, therefore, this chapter does not aim to offer a comprehensive account of the institutional, regional and regulatory history of ITV. Many important historical events and debates will inevitably be omitted here.[1] It *does* aim to offer one of the first attempts to think across the history of ITV and explore how it has changed over time. In doing so, this chapter focuses on those issues and debates that seem to recur across the history of ITV, but which have changed in quite distinct ways over time, focusing in particular on two issues that have been particularly pertinent: the relationship between commercial and public service broadcasting, and the relationship between national and regional broadcasting – issues that remain central to ITV.

Breaking the monopoly

The Report of the Broadcasting Committee, 1949 (Beveridge 1951) was delivered to the Labour government in January 1951. The report, which had been prepared under the chairmanship of Lord Beveridge, rejected outright any commercialization of British broadcasting, either in radio or television, although it was in favour of increased regional broadcasting from Scotland, Wales and Northern Ireland. Accepted by government, the BBC's monopoly of broadcasting in Britain, funded by a licence fee, was assured. Three years later, however, the Television Act 1954 was passed, which legislated for a new commercial television service in the UK. The following year, on Thursday 22 September 1955, the transmission of programmes by Associated-Rediffusion in the London area saw the start of Britain's first commercial television service, and the breaking of the BBC's monopoly. So what happened in these few short years to allow such a radical shift from the Beveridge Report to occur?

The debate that led to the establishment of ITV in Britain in the early 1950s could be characterized as a battle between those with commercial and ideological interests in the expansion of television services, and those who feared the impact of commercial forces on British cultural life and public service broadcasting. This was a debate that was to culminate with the establishment of commercial television as a *regulated public service*. The campaign for commercial television was facilitated in part by the major upturn in the British economy. By the early 1950s the postwar austerity of the years immediately following World War Two was waning, as the economy improved and incomes rose. This was accompanied by an expansion in production and the need for the creation of new markets for new and existing commodities. The impetus for a commercial television service or, at least, the expansion of television broadcasting, came partly, therefore, from the manufacturers of television receivers who wanted a reason for people to buy or rent new sets. The expansion of the economy also led advertisers to look for new media outlets to promote the expanded range of consumer goods, and individuals within the advertising lobby were very influential in the campaign for commercial television (Sendall 1982; Crisell 1997). At the same time, there was a handful of voices from within television, dissatisfied with the apparently slow development of television at the BBC.

Despite calls from manufacturers, advertisers and television insiders for an expansion of television, many in the British 'establishment' were ranged against a new commercial television service. Battle lines between those who were for and against commercial television were drawn around television distribution and television content (Sendall 1982; Crisell 1997). Those in favour, coalescing around the pressure group the Popular Television Association, saw commercial television as a new way to distribute and deliver new programmes and services. Their opponents, however, publicly and visibly manifested by the National Television Council were more concerned about television content. Labour MPs (in favour of nationalized and centralized social and cultural provision), many Conservative MPs, members of the Church and opinion formers in the media were fearful that commercially funded television programming would erode traditional values and morals. Many in authority believed in the concept of public service and the rigorously Reithian tradition of the BBC to 'inform, educate and entertain', and thought that the introduction of commercial values in broadcasting would mark an apparent trend towards to the 'Americanization' of British cultural life.

What ultimately drove through legislation for commercial television was a small handful of Conservative MPs. The Conservative government, elected to office in 1951 under the leadership of Winston Churchill, only had a majority of 16 seats in the House of Commons. A small, but cohesive group of Tory backbench MPs came from the world of business and believed in free enterprise and competition. These MPs, known as the 'One Nation Group', were opposed to any kind of monopoly, not just in broadcasting, and they were vociferous in their campaign for commercial television (Sendall 1982). Their success was predicated on two political factors. Firstly, the government's slim majority left it vulnerable to backbench revolt, and as a result the 'One Nation Group' was able to wield a disproportionate amount of power. Secondly, the group was able to strike a deal in the backrooms of government. The Conservative Party Chairman, Lord Woolton, agreed that government would legislate for the introduction of a commercial television service as long as the group did not threaten the BBC's monopoly of radio broadcasting. This was seen as a less controversial move because it was through radio that the BBC had earned prestige and respect, and at this stage television was still a new medium with a minority audience. As a result the Television Act was passed in 1954, which legislated the breaking of the BBC's monopoly and the start of commercial television, an event some came to see as an underhand capitalist conspiracy amongst businessmen and brokers (see for example Wilson 1961; and Jenkins 1961). Yet the legacy of the Beveridge Committee and the concerns expressed in public debates, led to a commercial system that was publicly regulated and regionally structured to counter the London-centric bias of the BBC.

Founding principles and early years

Despite being established as a commercial system, the new service marked a degree of continuity with principles that had governed BBC broadcasting (Goldie 1977; Briggs 1995; Turnock, forthcoming). In the first instance, the new service was subject to a degree of state control, operating under licence from the Postmaster General. It was legislated by an Act of Parliament which could be repealed, and indeed the Labour Party promised to repeal the Act when it was next elected to government, although it later changed its mind due to the service's apparent popularity with working-class voters (Milland 2004). The new service was also to be governed by a regulatory body, the Independent Television Authority (ITA), which was set up within weeks of the Act in 1954. The ITA's role was to build and operate transmitters across the country, to award licences to regional programme companies, and supervise programming and advertising. In one sense the ITA had a similar role to the governors of the BBC, and its 'members' were drawn from the same pool of people as the BBC's governors. The two men who headed the ITA both came from the public service and arts sectors. The first Director General of the ITA was Sir Robert Fraser, previously Director General of the Central Office of Information, and the first Chairman Sir Kenneth Clark, previously Chairman of the Arts Council and Director of the National Gallery (Sendall 1982). Therefore, although funded by the sale of advertising, the principles under which the new service operated were largely the same as the public service remit governing the BBC.

In particular, one of the ITA's key roles in the award and supervision of licences (of what came to be known as the 'programme companies' (Sendall 1982)) was maintaining an appropriate 'balance' of programming. Acknowledging fears of crass commercialism and 'Americanization', the Television Act charged the new service, in language borrowed from the BBC (Goldie 1977; Briggs 1995), to 'inform, educate and entertain'. In this the programme companies had to provide a range of programming within a mixed schedule, to include 'highbrow' forms of programming such as serious plays, classical music and arts programmes, as well as local, news, children's and religious programmes. In effect, to provide a mixed programme schedule along the lines of public service broadcasting established by the BBC in radio and television. Indeed, the award of licences to the regional programme companies on fixed-term contracts allowed the ITA to revoke licences when the time came for renewal, to ensure that public service standards were maintained. In fear, also, of 'Americanization' and in protection of British jobs, the ITA made a 'gentleman's agreement' to impose quotas on the amount of programming imported from abroad, which was set at an average of no more than seven hours per 50-hour broadcasting week (as it was then) (Sendall 1982). Furthermore, the ITA had, in theory, recourse to funds from the television licence fee paid by viewers to the Post Office. As part of the Television Act, the ITA could claim up to £750,000 from the licence fee in the new service's start-up years should any programme companies struggle financially to meet a balanced schedule. Although the first programme companies did, in fact, experience some serious financial concerns in the first year of the new service, the Post Office was reluctant to part with money during the height of the national crisis over Suez. After some negotiation the Post Office agreed to allocate £100,000 to the ITA for the following financial year, but after a bungled intervention by the programme companies the offer of money was withdrawn. The incident foreclosed the principle of any claim on the television licence fee in the future (see Sendall 1982).

The other area for which the ITA had supervisory responsibility was advertising. One of the principles behind the Beveridge Report's rejection of commercial television was the system of programme sponsorship that operated in the US in the 1940s. There, individual programmes were sponsored by a particular company/advertiser and the sponsor could exert direct editorial control on programme-makers. As a result of Beveridge's findings legislation was introduced that required the new commercial system in Britain to be funded by 'spot advertising', whereby advertising slots appeared in and between programmes. Spot advertising meant that theoretically advertising revenue was separated out from programme making. The ITA also had to enforce strict rules regarding how much advertising there could be (initially no more than an average of 6 minutes per hour of broadcasting) and what could be advertised (money-lenders, gambling associations and religions were, for example, banned).

As well as advertising, the institutional structure of ITV was significantly and deliberately different from the largely London-centric and metropolitan structure of the BBC, which had been criticized in the Beveridge Report. By contrast, ITV was set up along regional lines, with licences issued by the ITA to regional franchises charged with the responsibility of providing programming for that specific region of Britain. There were also commercial reasons for this regional structure as it was envisaged that regionalization could make the business of advertising and marketing more targeted to specific regional audiences (Curran and Seaton 1997).

After the first franchise round, licences were awarded in the main metropolitan areas of London, the Midlands and the north of England, to a group of companies that came to be known as the 'Big Four' (Associated-Rediffusion, Associated Television, ABC Television and Granada Television). As transmitters were constructed, ITV spread out across the country over the late-1950s, although the roll out of regional companies was not complete until Wales (West and North) Television (Teledu Cymru) went on air in 1962. When complete, ITV consisted of 15 programme companies operating in 14 franchise areas. These were complemented by the Independent Television News (ITN) service which had started broadcasting on the very first night of ITV and provided national news to all of the ITV companies (see Harrison in this volume).

Yet while these locally owned franchises provided a number of programmes with regional themes (in some cases even 'nationalist' – see Medhurst in this volume), it is debatable whether the ITV system, as constituted, truly provided a regional and competitive service as envisioned in the Television Act. Firstly, as Sendall (1982) has noted, London remained firmly the economic and talent capital in Britain. This was where the entertainment industry infrastructure was based. Many programmes made by the programme companies necessarily had to draw on this geographically located infrastructure. It was also the home of government, as well as the ITA and BBC television. Secondly, the regional structure of the ITV franchises was largely based on the location of transmitters, rather than on the assessment of cultural regions. In some cases ITV regional franchises actually covered wide and diverse regions with different needs. This is perhaps most apparent with TWW, which had bases in Cardiff and Bristol and a responsibility for broadcasting to the south-west of England and to the south of Wales, effectively crossing a regional and a national boundary.

Regionalism and competition were also undermined by what Sendall (1982) has described as the 'network carve-up'. In the very early days of ITV the first companies struggled to make money and there was serious anxiety that the commercial television enterprise would fail financially. As we will see below, this led to a programme policy that attracted negative criticism, yet it also had an impact on the structure of the ITV system. The Big Four, the first and largest ITV companies broadcasting to the most lucrative metropolitan centres, had made deals in terms of programme exchange and sales. Given the costs of television production it was deemed economically practical that the companies should share programmes, rather than each company producing its own original programming for its own schedules. This arrangement constituted a *de facto* network. As newer and smaller companies started up, it appeared economically sensible that they make affiliation agreements with one of the larger companies to provide a regular stream of programming. As the larger company would also have exchange agreements with the others, the smaller company could therefore benefit from an affordable supply of programmes coming from the existing network of arrangements between the Big Four. The smaller companies were often unhappy, however, with the quality and/or nature of the programmes provided to them. And there was further resentment as the smaller companies found it difficult to provide programmes back to the network. This effective 'carve-up' was, at the time, sanctioned by the ITA. It was felt that the big companies had taken large financial risks in setting up the network and that they should benefit from networking arrangements (Sendall 1982). At the same time, the ITA felt it was not the role of the smaller companies to have networking programme ambitions as they had been awarded licences to service their local areas. In the case of a number of franchises, such as Anglia Television, communication facilities for transmitting programmes back to London had not been included in their contracts (Sendall 1982).

The 'network carve-up' also marked a shift in ITV's philosophy of competition. Originally the ITA had envisaged that proper competition could only exist if viewers had the choice of watching two commercial services (as well as the BBC), and that there should be a minimum of two services covering each area (Sendall 1982). Initially this was not possible as the ITA had not had enough frequencies allocated to it, and the early anxiety about the financial viability of the commercial service had made sheer survival an economic necessity. In these early days at least, the ITA did not realize that competition would come to be regarded as supply of programming to a network in a duopoly rather than competition for audiences and revenue between programme companies (Sendall 1982).

The financial anxieties that had initially led to networking also had an impact on programming and this was to result in criticisms of the new service. In the first year of broadcasting, the ITV companies struggled financially, as audiences were initially slow to take up the new service (partly because viewers had to invest in new sets or aerials to receive ITV). The financial turning point for ITV seems to have been a conjunction of factors. The extension of the ITV network coincided with more people acquiring or adapting their television sets. This also coincided with a change in programming policy which moved away from programming that was regarded as more 'serious', towards more popular entertainment such as lavish quiz shows, which came to be known as the 'retreat from balance' (Sendall 1982). Audience figures started to rise, and this was accompanied by a certain amount of hyperbole on the part of the programme companies and the ITA that ITV programming was proving more popular than the BBC. Doubt has been cast over the extent to which ITV drove up the number of those who owned a television or the extent to which it stole the BBC's audience (see, for example, Curran and Seaton 1997; Hand 2003; Turnock, forthcoming), yet growing advertiser confidence nonetheless meant that the ITV companies started to attract more revenue. The apparent and increasing financial success of ITV was to be infamously characterized by Roy Thompson, the head of Scottish Television, declaring in 1957 that owning a television franchise was 'like having a licence to print money' (cf. Sendall 1982: 208).

The Pilkington legacy

In July 1960, before the ITV network had been completed and the ITA had awarded all of its contracts, the government established a Committee of Inquiry to examine broadcasting in Britain.[2] The Committee, chaired by Sir Harry Pilkington, had a broad remit to consider the future of broadcasting, to advise on the services that should be provided by the BBC and the ITA, and the nature of any additional services (Pilkington 1962: 1). At this time, the 'prevailing climate' towards ITV was hostile (see Sendall 1982: 371; Briggs 1995: 263–6; Milland 2004: 79–84). Criticisms in the press and amongst politicians centred on anxieties about the quality of ITV's public service broadcasting and the ITA's inability to enforce the quality provision of the Television Act 1954 in the face of what were seen as excessive profits for the contractors. Meanwhile, those (primarily Conservative) politicians in favour of ITV were frustrated at the consequences of networking, which had effectively created a monopoly in advertising and had failed to bring commercially competitive broadcasting to Britain (see Milland 2004: 88–9). This hostility towards ITV, and in particular, towards a commercially successful ITV, was reproduced in the final report produced by the Pilkington Committee in 1962.

Titled the Report of the Committee on Broadcasting, 1960, the Committee's findings were particularly critical of ITV for failing to recognize the full effect of television on its viewers, and not providing a fair and reflective balance of programmes. The report criticized ITV for the 'triviality' of its programming; a term that was used in the report to refer less to the subject matter itself than to 'the way a subject matter is approached and the manner in which it is presented' (Pilkington 1962: 34). In both regards ITV was unfavourably compared with the BBC, whose programmes were seen as 'serious' and of a higher quality in general, and which the committee felt took the responsibilities of broadcasting seriously. In its diagnosis of the 'triviality' of ITV's programmes, the report tended to devalue a number of the areas of programming in which ITV had been an initiator – such as light entertainment and, in particular, quiz shows (Pilkington 1962: 58–9). The report did recognize that ITV produced more programmes outside of London than the BBC. However, it argued that, despite this, ITV did not necessarily serve the needs of specific regions as its programmes tended to be 'local in origin rather than in appeal', while those programmes of local appeal were scarce and often scheduled outside of prime time (1962: 66). Ultimately the report argued that 'the decentralised structure [of ITV] has not resulted in an essentially regional or local service' (Pilkington 1962: 67). For the Pilkington Committee, it was not simply the service provided by ITV that was at fault; it was the very structure and ethos within which commercial television had been established in Britain. Essentially, the report argued that the responsibilities of a public service broadcaster could not be reconciled with the profit motive of commercial television. The Pilkington Report therefore challenged the very ethos of commercial broadcasting and, as a consequence, recommended a profound change to the structural organization of ITV (see especially, 1962: 168–70).

The report was to have a significant impact on broadcasting, but not in the way it was initially intended. The press had been critical of ITV when the Pilkington Committee was appointed in 1960, but the publication of the report saw a shift in focus as much of the British public and press leapt to the defence of ITV against what were seen as the 'elitist' judgements of the Committee and the undue favouritism accorded to the BBC, which received little criticism in the report (see Sendall 1983: 137–40). Sendall (1983: 134) claims that the appointment, in February 1962, of the Broadcasting and Television Committee to prepare a White Paper on broadcasting four months *before* the Pilkington Report was published on 27 June 1962 (in an attempt by government to get a new Broadcasting Bill through Parliament before a general election) reflected the government's lack of interest in the findings of the Pilkington Committee.

A second White Paper published in December 1962 rejected the Pilkington Committee's proposals for the structural reorganization of independent television. However, some of Pilkington's proposals were sanctioned by the subsequent Television Acts of 1963 and 1964, such as the allocation of a third channel (BBC 2) to the BBC on the higher quality 625-line UHF band. In relation to independent television, the Television Act 1963 sanctioned an increase in the powers of the ITA, in particular, to remove the rigidities of the current network arrangements, which favoured the Big Four. It also increased the ITA's control over content by giving it 'the power to vet programmes and schedules before transmission' (Milland 2004: 96). Finally, it recommended that the ITA rentals collected from the programme companies should include a levy on profits to be remitted to the Exchequer in order to minimize the 'excessive' profits gained from the contractors.[3]

Despite the levy, and increased rentals to fund the impending technical upgrading of the service from VHF to UHF and from black and white to colour, the ITV companies continued to operate profitably over the 1960s. All of the existing contracts were renewed in 1964, with the exception of Wales (West and North) Television (see Medhurst in this volume). Meanwhile, new networking arrangements were agreed in the summer of 1963 to attempt to restrict the effective oligopoly of the Big Four on networked programmes, which led to the cessation of the affiliation system. The impact of this legislation in practice was relatively limited as the Big Four continued to dominate networked programmes, and it certainly did not create the ITA's desired free competition for programme supply. As such, the legacy of the Pilkington Report is to be found less in the subsequent policy/structural changes than in the impact that its rhetoric had on broadcasting more broadly. As Jeffrey Milland (2004) and John Caughie (2000) have argued, Pilkington's insistence on the moral responsibilities of broadcasting to its audience (conceived as citizens rather than consumers) shaped the tenor by which public service broadcasting in Britain was evaluated in the following years. Indeed, over the 1960s the *ITA: Annual Report and Accounts* included a section devoted to 'The Development of Serious Programmes' across the ITV network in order to demonstrate that the channel's provision of informational, educational and critical programmes had grown since the publication of the Pilkington Report in 1962.

This emphasis on responsibility over commercial imperatives is further apparent in the renewal of the ITV franchises in 1968. For example, the ITA attempted to strengthen the regional representation of the programme companies by insisting on changes to the constitution and boards of a number of franchises.[4] The allocation of the London weekend contract to LWT, a new company comprised of experienced programme-makers including Michael Peacock (Controller of BBC1), broadcaster David Frost and former Head of ITN Aidan Crawley, has also been seen as an attempt by the ITA to put programme quality at the centre of its contract renewals (Sendall 1983). The stress placed in LWT's application on the applicants proven track record in programme making and their 'common belief that the quality of mass entertainment can be improved while retaining commercial viability' (reproduced in Smith 1974: 132), clearly resonates with the concerns expressed in the Pilkington Report. The subsequent financial difficulties suffered by LWT in the early 1970s, however, point to the difficult regulatory position for the ITA, which had to balance the need for strict enough controls on content and ownership against the need to have financially viable companies operating.

Overall, however, what emerged in the 1960s was a 'cosy' duopoly between the BBC and ITV in which the ITV programme companies were significantly protected from the marketplace. The unions ensured similar working practices in each institution and both institutions were regulated by a public service broadcasting remit interpreted by staff who had commonly worked for both the BBC and ITV. Over the 1970s the fears (evidenced in the Pilkington Report) that the commercial funding of ITV would prevent it from producing quality public service broadcasting receded and the ITV companies produced a number of critically acclaimed programmes. The increasing sense that there was less difference between ITV and BBC in terms of programmes, staff and approach did, however, lead to fears that the effective duopoly that the two broadcasters enjoyed was having a potentially negative effect on television. The BBC and ITV did not compete for revenue and, within the structure of ITV, there was no internal competition for revenue (as ITV companies had an effective monopoly on television advertising in their regions). There was also little competition between the two institutions for programme supply, as each functioned as a vertically integrated industry. As such, the BBC and ITV could quite happily coexist (see Goodwin 1998: 14–15). This raised a number of issues over the 1970s and 1980s, including fears of a lack of pluralism in the programming produced, but also disquiet about access to production, raised especially by those new and independent producers struggling to enter broadcasting.

From Annan to Peacock

Although the duopoly tended to protect ITV from the marketplace, the broader economic, industrial and political instability of the 1970s did affect the programme companies. A defining characteristic of the 1970s in the UK was an anxious economic climate, with instability, recession, high inflation and high unemployment. For the ITV companies this caused a series of short-term financial crises. However, of perhaps more significant impact at the time was the effect of government-enforced pay restraints, which contributed to a wider set of labour problems faced by ITV and the BBC into the 1980s. While both ITV and the BBC were affected by conflict with the unions, industrial action particularly hurt the profit margins of the commercial television companies.

At the same time, there were emerging dissident voices about the closed-shop nature of numerous media institutions, including the press, film industry and broadcasting. One group, the Free Communications Group (FCG), set up in 1968 and including members from across a range of media industries, campaigned for greater access to and control of the media by the public and workers in the industry. The FCG was particularly critical of the way in which ITV programme companies had been allowed to control a wide range of media (and non-media) business interests and the way union rules restricted entry for workers into the commercial television industry (see Darlow 2004: 35). The FCG also criticized the lack of effective powers that the ITA (and later the Independent Broadcasting Authority) had in policing ITV franchise contracts, especially in the wake of an apparent retreat from quality in LWT's programmes at the beginning of the 1970s (see Darlow 2004: 99–102).[5]

In addition to this, broadcasting in general was subject to political hostility, and when the Labour government originally set up a committee of inquiry under Lord Annan in 1970, its remit did not assume (as the remit for the Pilkington Committee had done) the continued existence of the BBC and the ITA (see Goldie 1977: 304). However, the Annan Committee was postponed when the Conservative Party won the 1970 general election, and did not resurface again until the Labour Party was back in power in 1974. The Committee had a broad remit to consider the future of broadcasting in Britain, including the recommendation of *additional* services, and 'to propose what constitutional, organizational and financial arrangements and what conditions should apply to the conduct of all these services' (Annan 1977: 3).

When the Annan Committee reported in 1977 its attitude towards ITV was very different from the criticisms found in the Pilkington Report. The Annan Report was not only positive in its praise of ITV programming (particularly news); it also made few objections to advertising, which had become an accepted way to fund public service television. Despite this, the report did not favour allocating a fourth channel to ITV, and rather made recommendations designed to remove what was seen as the 'straightjacket' that the duopoly placed on broadcasting (Annan 1977: 471), such as the implementation of a new broadcasting authority to run a fourth channel. In fact, one of the characteristics of the Annan Report was a call for greater pluralism and diversity in television programming and production than was then possible under the duopoly, to respond to the development of an increasingly pluralist and multiracial society in Britain (Annan 1977: 30).

A number of the Annan Report's recommendations, including the establishment of a new regulator (the Open Broadcasting Authority) to oversee a fourth television channel, were included in a government White Paper published on 26 July 1978, but were not implemented before Labour lost the general election in 1979 to Thatcher's Conservative government. The Conservative government's initial response to broadcasting in the Broadcasting Act 1980 left the BBC and ITV largely unchanged, and instead extended the IBA's responsibilities to include the provision of a fourth channel (Channel 4).[6] Channel 4 was established as a wholly owned subsidiary of the IBA funded by subscriptions from the ITV programme companies, who in return sold advertising on the channel. In addition, Channel 4 took half of its programmes from the independent sector (the other half coming from ITV), and had a specific remit to offer a diversity of programming that was not found on the other channels. As such, although regulated by the IBA (contra Annan's recommendations), the establishment of Channel 4 did tackle concerns about the duopoly by increasing the diversity of television programming, introducing economic competition into television production, weakening the vertical integration of the duopoly, and weakening the hold of the trade unions on the industry. Meanwhile, all but two of the ITV franchises were renewed in 1982, and television hours were expanded with the introduction of breakfast-time services on both the BBC and ITV.[7]

However, after winning a second election victory in 1983, the Conservative government turned its attention more specifically to reforming the BBC in line with their broader free-market policies (see Goodwin 1998: 69–70). In March 1985 the government established a committee of inquiry under Sir Alan Peacock on the alternatives to funding the BBC, in particular the introduction of advertising. Peacock himself was a free-market economist, and as Goodwin (1998: 78, fn1) argues the Committee's report was the first report in the history of broadcasting to see the market rather than public service broadcasting as the underlying principle of broadcasting. When the report was published a year later, however, it recommended, contrary to the government's wishes and expectations, against the introduction of advertising on the BBC, fearing that it would reduce consumer choice. In fact, 'consumer sovereignty' was central to the Peacock Report's understanding of broadcasting, and its recommendations were based on moving broadcasting towards 'a system which recognises that viewers and listeners are the best ultimate judges of their own interests, which they can best satisfy if they have the option of purchasing the broadcasting services they require from as many alternative sources of supply as possible' (Peacock 1986: 133). The report was not opposed to the regulation of public service broadcasting, but argued for the active encouragement of technological developments that would enable television to expand and diversify. Furthermore, the report argued that despite the introduction of Channel 4, there remained a 'comfortable duopoly' between ITV and BBC that reduced efficiency in each organization and limited the development of the independent sector and competition for programme supply (Peacock 1986: 124). Amongst a range of recommendations to counter this, Peacock proposed that the BBC and ITV increase the number of programmes that they commission from independent producers. Furthermore, and perhaps more radically, Peacock recommended that the ITV franchises be put to competitive tender and allocated to the highest bidder. While the levy had been introduced in 1964 to reduce the profits gained by the ITV contractors from the scarce national resource of the airwaves, the Peacock Report argued that it provided no incentive to the companies to economize in costs. Rather it claimed that an auction system in which companies pay in advance for the use of the airwaves would increase subsequent efficiency in the use of resources (Peacock 1986: 143).

Towards consolidation

Subsequent reform to expand choice in broadcasting through new technological developments was a significant part of the Conservative Party's 1987 election manifesto (see MacDonald 1994: 27). After they returned to power in 1987 the Conservatives put forward a number of proposals for broadcasting leading to the Broadcasting Act 1990, which came into effect in 1992. With some amendments, the principle of competition became a major cornerstone of the Broadcasting Act, which implemented the auction of the ITV contracts, but did allow for licences not to be awarded to the highest bidder under 'exceptional circumstances' where 'the quality of the service proposed by such an application is exceptionally high'.[8] Included within the Act was a statutory requirement that both BBC and ITV take 25 per cent of their programming from independent production.[9] At the same time, broadcasting was to be deregulated with the establishment of a 'light touch regulator', as the IBA was replaced by the Independent Television Commission (ITC) and Radio Authority. The ITC was no longer in charge of the national network of transmitters,[10] and was unable to view and vet programmes in advance or to dictate schedules. As a consequence over the 1990s, a number of ITV's mandated 'public service' programmes (such as religious programming and news) were moved from primetime into less ratings friendly slots, often amid significant controversy.[11] However, despite the relaxation of ITC's regulatory responsibilities, it has been argued that it was much tougher than expected (Goodwin 1998). The Commission was allowed a large amount of discretion, and was charged with deciding how the ITV structure (now also known as Channel 3) was to be shaped. It decided that there should be exactly the same number of licences as before, drawn up along the same regional boundaries, including a licence for a national breakfast television service and the separation of the weekday and weekend London franchises. Meanwhile ITN became a profit-making business, and was nominated as the sole provider of news to the Channel 3 licensees for their first 5 years (see Harrison in this volume). In another major change, and in contrast to the 1968 franchise round for example, licence applicants did not need a regional base. This was because new applicants could work on a 'publisher-contractor' model relying on programming from the independent sector (Goodwin 1998).

In October 1991 the ITC announced that it had awarded licences to 12 of the incumbent licence holders, and replaced four of the licensees with new companies. On 1 December 1992 the ITV Network Centre was established, with responsibility for commissioning and scheduling programmes for the ITV network. The Network Centre was designed to create a more equal market for the supply of programmes to the network by separating out the function of the licensees as programme-makers and broadcasters, and making it easier for smaller companies to provide programmes for the network. However, in negotiations prior to the start of the new system, independent production companies were initially denied direct access to the Network Centre and instead had to have their programmes commissioned through one of the ITV licensees, enabling the larger ITV companies to maintain significant control over networked programming. In December 1992 the Office of Fair Trading ruled that these arrangements were anti-competitive, and amendments were made to allow the independents to contract with the ITV Network Centre directly.

In addition to increased competition, the 1990s also saw increasing consolidation of ownership across ITV. Although supplementary legislation following the Broadcasting Act 1990 prevented any company from owning or controlling more than two licences (Bonner 1998: 411), some of the programme companies lobbied for change, particularly in the face of increasing competition from the cable and satellite sector and, from 1997, the new commercial terrestrial service Channel 5. Partly because of fears of European takeovers of British companies, and because larger companies could operate more effectively and economically against competition, the rules were relaxed at the end of 1993 to allow companies to own up to two large franchises (but not both London franchises), leading to a number of corporate takeovers. The Broadcasting Act 1996 made further amendments to rules of ownership, allowing mergers as long as they did not negatively influence the quality and range of programmes available to the public, and the regional representation of the company and its programming.[12] Significantly, the Act redefined media ownership in relation to the 'share' of the audience gained, rather than simply the number or size of the companies owned. Specifically it allowed newspaper groups with less than 20 per cent of the national newspaper circulation to control television broadcasters with up to 15 per cent of the market (defined as audience share) (see Goodwin 1998: 147–53). As a consequence of this deregulation, by the end of the 1990s, ownership of ITV was effectively divided between three main players, Granada, Carlton, and United News and Media (UNM), with a handful of smaller companies remaining. Further consolidation followed in July 2000 when Granada bought Meridian and Anglia from UNM, making Granada the key shareholder of ITV, with Carlton second.[13]

Increasing competition, with multi-channel television reaching 50 per cent of homes (*ITC Annual Report 2002*) and a downturn in advertising revenue at the start of the twenty-first century made a consolidated, single ITV more likely. In October 2002, a plan was established for the merger of Granada and Carlton, but there remained anxieties about how much of the advertising market the merged ITV would corner – estimated at around 55 per cent (Milmo 2002). There were also regulatory hurdles, with the ongoing restriction that no company could own two London licences, and there were fears that a Granada and Carlton merger would devalue the remaining ITV franchises, Grampian and Scottish (owned by SMG), Ulster and Channel. After a six-month inquiry by the competition watchdog and consultation with the Department for Trade and Industry, the merger finally took place on 2 February 2004 creating ITV plc, a £5.8 billion broadcasting giant.[14] In the first year of the merged company, ITV's audience share was still being battered by competition, and BBC1 was the most popular television channel for a fourth consecutive year. Yet ITV plc still remained an economic force to be reckoned with, making £1.67 million in advertising, with a 48.9 per cent share of the advertising market (Brown and Martinson 2005). In 2005, ITV plc not only owned 11 of the ITV programme companies that made up ITV1, but also the cable, satellite and digital channels ITV2 (launched in 1998), ITV3 (launched in 2004) and the ITV News Channel (launched in 2000).[15]

During this period, consolidation not only characterized ownership of ITV licences, but also of regulatory bodies. In December 2003 Ofcom officially came together out of five different regulators, the Broadcasting Standards Commission, the Independent Television Commission, the Office of Telecommunications, the Radiocommunications Agency and the Radio Authority. The new organization, the Office of Communications (Ofcom) was legislated by the Communications Act 2003, 'to further the interests of citizens in relations to communications matters' and 'to further the interests of consumers in relevant markets, where appropriate by promoting competition'.[16] As an enlarged regulator, the new organization had a wide range of responsibilities relating to broadcasting and telecommunications. In relation to television broadcasting, Ofcom inherited the ITC's licensing responsibilities and retained its sanctioning powers as laid down by the Broadcasting Act 1990. Yet Ofcom's operational philosophy seems finely balanced between intervention and non-intervention in broadcasting issues. As indicated on its web site, Ofcom's regulatory principles dictate that the organization 'will operate with a bias against intervention', and 'will always seek the least intrusive regulatory mechanisms to achieve its policy objectives'. Yet the regulator also spells a willingness to act 'promptly and effectively where required' and 'intervene where there is a specific statutory duty to work towards a public policy goal which markets alone cannot achieve'.[17]

'Competition for quality'

One of the first interventionist, statutory duties for Ofcom, charged under the terms of the Communications Act 2003, was to assess the 'effectiveness' of the terrestrial broadcasters (BBC, Channel 3, Channel 4, 5, S4C and Telextext) in delivering public service broadcasting and how to maintain or improve it (Ofcom 2005). Ofcom also had to take into account the increasing number of households switching over to multi-channel television, and digital and broadband technologies. So not only was Ofcom charged with assessing the provision of public service broadcasting (PSB) in Britain at the beginning of the new century, it had to assess how PSB had to adapt to technological, market and consumer change.

Ofcom's PSB review was conducted in three phases, with a third and final report (consolidating the findings of the first two) being published in February 2005. Both the title and overarching theme of the Phase 3 Report was *Competition for Quality*. Under this theme the report proposed a new definition of PSB (see Ofcom 2005 for details) and identified four key characteristics of public service broadcasting. These were high quality, well funded and produced programming; original UK programming, rather than repeats or programmes bought from abroad; innovative programming; and challenging programming – 'making viewers think' (Ofcom 2005: 7). In the first instance, this is to be achieved in a competitive marketplace, with the increasing number of digital and broadband services providing a wider range of quality than existing analogue services. Secondly, while the increased number of commercial broadcasters would provide a wide range of programming, Ofcom found that there would be under-provision of certain programme forms in a purely commercial marketplace. This meant that 'intervention is needed to ensure that there is sufficient range, volume and quality of programming made in the UK and for UK audiences' (Ofcom 2005: 3). As a result, there would need to be a plurality of outlets, of commissioning, and of production to ensure adequate public service provision (Ofcom 2005: 31). While recognizing that the BBC had been, historically, central to PSB, Ofcom argues that there needs to be a range of broadcasters to provide public service programming, with different sources of funding. This would necessarily include ITV. Yet Ofcom also acknowledges that commercial PSBs are subject to increasing competition for advertising revenue which in turn affects their ability to produce some elements of PSB programming. At the same time Ofcom argues that the value of the analogue system will decline in the face of digital expansion, making broadcasters less inclined to own analogue licences in return for providing PSB programming. So Ofcom admits that it will be unable to ensure that commercial PSBs like ITV meet public service obligations after digital switchover – the point at which broadcasting no longer operates on analogue systems. With broadcasting experiencing a period of profound change, Ofcom's third proposal is for a more 'robust' PSB system to be flexible enough to meet these changes, in the guise of a new Public Service Publisher (PSP), a publicly funded body to deliver distinct and high quality content to 'citizens and consumers' using a range of media.[18]

The effects of this report for ITV are numerous. According to the report (Ofcom 2005: 9) ITV 'should focus on its strengths of news and high production value origination from around the UK'. ITV, along with 5, is expected to provide a range of high quality, original content across a number of genres in competition with BBC and Channel 4. However, recognizing the difficulties for commercial public service broadcasters to sustain a wide range of obligations in a highly competitive marketplace, Ofcom (2005: 9) also argues that 'it is better for ITV1 to prepare for its future role as soon as possible, rather than to be asked to preserve in full a range of commitments designed originally for a very different analogue world'. This in particular reduces ITV's responsibilities in certain programme areas such as children's and religious programming (Brown 2005: 10). A reduction in these programmes was the first time the 'taken together test' from the Communications Act 2003 had been applied, where Ofcom assessed provision of programme forms across the public service broadcasting networks, rather than within a single network or channel (Brown 2005: 10). Furthermore, the report proposes changes to ITV's regional programming, striking at one of the original founding principles of commercial television in the UK. In particular, the report argues for a reduction in ITV1's obligations for non-news regional programming, arguing that 'it is better to move to a more realistic and sustainable approach [to regional programming] now, and to require ITV1 to commission increased levels of high-value network production from the regions, rather than to preserve low-budget regional programming which is not as highly valued by audiences' (Ofcom 2005: 14).

In its proposals for broadcasting more generally and ITV specifically, Ofcom's Phase 3 Report is clearly inflected with the rhetoric of the Peacock Report, particularly in its arguments for the need to expand and increase competition in the broadcasting marketplace. Yet Ofcom does not simply conceive of broadcasting in commercial terms, and its broader remit to further the interests of citizens *and* consumers reflects the understanding of broadcasting as a social responsibility that has inflected the entire history of ITV over the past 50 years. The role that ITV will have in the future in fulfilling this responsibility, however, is open for debate. In the very title of its Phase 3 Report, *Competition for Quality*, Ofcom hits on an argument that has been present from the early 1950s and formed the foundations of ITV – that competition can enable the provision of quality programming. The competition of a multi-channel digital broadcasting landscape, however, is a far cry from what was envisaged when ITV first broke the BBC's monopoly in 1955. Yet the question still remains as to whether a commercially funded, regionally structured broadcaster can function as an effective and viable public service broadcaster. In an increasingly competitive and *digital* future, it seems as if Ofcom's answer might be a qualified 'no'.

Bibliography

Annan, Lord (Chair) (1977) *Report of the Committee on the Future of Broadcasting* [1974], Cmd 6753. London: HMSO.

Beveridge, Lord (Chair) (1951) *Report of the Broadcasting Committee, 1949*, Cmd 8117. London: HMSO.

Bonner, P. (with Aston, L.) (1998) *Independent Television in Britain, Volume 5, ITV and IBA, 1981–92: The Old Relationship Changes.* London: Macmillan.

Briggs, A. (1995) *The History of Broadcasting in the United Kingdom, Volume 5, Competition.* Oxford: Oxford University Press.

Brown, M. (2005) A clerical error? *Guardian*, 7 March.

Brown, M. and Martinson, J. (2005) Warming to a shotgun wedding, *Guardian*, 7 February.

Caughie, J. (2000) *Television Drama: Realism, Modernism, and British Culture.* Oxford: Oxford University Press.

Crisell, A. (1997) *An Introductory History of British Broadcasting.* London: Routledge.

Curran, J. and Seaton, J. (1997) *Power Without Responsibility: The Press and Broadcasting in Britain.* London: Routledge.

Darlow, M. (2004) *Independents Struggle: The Programme Makers Who Took on the TV Establishment.* London: Quartet Books.

Goldie, G.W. (1977) *Facing the Nation: Television and Politics 1936–76*. London: Bodley Head.

Goodwin, P. (1998) *Television under the Tories: Broadcasting Policy 1979–1997*. London: British Film Institute.

Hand, C. (2003) *Television Ownership in Britain and the Coming of ITV: What do the Statistics Show?* www.rhul.ac.uk/Media-Arts/staff/Television%20Owenership.pdf (accessed 10 June 2004).

Horsman, M. (1999) Tomorrow's world, *Guardian*, 29 November.

Jenkins, C. (1961) *Power Behind the Screen: Ownership, Control and Motivation in British Commercial Television*. London: MacGibbon & Kee.

MacDonald, B. (1994) *Broadcasting in the United Kingdom: A Guide to Information Sources*, 2nd revised edition. London: Mansell.

Medhurst, J. (2002) 'Servant of Two Tongues': the demise of TWW, *Llafur: Welsh Labour History*, October.

Milland, J. (2004) Courting Malvolio: The Background to the Pilkington Committee on Broadcasting, 1960–62, *Contemporary British History*, 18(2): 76–102.

Milmo, D (2002) £2.6bn ITV merger agreed, *Guardian*, 16 October.

Office of Communications (Ofcom) (2005) *Ofcom Review of Public Service Television Broadcasting Phase 3 – Competition for Quality*, 8 February, www.ofcom.org.uk/consult/condocs/psb3/psb3.pdf (accessed 14 March 2005).

Peacock, Alan (Chair) (1986) *Report of the Committee on Financing the BBC*, Cmd 9824. London: HMSO.

Pilkington, H. (Chair) (1962) *Report of the Committee on Broadcasting, 1960*, Cmd 1753. London: HMSO.

Sendall, B. (1982) *Independent Television in Britain: Volume 1, Origin and Foundation, 1946–62*. London: Macmillan.

Sendall, B. (1983) *Independent Television in Britain: Volume 2, Expansion and Change, 1958–68*. London: Macmillan.

Smith, A. (ed.) (1974) *British Broadcasting*. Newton Abbot: David & Charles.

Turnock, R. (forthcoming) *Television and Consumer Culture: Britain and the Transformation of Modernity*. London: I.B. Tauris.

Wilson, H.H. (1961) *Pressure Group: The Campaign for Commercial Television*. London: Secker & Warburg.

Notes

1 The timeline at the end of this book offers a chronology of the dates of the various Acts of Parliament and the institutional/regulatory changes (such as franchise renewals) over ITV's history.

2 As Milland (2004) points out, the Committee was necessary because

ITV was due to expire in 1964 (a condition made in the Television Act 1954 to keep the opposition to ITV quiet), and the BBC charter was up for renewal in 1962.

3 Over the 1960s, 1970s and 1980s the precise nature and amount of the levy (whether on profits or revenue, for example) was subject to change.

4 The allocation of TWW's contract for Wales to a new programme company HTV can also be seen as part of the ITA's concern that its programme contracts should be more regionally representative after HTV had made an issue in their application of the fact that TWW had its offices in London (see Medhurst 2002).

5 The ITA was replaced by the Independent Broadcasting Authority (IBA), to take regulatory responsibility for the start of commercial radio in the UK, under the legislation of the Sound Broadcasting Act 1972.

6 The fourth channel covered all of the UK except Wales, which was allocated a separate fourth channel with a substantial number of Welsh language programmes regulated by the Welsh Fourth Channel Authority, leading to the establishment of S4C. The Bill also established the independent Broadcasting Complaints Commission.

7 ITV's breakfast time broadcasting was contracted to a single company responsible for broadcasting in this slot across the network, and initially awarded to TV-am. The concern in the 1968 contract renewals that the programme companies be regionally representative was echoed in the insistence that ATV base itself more firmly within the Midlands region, and the company was restructured as Central Independent Television.

8 Broadcasting Act 1990, London: HMSO, p. 17. The 'exceptional circumstances' clause was the subject of much debate in Parliament leading up to the passing of the Act (see Bonner 1998: 410–11; Goodwin 1998).

9 In addition, as a consequence of the Broadcasting Act 1990 Channel 4 was required to sell its own advertising (with a financial safety net provided by the Channel 3 licences), although its remit was unchanged.

10 The transmission system, previously the responsibility of the IBA, was privatized, as National Transcommunications Ltd (NTL) became the sole provider of transmission services to the ITV franchises in 1991 (see Bonner 1998: 307–12).

11 See Harrison in this volume for a more detailed discussion of the changing scheduling of ITV's news programmes in the 1990s and 2000s.

12 Broadcasting Act 1996, London: HMSO, pp. 72–4.

13 Carlton and UNM had initially proposed a merger in 1999, and Granada had stepped in to bid for UNM. However, any merger or takeover

would have breached ownership rules, which also prevented Granada from owning UNM's third ITV franchise HTV (Horsman 1999).

14 The Communications Act 2003 removed the regulatory hurdles to a single, merged ITV.

15 The ITV News Channel was initially launched in 2000 as the ITN News Channel, a joint venture between NTL and ITN. However, Carlton and Granada bought out ITN in 2002, and in 2004 ITV plc bought out NTL's remaining shares to make the channel wholly owned by ITV plc. Carlton and Granada were also the main shareholders in ONdigital, the first digital terrestrial television network, launched in 1998. After suffering financial difficulties, and despite rebranding as ITV Digital in 2001, the company went into administration on 27 March 2002, and its licence was allocated to a consortium, including the BBC, which launched the Freeview service on 30 October 2002.

16 Communications Act 2003, www.legislation.hmso.gov.uk/acts/acts2003/20030021.htm (accessed 14 March 2005).

17 See www.ofcom.org.uk/about/sdrp/ (accessed 14 March 2005).

18 At the time of writing, how PSP could operate and be funded is under discussion.

2 IMPORTANCE, SIGNIFICANCE, COST AND VALUE: IS AN ITV CANON POSSIBLE?

John Ellis

What is a canon?

Once there was just television: everyone enjoyed it but nobody thought it had much enduring value. Now there is so much television and it has clearly lasted, so the question of value has become inescapable. It seems we need a canon to sort out the wheat from the chaff, just like they do in literature. But just as television studies feels that it needs such canons, the literary notions are falling into disrepute. The attempts by Harold Bloom to codify the working assumptions of many of his colleagues into an explicit canon met with a storm of criticism about the explicit and implicit criteria he used (Bloom 1994; 2001; 2003).[1] Canons are essentially map-making exercises, charting a field and indicating the points that are worthy of attention. Too cluttered a map, and it becomes useless. Too many details omitted that people think worthy of attention and it becomes controversial and risks not being used at all. So it was with Bloom, criticized for his neglect of non-Western traditions and the literature of the oppressed within the Western tradition. When Bloom produced a sturdy defence of a traditional literary canon, this crystallized a growing feeling that the criteria for literary value were no longer shared by those engaged in the production and promulgation of literature. The criteria of value had multiplied and become more diverse and even irreconcilable under the impact of increasing cultural diversity and wider circulation of literary texts.

Bloom's canon implied a hierarchy of importance, and any such list is immediately seized upon for marketing purposes. The device has proved successful for selling books and magazines and even as the basis for television shows.[2] Such lists have a particular function in a culture that has a minor obsession with hierarchical lists, and ITV's fiftieth anniversary in 2005 will doubtless prompt a flurry of list-making activity. Such lists provide one way of dealing with the superabundance of information and entertainment opportunities in contemporary culture. As a means of selection, any established canon or list will guide the dissemination of texts. The canon will determine what is reprinted and what is not; what is distributed; what is taught; what enters into the common stock of knowledge and reference that we share with particular groups of our fellow humans.

Hovering behind these considerations is the real difficulty of actually getting to see old television programmes. The vagaries of archival survival, plus those of current tastes govern what is easily available. A large but relatively homogenous list of ITV programmes are in current circulation, being sold on DVD or video, and the existing canons or lists powerfully influence the selection of them. They tend towards drama or comedy (there are few documentaries beyond the legendary *World at War* series), and include a high number of cult or nostalgia-inducing programmes like *The Avengers*, *The Prisoner*, and *The Adventures of Robin Hood*. It is scarcely surprising that this should be so.

But when it comes to constructing new canons or even elaborating the existing ones, the problem of archival sources becomes crucial. From the pioneering ITV drama anthology series *Armchair Theatre*, 'Lena oh My Lena' (1960) is comparatively well known as it has appeared on several television history courses since it was re-screened in 1985. However, 'No Tram to Lime Street' (1959), written by Alun Owen, is listed as 'one of the twenty most important missing programmes' (Fiddy 2001). The more distant the date of the creation of a programme, the more important it is to see and re-evaluate its reputation. Unfortunately, the more distant the date, the more likely it is that the programme has ceased to exist. Any attempt at constructing an ITV canon will be at the mercy of this problem of physical survival. No regular editions of the advertising magazine *Jim's Inn* seem to survive, although there were over 250 episodes of 15 minutes between 1957 and 1963. So all I have are uncertain childhood memories to argue why it should be remembered in any way as a signature programme other than the infamous phrase of the Pilkington Report 'the distinction insisted on by the [Television] Act [1954] – between the programme and the advertisement – is blurred; . . . and we conclude that the spirit of the Act would be better served if advertising magazines were prohibited' (Pilkington 1962: 81, 83).

Canons become self-fulfilling prophecies as they consign most texts to the hinterland of critical neglect, dwindling market value and lack of preservation, whilst promoting others to a continued prominence. Canons, then, can spur rediscovery of hitherto neglected texts or activities, where those texts continue to exist. For canons, unfortunately, can imply destruction of material that, in the eyes of those running archives, is not only excluded from current canons but could not conceivably find their way into any that future generations might construct. So the construction of a canon for ITV would carry some grave responsibilities.

At best, this produces (or enforces) a common inheritance, summed up by the assumption that all the *Desert Island Discs*' castaways have to choose one book 'other than the Bible or Shakespeare' because those two books form the core of 'our' inheritance. At one level, of course they do: their styles and references still pervade much of British society's formal linguistic discourse. But on another level, why would a convinced atheist like Jonathan Miller or someone with two other religious traditions in her background like Meera Syal ever dream of taking the Bible with them? Such are the problems of creating canons. They make explicit consensual cultural assumptions, and in doing so render them more open to challenge. At worst, of course, the choices made can be deliberately tendentious, putting in things just to get a reaction, and leaving out the work of writers who have somehow offended the compiler of the canon, either personally or morally.

Television canons

The television industry and television studies have both recently embarked on a voyage of canon building. They usually base themselves on some kind of a survey, using memory as the only viable way of gathering data. The trade magazine *Broadcast* in July 2004 tried to establish the 50 most influential television shows, while in the same year Glen Creeber (2004) edited a collection of essays entitled *Fifty Key Television Shows*. Neither of these lists specifically addressed ITV, but the same ITV titles tend to recur: *Coronation Street*, *Blind Date*, *The Prisoner*, *World in Action*, *Prime Suspect*. Both lists make no formal distinction between the major genres of television, beyond providing a general spread. In 2000, the British Film Institute (BFI) undertook a poll to establish the 100 best television programmes, which was based on genre distinctions. As the then BFI Director, John Teckman, outlined it, this made some pretty bold assumptions:

> we sent voting booklets to the professional experts – programme makers, actors, technicians, executives, critics, academics – altogether some 1,600 members of the television industry UK-wide, each of whom was invited to make up to 30 choices across six genre categories (with at least three votes per category): Comedy & variety; Single drama; Drama series & serials; Factual; Children's & youth; Lifestyle & light entertainment. News and sport were omitted from this poll at the outset (is it the event itself, rather than the coverage, which is most important?). We also excluded classic shows which were wiped or discarded (or broadcast live and not recorded in the first place), so that every programme in the BFI TV 100 still exists and can be viewed today. (Teckman 2000)

Leaving out missing or destroyed programmes was a controversial exercise because many are still remembered. The decision to use explicit genre categories leads to the problem that they have traditionally been given very different cultural weight. The BFI web site is frankly apologetic for having included a genre that it has invented itself from a rather unhappy merger of two different television traditions, 'lifestyle and light entertainment':

> Not only did we want the BFI TV 100 to embrace popular programmes alongside those critically acclaimed, but we also wanted to show that the programmes in this genre are an important record of the ordinary, everyday viewing of millions of people, and serve as increasingly important weapons in the ratings battle. Those that remain in the memory are surely worth celebrating and preserving as they add to our and future generations' understanding of how we live. (Rostron 2000)

The decision to omit news and sport and yet to include the single drama as a separate category is also an indicator of the criteria for cultural value that are being used. The importance of the regularity and 'dailiness' of television is downgraded by omitting two of television's most time-sensitive genres. However controversial it is in execution, the BFI's decision to opt for genre categories does demonstrate the problem of any television canon compared to that of literature. The range of work, of types of text, is far wider than the canonical literary forms of epic, poem, novel and play. Any television canon has to include forms of textuality that the institution of 'the literary' is designed to exclude: ephemeral forms like journalism and reportage; interview and discussion; sketches and gags; and huge series of roughly similar things.

Whilst acknowledging the desire and even need for a canon of ITV programmes, I do not want to construct one here. Rather I will look at ITV and my experience of its history to bring out the problems of any canon construction around television. The nature of television itself would seem to make it impossible to construct a canon of ITV programmes. It would take 35 years round-the-clock viewing to see all of ITV's output again,[3] but on the other hand most of the programmes no longer exist. So a canon has to be constructed largely from memories and received wisdom. I have those memories, from 'Pussy Cat Willum'[4] to *Prime Suspect Six*, but so do many others. What mattered intensely to me was of little or no interest to many others.

The importance of memory and the moment

The importance of memories of the viewing experience of broadcast television poses huge problems for the construction of any canon.

Broadcast television is both huge and intimate. The tide of programming rolls on, yet everyone has particular series and moments that have become a special part of their lives. These consist of the intersection of programmes and lived experience, and so would mean little as programmes to succeeding generations. This is most clear with children's programmes: there is a *Tiswas* generation and an Ant and Dec generation, and even a *Twizzle* generation. Each show is simply quaint to succeeding generations for whom it was not central (either as children or as parents of those children). Similarly, regional programmes with their affirmation of locality, accent and preoccupations will be intensely important to some and unknown to others. Even the choice of channels was at one time a deciding factor, as households late to television tended to shun ITV in favour of BBC out of a sense of commitment to civilized, non-Americanized, cultural values. This was a pity since they missed the high cultural treats that ITV's public service requirements forced it to produce, like Sunday afternoon's *Tempo* (1961–7) from ATV.

My personal ITV canon would include early quiz shows like *Double Your Money*; the first season of *Hill Street Blues* shown out of order late at night; despised advertorial programmes like *Jim's Inn*; as well as more acclaimed programming like *Cracker*, *The Avengers*, *World at War*, and *Morecambe and Wise*. The double act of Morecambe and Wise worked just as well, and arguable better, for the BBC, and this, incidentally, indicates one of the perils of canon building on the basis of a single channel. My canon would be richly nostalgic about comedy series like *Mrs Thursday* (1966–7) where Kathleen Harrison's charwoman had inherited a property company that she ran (through a frontman) with considerable business nous; or *Do Not Adjust Your Set* (1967–9), the best of the pre-Python series that teamed Palin, Jones and Idle with David Jason and Denise Coffey. It would exclude genres that do not interest me much, like sport, and the soap opera *Coronation Street*, which has never drawn me in particularly. My personal ITV canon is made up, like anyone else's, of memories and programmes, not of programmes alone. I can remember my father's keen interest in *Jim's Inn*, his pleasure at being able to spot how television was 'trying to pull a fast one', the same television that had given him the straightforward pleasure of those early game shows. I can remember the revelation that was *Hill Street*, even in the strange treatment it received in the schedules at the time. I can remember encountering a whole new world of music and style in *Oh Boy!* and *Ready Steady Go*, and family enjoyment of *Morecambe and Wise*. My personal canon emerges from how television intersected with my life.

The cultural importance of television lies in the sum of these personal experiences.[5] The real significance of television in popular culture is its role in everyday life, providing entertainment and solace, information and enlightenment, togetherness both real and imaginary, boredom, irritation and outrage. Sometimes it can be used to provide dramatic illustrations of the assumptions of historical moments that have now gone. Popular shows embed those assumptions, both social and generational. They made *Highway*, a religious music series with Harry Secombe, or *Love Thy Neighbour* (1972–76), a sitcom that pitched ill-matched black and white neighbours against each other, into the programmes that they were. But personal importance is more than this: it is what gave a brief and vivid social life to texts that nowadays seem inert.

Television in this perspective is not a series of portrayals of 'us' (or 'them' or 'our society') but a universe of meanings and instant connections to others. It emerges in the shared references to Morecambe and Wise jokes, or speculations about the attractions of Roger Moore as *The Saint* or the exact nature of the relationship between Hughie Green and Monica.[6] It is this feeling of connection with television that a canon should seek to address. It is equally something that any list or catalogue will fail to capture unless it is generationally based. The programmes are not the 'best' programmes by any objective criteria of aesthetic or technical merit, and they are often tedious to viewers who did not experience them in their period of contemporaneity. Yet they have a cultural importance because they were part of that shared moment of contemporaneity. Their status in this respect is little different from that of the Bible or Shakespeare.

As the original moment of transmission recedes, the relationship between programmes and time becomes more complex. Key series are lost to the archive and so to rediscovery like most of the 900 episodes of the ITV soap *Emergency Ward Ten* (1955–57), which no longer exist. Those that do exist can be rediscovered and re-evaluated. Telefantasy of the 1960s, like *The Avengers,* has been explored by a generation of scholars who were not even born when the shows went out, let alone impressionable teenagers comparing the allures of Honor Blackman and Diana Rigg. Such scholars are rediscovering and re-evaluating these programmes as texts, no longer firmly embedded in their moment of transmission as they always will be for me. Their relation to the effects of Blackman and Rigg are not those of impressionable teenagers like I was. The dimension of sexuality is altogether more coolly addressed. The moment of transmission is itself the object of study, but a difficult object as so much of it is extra-textual, to be found in contemporary popular references. It is often a more viable form of study to take the texts as free-standing, in the same way any present-day viewer would do on coming upon them for the first time.

There is, therefore, a tension in the study of television between an historically based and a text-based study. Such a tension exists for literary criticism as well, but it is more pronounced in relation to television. The distinguishing feature for television is the ephemeral nature of the medium in the most positive sense of that word. Television programmes were (and often still are) made for a particular moment in time and for a huge audience. The element of the synchronic in their meaning systems is correspondingly important, and a large amount of television exists primarily for its synchronicity. That is why so few editions of key shows like *Opportunity Knocks*, *Thank Your Lucky Stars* or *Sunday Night at the London Palladium* exist any more, let alone less remembered works like the sci-fi series *Out of This World*.[7] So many programmes were discarded because they were perceived at the time to have been used up by their initial moment of synchronicity, their brief evening of blanket fame. That moment endures in the memory of individuals and the heritage of the society that evolved from that moment. So an ITV canon based on the revaluation of texts for their durability alone would be a misguided project as it would emphasize genres and styles from very specific parts of the wide ITV output.[8] 'Worth watching now' is a treacherous criterion of value in relation to television.

Typicality and the canon

One way of dealing with this problem would be to create a canon based to a considerable degree on the principle of including those programmes that best summarize the character of ITV. Shows do not sum up a whole channel but they can indicate one aspect of its character at a particular time. *News at Ten*, *World of Sport* and *Opportunity Knocks* would all appear quite naturally, as would *Emergency Ward Ten*. This may in the long term be a solution, but for the moment it runs up against two problems. First there is an ongoing polemic about the nature and future of ITV; and second there has been very little work directed towards summarizing the 'nature' of a channel, especially one established and run for many years on the principle of a diverse schedule with substantial public service values. At the time of ITV's fiftieth anniversary, these two issues are profoundly intertwined. For instance David Plowright, formerly Programme Controller, Managing Director, and Chair of Granada, commented on 13 October 2003, 'ITV used to be an industry for programme production but has changed out of all recognition to one about profits above all else' (*Guardian*, 13 October 2003, cf Darlow 2004: 603). The occasion was the merger of Granada and Carlton, which brought together ITV in England and Wales (apart from the Channel Islands) into one company that then went on to seek a reduction in its public service commitments from the new regulator, Ofcom. The commitments that ITV sought to reduce include religious programming, regional programming and the principle of a mixed and balanced schedule in peak time. This went along with an increasing investment in repeatable series drama and the launch in 2004 of the drama-based free-to-air digital channel ITV3.

So is it possible to characterize ITV as an entity and to deduce from that the list of programmes that most aptly summarize its nature at any given point? Helen Wheatley (2003: 79) offers a sketch of a channel where 'In short, the entertainment culture on ITV of the 1950s and early 1960s gave way to a journalistic culture in the later 1960s and 1970s.' To this could be added a decisive shift towards original drama in the 1990s. But this sketch might be more perception than reality, the result of the preoccupations of discourses around the channel as much as the real pattern of its output. These characteristics are defined in relation to the activities of other channels, so the perception that ITV had an early entertainment bias might be the result of the character of the entertainment that it offered rather than the amount of it compared to the BBC. The shift towards UK-originated drama in the 1990s, which was the subject of big public announcements, can similarly be seen as a response to increasing competition, replacing feature films (which were becoming prohibitively expensive) with 90-minute drama, which had the added advantage of creating a highly saleable asset for the future. Similarly the perception of a journalistic culture might be a reflection of regulatory concerns along with the preoccupations and background of senior management[9] rather than the nature of programming. Early ITV seems to have resorted to light magazine formats as a way of filling hours. The later 1960s saw the (regulator-driven) entrenchment of flagship current affairs and the 30-minute *News at Ten*, but a retrenchment in magazine programming. So there might well have been journalists in charge, but a less journalistic (but more visible) emphasis in the overall output.

Some programmes do still impose themselves as summarizing the channel in particular phases of its development. Wrestling proved to be a long-running feature of ITV. Starting with the national finals from the Caledonian Baths on 14 December 1955, it was originally a mid-evening entertainment at 8.30 p.m. It then settled into a tenancy on Saturday afternoons for an hour or so, with commentary by Kent Walton. Through the 1960s it was a key factor in forming ITV's working-class identity. Such signature shows are ones that recur, which have long runs and have a prominent place in the schedule. *Coronation Street* remains a constant through almost the whole half-century of ITV's history to 2005. *The Bill* has been around since 1984, but in varying formats: sometimes a half-hour police soap, sometimes an hour self-contained narrative, sometimes a mixture of the two. *Who Wants to be a Millionaire?* seems to inherit the mantle of early primetime quiz shows and represents the resurrection of the genre from a marginal role on ITV. Yet when the show became a huge ratings success for a few months, some argued that *Millionaire* was a signature show for ITV because it summarized a change in the channel's direction. It seemed to indicate that ITV was moving away from expensive and significant work like *Inspector Morse* or *Winston Churchill the Wilderness Years* or even *Minder*, and towards the lightweight and ephemeral. Such polemics do not compare like with like, however. They imply that resources have moved away from the list of 'good' programmes to those disdained by the speaker. In fact, resources in the early evening slots between 7.00 p.m. and 9.00 p.m. have been fairly consistently applied to programmes like *Millionaire*. The early quiz shows like *Take Your Pick* gave way to *Celebrity Squares* and *Sale of the Century* in the 1970s and *Play Your Cards Right* in the 1980s. After a relatively brief spell of docu-soaps and light documentary like *Airport* and the *From Hell* series (Drivers, Holidays and so on), ITV rediscovered the ratings potential of that rare thing, a good game show format in *Millionaire*. It is now supplemented by the challenge reality format of *I'm a Celebrity Get Me Out of Here*. There is a genre shift in this series of successive signature shows, but they have a great deal in common as well. Ordinary events and skills are constructed into a challenge in the course of which there are opportunities for plenty of good-natured joshing and teasing as well as tension and suspense.

Generalizations about ITV's character and its signature shows, necessary though they are, will be substantiated only when research is carried out to compare the balance of genres across output over time with the shifting public characterizations (the brand image) of ITV. Until then, the question 'is ITV remotely the same channel as it was in the 1960s?' can be answered only anecdotally and polemically.

Polemical and problematic canons

Polemical list-making intends to send a message to those currently running the television industry.[10] So *Broadcast*'s list of 'TV's 50 most influential shows' includes *World In Action* (1963–98):

> 'always a thorn in the side of the powers-that-be – whether state or private business', says [Roger] Graef. 'It was full of bravery and bravado – often a wake-up call for outrages and scandals, and it spoke in clear and vivid terms to the whole nation. It was tabloid telly at its best'. Its axing in 1998 caused a massive row – evidence of its credentials.[11]

Projected in this commentary is a clear vision of what ITV used to be and is no more: a channel that, though funded by commercials, was not afraid to use its public service role to take on all comers. It did so in terms that were readily accessible to the nation as a whole. The tone of regret at the passing of this ITV is unmistakable.

Polemics have their uses in reminding us of neglected parts of ITV's heritage, particularly that of the free-standing single programme. This is demonstrated in concerns expressed by many of those canvassed for the BFI's list of 100 best television programmes. The extensiveness and ubiquity of broadcast television make the definition of the size of entry to be selected almost impossible. Some single programmes stand out. So should an ITV canon include 'Death on the Rock?' It was not a free-standing programme but a particular edition of Thames' *This Week* series. Yet it is a notorious programme and hugely influential in the history of ITV and its relations with the government. It demonstrated in a painstaking manner how British SAS men had in effect assassinated three members of an IRA active service unit in Gibraltar. The scandal that ensued is often put forward as the reason why Thames lost its licence for the ITV London weekday franchise, if only because it took up so much senior executive time that the bid for franchise renewal was fatally flawed. However, formally and aesthetically 'Death on the Rock' was, deliberately, no way exceptional at the time and is even less so in retrospect. So its inclusion or exclusion from any ITV canon would require a closely reasoned explanation.

The size of different programme concepts is one of the most frequent problems. It seems impossible to compare the 40 years of *Coronation Street* with a single drama like *The Naked Civil Servant*, Jack Gold's 1975 film for Thames. Gold's film has somehow become the totemic example of the long tradition of single dramas that has virtually died out on British television as a whole, rather than just ITV. Again, how is it possible to compare a single documentary like Frank Cvitanovich's wordless, celebratory *Victoria Park* (1982) with long-running but ever-changing series like *World in Action* (current affairs), *Survival* (nature) or *Disappearing World* (anthropology)? And what is meant by including such portmanteau series when individual films within them took very different approaches? *World in Action* experimented with observational documentary in the late 1960s, most notably in Northern Ireland at the start of the Troubles. For *Disappearing World*, 'Some Women of Marrakech' (1976) was probably the first British film to have been made entirely by women; Mike Grigsby's 'Eskimos of Pond Inlet' (1975) was an outstanding attempt to let the subjects structure the film for themselves. Any canon that included these would have a polemical edge, as they would be hard to conceive as productions for ITV in 2005.

Perhaps programmes are the wrong category for a canon anyway. One powerful means of identifying ITV at any one moment is by its faces rather than the shows in which they appear. Recent on-screen promotion has exploited this with a series of 'stings', which simply consist of relaxed stars, out of role, looking into camera. So ITV is at the time of writing the channel of Ross Kemp and David Jason.[12] ITV has been the channel of Bruce Forsyth, Jonathan Routh, Jeremy Beadle, Bob Monkhouse, Russ Conway, Liberace, Ted Rogers, Les Dawson, Tommy Cooper and Benny Hill. It is more recently the channel of Amanda Burton and Tamsin Outhwaite. It has been the channel of Little and Large, Hale and Pace, Mike and Bernie Winters and all those double acts after whom Ant and Dec seem a positive relief. It teamed Dennis Waterman with John Thaw and then with George Cole. It kept giving us Leo McKern as *Rumpole of the Bailey*. It was equally the channel of Reginald Bosanquet and Andrew Gardner, Anna Ford and Pamela Armstrong, Sandy Gall, Michael Nicholson and the inimitable Trevor Macdonald on the news. Current affairs used Brian Connell, Brian Walden, David Frost, John Pilger and Roland Rat. It was the channel of Violet Carson and Noele Gordon presiding over their soaps; Diana Dors and Trisha Goddard over chat; Fanny Craddock (and Johnnie of course) over the kitchen; Dickie Davis and Jimmy Hill over the world of sport; Cilla Black over dating; Matthew Kelly over amateur nights. It gave us Hughie Green and Chris Tarrant, and Mark McManus as the original *Taggart*. It was also the channel that brought out the grotesqueries of on-screen celebrity in the political satire *Spitting Image* (1984–96) and its latex puppets.

Implied in all these considerations is the idea that any canon of ITV programmes would be one of its own productions. But ITV has also been a channel of imported programming: from the beginning it gave us *The Lucy Show*; it also treated us to *Rich Man, Poor Man*, *Hawaii Five-O* and the *A-Team*. These are canonical shows, but in whose canon should they appear? One driven by the synchronic concerns of the contemporary audience would have to include them; one more focused on the question of enduring texts should exclude them from a canon of British television, preferring instead to include them in a text-oriented canon of US television.

Things don't look the same

The greatest problem of constructing any canon is the rapid change in the nature of programming and the resources that programme-makers could command. As John Caughie (2000: 13) says: '"old television" presents itself like the family album, inviting us to gather round and be amused by the way we once were' and this attitude extends not only to differences in costume, hair length, attitudes and behaviour, but also because the programmes are materially different.

In the beginning ITV was a medium of standard frame, black-and-white mono-sound programmes with analogue transmission on 405 lines. It is currently moving towards widescreen high-definition colour stereo or surroundsound digital transmission. The technological basis of programme-making has changed so that the current makers of the cheapest programming now have resources for sound and image creation and manipulation that were not available to the makers of even the most expensive programmes in the first 25 years of ITV's history. Programmes from that first era have different production values, different pace and different performances. This presents a problem for the creation of any canon. These programmes seem at first sight poorer than their contemporary equivalents. It is even difficult to compare series shot on film like *The Adventures of Robin Hood* (1955–59) or with what were, at the time, high production values like *Bouquet of Barbed Wire* (1976) with their later equivalents like *Cadfael* (1994–99) or *Cold Feet* (1997–2001). Or take the examples of *Midsomer Murders* (1997–) and *Inspector Morse* (1987–). These series have similar visual qualities to each other. They both feel very different from *Sergeant Cork* (1963–66) and *Gideon's Way* (1964–65). Yet all these four detective series, with differing contemporary production values, belong to the same drama niche. They all occupy the prestige end of long series production, destined for key schedule slots, traditionally 9 p.m., and pulling in a wide audience with a middle-class core.

The history of ITV has seen subtle changes in the level of production values, in the range of locations, sophistication of camerawork, modulation of performance, speed of cutting and extent of post-production (especially sound design), so that programmes from various periods feel very different to us viewing them now. The changes are most marked in the use of video. The early years of ITV saw the extensive use of studios recording onto video, using limited editing even for prestige drama. Film was used only for those series that had obvious international sale potential. Changes in the cost and potential of film technology meant that during the late 1960s and through the 1970s, drama production moved across to 16 mm film, a medium that documentary had been using for some time. But most ITV productions from sitcoms to light entertainment remained on video. Video technology became more miniaturized and location-friendly in the 1980s, so that documentary in particular adopted it to take advantage of the longer shooting time and more unobtrusive access that it seemed to promise. In other words, production technology and hence what has been available and affordable has changed hugely in ITV's history.

Yet if we are able to look beyond the production values, the programmes remain remarkably similar. What now looks 'quaint' or 'cheap' was not so when it enthralled contemporary audiences. And ITV in 2005 still maintained the same hierarchy of production costs as 50 years before. *Coronation Street* has remained a half-hour early evening soap. It shows a more marked evolution in character and plot than in production values. There are still sitcoms, short and long drama series, prestige and low-cost drama, news, current affairs, quiz shows, factual programmes, spot advertisements and the rest on ITV. It is recognizably the same phenomenon: a linear broadcast television channel, carrying the typical productions of the medium. So one of the challenges in creating any canon is to take account of the fluctuations in production values so as to be sure of comparing like with like. This issue has scarcely been explored, yet is particularly marked in the genre of television drama. The following case study demonstrates that in this area, a sea change took place in the level of resources that drama could command at the end of the 1970s.

The case of drama production values

There appears to have been a fairly abrupt transition in production values at the end of the 1970s. Suddenly the top range of productions was being allocated proportionately greater resources than before, or, to put it another way, the prestige output began to look really expensive. This fits well with other periodizations of broadcasting, both the model of scarcity/availability/plenty that I put forward in *Seeing Things* (Ellis 2000) and that of the development of televisuality explored by Caldwell (1995). Proof can be found in the minutes of a confidential discussion that took place within ITV at that period. In July 1979, the Independent Broadcasting Authority, the regulatory body for ITV, called together senior executives for a 'consultation' in St Andrews. The detailed minutes survive in the BFI library. This was something of a crisis meeting. The IBA was concerned that ITV drama was failing to innovate, and tended to blame the decline of the single drama. The ITV executives were concerned about escalating costs, and were on the brink of what turned out to be the most damaging of their many labour disputes, which blacked out the channel for a total of ten weeks in September and October 1979 (Darlow 2004: 209, 234–5).

In a paper for this meeting, David Plowright, Granada's Managing Director, produced a historic comparison of costs for drama.[13] The minutes report him as saying that at that time on 16 mm film 'above the line budgets hovered around £100–150,000 an hour direct for 60-minute films, plays or series as against £50,000 all studio and £60, 000 for combination tape and film'.[14] He then compared these figures with a range of named examples from the end of 1959 and the beginning of 1960:

£3,100: *Knight Errant* (1959, 1960), a 55-minute high range drama for mid-evening with a variety of (studio-constructed) locations.

£2,100: *Skyport* (1959–60), a 30-minute series of stories set in an airport.

£3,500: *Family Solicitor* (1961), an ambitious, prestige 55-minute drama based on legal stories passing through the precinct of a busy solicitor's firm.

£1,800: *Biggles* (1960), a 30-minute series primarily for children shown in the early evening.

£1,350: *Coronation Street* (1960–), a half-hour soap opera that still continues at the time of writing.

Plowright further asserted that he 'suspects' *Armchair Theatre* cost around £4,000 per hour. He then added generalized figures for 1975, four years before the meeting, to illustrate his argument that a sudden inflation in costs was taking place in the late 1970s.

The most immediately remarkable thing to contemporary eyes is the relatively narrow range of costs he cites for 1959/60. The prestige one-off drama series *Armchair Theatre* cost only three times as much as the soap *Coronation Street* at the turn of the 1960s. A prestige drama series episode currently costs five or six times the cost of *Coronation Street*, and a single drama would be made more like a cinema film with a considerably larger budget. So it is immediately clear that the range of available budgets for producers has substantially increased.

However, such figures as Plowright's do come with certain caveats. First they are the product of what can be called 'producer's rule of thumb'. Levels of price within the market at any one time are necessary working knowledge for a producer, and they should be able to identify with considerable accuracy the budget range of any given production that they see. Plowright is simply giving these guideline figures and comparing to a moment that was probably vivid in his mind: the early years of Granada when he entered television management as head of Granada's local news in 1959. Thus we can be confident that the illustrative figures have a high degree of accuracy. The only moment where he becomes elusive is the cost of *Brideshead Revisited*, a lavish filmed drama series in production at that moment and already regarded a something of a financial folly (see Darlow 2004: 302–3).

Second, he uses the phrase 'above the line' to indicate the nature of the figures given. These are the amounts expended by Granada specifically on those productions. This was the standard form of accounting within the television industry at the time, a form that suited the vertically integrated structure that combined production and broadcasting into one organization.[15] So they do not include general Granada expenditure on its core operation: the salaries of staff producers, the hire of Granada studios, the background legal or publicity staff and so on.[16]

Plowright's figures show that a dramatic change in the cost of television drama took place towards the end of the 1970s. In his presentation, he attributes it to the increasing use of 16 mm film as the standard format rather than studio-oriented video, often transmitted live or 'done as live' onto videotape. The adoption of 16 mm film extended the physical reach of television drama productions into real locations. Video at that time was not the portable format that it became in the 1980s, so effectively producers had the choice between two production routes: studio/video or location/film. Frequently, productions would mix the two, producing what today seems a rather strange unevenness of texture.

For a number of reasons, drama production moved decisively towards film in the late 1970s. This also initiated a marked rise in production values, the amounts expended on the look, feel and atmosphere of a drama. During the late 1970s studio production was abandoned for all but routine drama production. It had been the only affordable and viable format in the late 1950s and early 1960s until the introduction of 16 mm film. And as late as 1971, studio production was still the natural choice for a prestige series like *Upstairs Downstairs,* which ran until 1975.

By the mid-1980s, a series like *Upstairs Downstairs* would have been shot on film, as were ITV series like the prestige *The Jewel in the Crown* (1984) or the quality crime series *Widows* (1983). It would have produced the look and feel that audiences by that time would have expected, not least because of expectations created by increasing production values in commercials and the presence of US mini-series on UK screens. Drama in the 1980s both looked very different and cost a lot more than 10 years before. This sea-change in the costs of television drama is clearly illustrated by Plowright's figures, even when (as is necessary) they are adjusted for inflation.

The series *Knight Errant* in 1959–60 cost £3,100 for a 55-minute episode. As such it represents the higher end of series drama, as its premise clearly required a greater variety of sets than *Skyport,* and it was scheduled as mid-evening peak viewing as opposed to the early evening *Biggles.* These figures can now be compared with Plowright's (1979) claims that in 1979 'budgets hover around £100 to £150 thousand an hour direct for 60 minute films, plays or serials' but that in 1970–75 the 'above the line costs of series was £12,000 to 20,000'. Before completing the comparison, the figures have to be inflation adjusted, as the 1970s in particular saw significant inflation.[17] As Table 2.1 shows, the inflation adjusted above the line cost of *Knight Errant* in 1959 was the equivalent of more than half that of an average drama in 1975. But only 4 years later the real, inflation adjusted cost of such drama had quadrupled. The average above the line cost of an hour's drama in 1975 would have bought only 15 minutes worth just 4 years later. The cost of an hour's drama in 1979, however, would buy almost 45 minutes of drama at 2003 above-the-line prices.

Table 2.1 Inflation-adjusted cost as percentage of equivalent programme

	1959	1975	1979	2004
	Knight Errant	Plowright's estimated equivalent programme	Plowright's estimated equivalent programme	Author's estimated equivalent programme
1959	**£3,100**			
1975	£8,467	**£15,000**		
1979	£14,037	£29,327	**£125,000**	
2003	£43,649	£91,190	£388,687	**£500,000**
Knight Errant	100%	56%	11%	8.7%

It is clear that drama production costs grew at a faster rate in the period 1975–80 than at any time before or since. This was the result of two processes taking place simultaneously, only one of which was really visible at the time. Any observer in the period would have pointed to the difficult political and economic problems of the time, which were eventually and brutally resolved by the Thatcher government of the 1980s. Throughout the 1970s an old-fashioned management culture had confronted labour unions of growing strength. Successive governments had failed to produce a working compromise between the two, especially as management refused to modernize and unions refused to contemplate political rather than economic demands. The result was an escalating series of strikes for better wages and conditions. ITV was particularly vulnerable to such strikes, and was well known for its chronic labour problems. Its management caved in to union demands because of a number of strikes that blacked out the channel for weeks at a time, and it simply increased wages and overtime payments. The year 1979 represents an all-time high for production costs, and is the real reason for the IBA's summit.

These stormy labour relations effectively mask a second process: the increasing sophistication of television drama at the more expensive end of the scale. It is not just that ITV was paying inflated wages to certain classes of technician in order to stay on air. It is also that television drama was increasing in its range and ambition during the period. The comparison with 2003 prices shows that a quantum leap occurred at the end of the 1970s at the higher end of drama costs. This is supported by Plowright's costing for a 1960 episode of *Coronation Street*. At £1,350 per episode, it cost 43 per cent of an episode of *Knight Errant*. This, adjusted for inflation, is £19,000 at 2003 prices. Above the line costs of an episode of *Coronation Street* today would be something like £90,000. So the purchasing power of the 1959 *Coronation Street* budget would still purchase 21 per cent of an episode today, whereas in series drama, *Knight Errant's* hourly budget would buy just 8.7 per cent of an episode of an equivalent series in a similar slot today. The difference here is that *Coronation Street* has consistently been a studio-based multi-camera production, first live from indoors and then on video from a complex of standing sets. It would appear, then, that the changes in production values were more far-reaching for middle and top-range drama than for the more explicitly factory or studio-based products like soaps. To put it simply, soaps cost 4.7 times as much as they did in 1959, but substantial peaktime drama series cost 11.5 times as much.

So although a redistribution of costs away from wages has occurred during the 1980s and 1990s,[18] it would be reasonable to say that the scale of costs is comparable between 1979 and the present, and that the period 1959–75 represents a different era of television drama production. This second era was reached through a rapid and destabilizing transition in the late 1970s, the extent of which was masked both by in-house accounting methods and by the prevailing national process of intense labour relations conflicts.

This second era of production is aptly named 'televisuality' by Caldwell (1995). It was a period when the look of a television programme became more important. He describes the 1980s as a period when there developed a movie-like attitude to the *mise-en-scène* of television, expending more time and money on creating a distinct 'look' for each drama series, as well as on props, location and the sense of visual luxuriance. As video technology developed decisively in the 1980s into a much more flexible tool, both on location and in post-production, it too became a tool for creating more visually ambitious work at all levels in the television system.

As a result, drama from pre-1975 now feels very distant. To the uninformed observer, it simply looks 'cheap' or 'tacky'. This is the case with an episode of the well-resourced and successful ITV series drama *The Power Game* (1965–66) that I was able to revisit recently. It has an utterly different look to its equivalent contemporary drama, like the BBC's *Spooks*, but I remember watching it in 1966 with great intensity and enjoyment. For a 13 year old, it seemed to uncover important facts about the adult world, and it seemed utterly modern and convincing. The distinctive look and atmosphere is the result of a different prevalent aesthetic allied to a different economics. Actors and lines predominate over action and mood. The *mise-en-scène* sometimes gives the feeling that the actors have waited for the equipment to be ready before pitching into a scene. This is balanced by a marked tendency to write scenes as though the audience were joining them half way through the action. The scenes tend to be played long, as the scripting concentrates as much into single locations and time spans as possible, leavened by some crucial short inserts and single camera shots. There is a distinct studio acoustic with very little in the way of sound effects.

Nevertheless the ambitious structure is much closer to those of contemporary series drama. This seems to contradict claims that multi-stranded drama is a relatively recent phenomenon and was originated in the US (see for example, Nelson 1997). In the episode 'Persons and papers' shown on 15 February 1966 at 8 p.m., there are four interlocking plot lines, all of which centre on Sir John Wilder, the ruthless managing director of a construction company. Plot one concerns Wilder's decision to bid for the M27 construction contract with another company; plot two, his relationship with his wife and her past affair with Frank Hagedan; plot three, his continuing affair with Susan Weldon at the National Export Board, which has been the subject of a security enquiry; plot four, his continuing efforts to outsmart Sir Caswell Bligh, whose son Kenneth is his number two (a fact nowhere mentioned as we are assumed to know it). Plot three picks up from an earlier episode of the series (again assuming audience knowledge), and does not involve Sir John directly, being a series of scenes between Susan Weldon and two civil servants, both of whom are playing their own power games. Plots one and two collide when Wilder discovers that his only possible partners in the M27 bid have employed none other than Hagedan as their project manager. He then persuades his wife to humiliate Hagedan by breaking definitively with him, whilst he cold-shoulders the unfortunate Susan Weldon. In its structure and its adult, if not cynical, view of human relations, this is strikingly modern. The complexity of plotting compares with that of more recent long-running US dramas like *The Sopranos* or *NYPD Blue*. But as this is the UK and 1966, the production values are entirely different.

The structure of *The Power Game* is very modern, but the look, pace and feel is not, so how might this series be selected for an ITV canon? Any canon of ITV programmes has to negotiate its way around the fact of these obvious differences combined with striking similarities. To be meaningful, comparisons would have to make allowances for the material circumstances of each production. This means taking into account the available resources and budget, and the prevailing aesthetic of the time.

Is a canon possible?

Any canon seeks to compare examples across time, and to abstract particular exemplars of a period from the flow of history. The difficulties with such a process in relation to television are the result of the nature of television itself. The kind of broadcast channel that ITV has been for its first half century has a strong synchronic relationship with its audience. It shares their present moment, and the programmes gain in significance as they reach further into everyday life. So a canon could be created just as meaningfully from ITV faces as it could from ITV's programmes. Yet the programmes endure physically (at least in some cases), and canons can also be constructed on the entirely valid principle of 'I'm a busy person, what *must* I see?' Busy people, as we all are, would be unwilling or unable to see television's most typical product, the series of broadly similar episodes that lasts for weeks, coming at a regular moment in the schedule and hence the everyday lives of its viewers. Beyond this consideration, problems emerge with the often conflicting criteria of the social importance of entertainment as against the aesthetic importance of quality drama. There are also the problems of huge changes in production values during the first 50 years. So television resists canons, unless they are constructed polemically on the principle of 'things aren't as good as they were'. Fortunately, all canons are unstable, subject to rediscoveries, and the re-evaluation of successive generations. If a useful ITV canon is to emerge, it will have to balance the competing influences of personal importance, typicality, historical importance, industry polemic, the nature of broadcasting and changes in the aesthetics of television itself. All this whilst the material to choose from expands by more than 150 hours a week, almost all of which is now archived.

Bibliography

Bloom, H. (1994) *The Western Canon: The Books and School of the Ages*. New York: Harcourt Brace.

Bloom, H. (2001) *How to Read and Why*. New York: Fourth Estate.

Bloom, H. (2003) *Genius: A Mosaic of One Hundred Exemplary Creative Minds*. New York: Warner Books.

Caldwell, J.T. (1995) *Televisuality: Style, Crisis, and Authority in American Television*. New Jersey: Rutgers University Press.

Caughie, J. (2000) *Television Drama: Realism, Modernism, and British Culture*. Oxford: Oxford University Press.

Creeber, G. (2004) *Fifty Key Television Programmes*. London: Hodder Arnold.

Darlow, M. (2004) *Independents Struggle: The Programme Makers Who Took on the TV Establishment*. London: Quartet Books.

Ellis, J. (2000) *Seeing Things: Television in the Age of Uncertainty*. London: I.B. Tauris.

Fiddy, D. (2001) *Missing Believed Wiped: Searching for the Lost Treasures of British Television*. London: British Film Institute.

Hughes, R. (1993) *The Culture of Complaint*. New York: Oxford University Press.

Nelson, R. (1997) *TV Drama in Transition: Forms, Values and Cultural Change*. London: Palgrave Macmillan.

O'Sullivan, T. (1991) Television memories and cultures of viewing 1950–65, in J. Corner (ed.) *Popular Television in Britain: Studies in Cultural History*. London: British Film Institute.

Pilkington, H. (Chair) (1962) *Report of the Committee on Broadcasting, 1960*, Cmd 1753. London: HMSO.

Rostron, P. (2000) Lifestyle and light entertainment, *BFI TV 100*, http://www.bfi.org.uk/features/tv/100/articles/lifestyle.html (accessed 1 Feb. 2005).

Teckman, J. (2000) Foreword, *BFI TV 100*, http://www.bfi.org.uk/features/tv/100/articles/foreword.html (accessed 1 Feb. 2005).

Wheatley, H. (2003) ITV: 1955–89: populism and experimentation, in M. Hilmes (ed.) *The Television History Book*. London: British Film Institute.

Notes

1. The furore around Bloom's exercises and those of others was particularly bad tempered, and triggered such defences of canon-building as Hughes (1993). The issue of value has not been tackled until recently in television studies, as Caughie points out (2000: 21–4).
2. For a number of years various television formats exploited this, such as *TV Heaven*, and more recently the explicit listing format adopted particularly on Channels 4 and 5 in the UK, with *100 Best TV Moments*, *100 Worst TV Moments* and so on.
3. This estimate is based on the fact that 24-hour transmission was introduced only in the 1980s. Prior to the arrival of breakfast television on ITV in 1983, broadcast hours had been slowly extending from its original two periods, lunch-time and evening. Schools broadcasting took place in the mornings in term time.
4. This is how I referred to *Small Time* (1959–65), by the name of what seemed to me to be its central character, a puppet cat.
5. One of the few pieces of research that addresses this is O'Sullivan (1991).
6. Monica Rose was a cheeky contestant who became a fixture on *Double Your Money* from 1964–68.
7. A 13-part anthology series made for ABC in 1962. One episode survives (see Fiddy 2001: 98–106).
8. A text-based exploration carries its own implicit values. Most of the current work on ITV programmes looks at drama made on film. There are obvious issues about favouring an accessible genre here, but more silently there is a question of the history of television production values, of which more later.
9. Top-level management in British television has tended to be drawn from news, current affairs and documentary rather than entertainment.
10. There are many reasons why particular past programmes come forward in such exercises, and not all of these are to do with the intrinsic qualities of the programme concerned. Acclaim at the time, either popular or professional, will tend to ensure that a series becomes a candidate, all the more so if it is promoted as an index of quality. Such is the case with the drama series *Brideshead Revisited*, still claimed by Granada's web site in 2005 as an index of its reputation for quality (along with *World in Action* and *Disappearing World*). Even at the time it was seen as something done despite ITV, a folly possibly, rather than a pinnacle of achievement. Now it has become the symbol of a lost era of commercial television in Britain.
11. TV's 50 most influential shows, *Broadcast*, 22 July 2004.
12. Both were made television stars by the BBC. Kemp by *Eastenders* and Jason in *Only Fools and Horses*. ITV has made a different Jason, the

successful wideboy of *Darling Buds of May* and the quirky detective Jack Frost. Kemp has failed to find a durable format and gallery of characters, and so may not last as an 'ITV face'.

13 Plowright's purpose was to demonstrate that the move to production on 16 mm film was responsible for much of the cost inflation which was then rampant in ITV. However with hindsight, his figures can be used to demonstrate a more general argument about the changing nature of television aesthetics and production methods.

14 Held at the BFI Library as ITV, 1979 (p. 5). The '£' indicators of currency have been inserted by the present writer.

15 Since the expansion of the independent sector in the early 1990s, full cost budgeting (combining above and below the line costs) has become the norm and therefore constitutes the 'rule-of-thumb' figures offered by producers.

16 Michael Darlow (2004: 273) quotes a key speech by BBC Director General Michael Checkland in 1980 that illustrates the nature of these figures.

17 John J. McCusker provides such a tool at www.eh.net/hmit/ppowerbp/.

18 The skills and equipment to produce television-like material are more widespread now than in the 1970s. So a redistribution of costs has been carried out within the television industry under the banner of 'seeing the costs on the screen' or 'more bang for the buck' – investing in the look rather than technicians or equipment. It is probably true to say that both behind-the-camera labour costs and the initial costs of technology both declined during the 1990s and that in drama some, but not all, of these savings have been translated into enhanced production values.

3 AND THE REST IS HISTORY: LEW GRADE, CREATION NARRATIVES AND TELEVISION HISTORIOGRAPHY

Jonathan Bignell

Lew Grade is an iconic figure in British television history, representing simultaneous but divergent attitudes to independent television as an industry, institution, programme-maker and facet of British culture. He had a prominent role in one of the three companies dominating ITV at its foundation, and in programme supply to the commercial network. Grade's given name was Lovat Winogradsky, and he was born in the Ukraine in 1906, the son of semi-professional singers.[1] His family migrated to Britain in 1912 and after working in the clothing industry he became a dancer touring the music halls. He then worked as a theatrical agent, booking British and European acts. In 1954 he formed the Incorporated Television Company (ITC) to produce filmed programmes for television, having lost in the first round of bids for ITV broadcasting licences because the Independent Television Authority (ITA) regarded Grade's consortium of cinema chains, theatres and music halls as too powerful in the British entertainment industry. Precisely because Grade and his collaborators 'seemed to have all the characteristics of a great show-business monopoly ... it would surely not do for them to be given the chance to swallow up Independent Television right from the outset' (Sendall 1982: 78). But ITC was invited to contribute its financial strength to the under-funded ITV broadcasting contractor that won the Midlands region, Associated Television (ATV). At ATV, as Deputy Managing Director from 1955 to 1962 and thereafter its Managing Director, Grade worked with executives who were fellow entertainment impresarios and theatre owners, including Val Parnell and Prince Littler, as well as directors from the newspaper business. ATV bought ITC, which immediately became a supplier of popular and lucrative programmes: it was at the forefront of programme export to the US, a strategy for which

Grade himself took credit (Bakewell and Garnham 1970: 275). Grade's reputation was built on his apparent ability to identify potential stars and ideas for successful programmes, and his skill in business relationships. Recognition of his personal contribution to commercial television was given when ATV gained two Queen's Awards to Industry for export achievement in 1967 and 1969. Grade was knighted in 1968, and given a peerage in 1976 before retiring from the directorship of the company. He pursued other ventures through his film-making company Associated Communications Corporation, and died in 1998.

This chapter focuses on how Grade has been represented, and begins from the assumption that the writing of television history necessarily pinpoints key individuals, programmes, and moments in time. The way that different representative people, historical turning-points and texts are presented reveals much about how histories are framed and patterned (Bignell 2005). Moreover, histories often cite and emphasize the same components in different ways, so the weave of historiographic writing in its multiple forms can be understood as a multi-dimensional space in which competing and complementary narratives overlap, coalesce and leave gaps. By examining the roles that references to and stories about Lew Grade play in the writing of television history, some of the problems and insistences in those histories can be examined. In particular, the conceptualization of ITV can be analysed by taking the adoption of Grade as its icon and totem as symptomatic of attitudes to ITV by contemporaneous commentators in British television's 'Golden Age' and by television historiographers in subsequent periods.

Clearly, constraints of space prevent an extended discussion of historiographic discourses that analyse independent television in Britain, but my argument is that since Grade stands in for ITV as a totemic figure then an analysis of his role in television historiography offers an insight that goes further than the focus on a single individual might suggest. Secondly, because Grade is placed at the centre of characteristic ways of representing ITV history, this methodology leads to a further project of analysing his own role in accounts of the origination of significant programmes. Discourses about ITV programmes that have been regarded as representative, important or valuable mention Grade as a facilitator and sometimes an obstacle to their creation. So Grade is not only discursively positioned at the heart of ITV, as a brief sketch of his role in the formation of the network suggests, but also at the birth of some of its most-discussed programme output. By analysing how these creation stories deal with Grade, an insight can be gained into how programmes' origins are said to depend on his persona and position him as their midwife at the moment they emerge. Questions of origin, representativeness and historiographic writing bring together the focus on Grade and the focus on programme examples.

However, there are three methodological issues that this project immediately raises. The first is the focus on Grade as an individual, which suggests a model of history as being driven by 'great men'. This chapter explores the tension between Grade as an agent or driver of events, policies and decisions, and Grade as a point of confluence for broader social, economic and institutional structures that shaped the parameters of British television. The second problem is the question of representativeness in relation to selected programmes. Plucking brief examples of Grade's involvement in programme creation means allowing these programmes to stand in for an absent multitude of other possible choices of example. The examples chosen for this chapter are representative, in that they illuminate larger questions of programme creation, form, technological and aesthetic contexts, and economic and institutional issues. But, conversely, they are unrepresentative in that by their very presence they exclude the surrounding field of both similar and different examples. In discussing programmes where Grade apparently had an originating role, this chapter will engage with the ways in which those programmes lead outwards to broader questions as well as possible studies of more detailed programme-specific issues. Thirdly, the lack of homogeneity in historiographic discourse itself affects the kinds of evidence with which this project engages. The writing referred to here ranges from 'official' histories of independent television represented by the work of Jeremy Potter (1989, 1990) and Bernard Sendall (1982, 1983), to academic studies of programmes and genres, to publications written primarily by and for television enthusiasts. These categories overlap, especially the latter two, and this discussion ranges across different ways of approaching television history.

Entertainment and commerce

In the 1950s and 1960s Grade aimed to offset the costs of television production by making programmes that would be offered to the UK ITV network, thus covering the greater part of their costs, but also sold to the US as a means of raising ATV/ITC's profitability. This system of domestic production at marginal profit, followed by overseas sale at much greater profit margins, was already what US television companies did. So Grade's companies were praised for competing with Hollywood at its own game, but were also tainted by suspicions of Americanization, as discussed below. ATV/ITC began with the filmed drama series *The Adventures of Robin Hood*, a co-production with the US company Sapphire, which was broadcast in Britain and sold to CBS in 1955 (see Neale in this volume). Further sales to US networks followed with *The Buccaneers* (CBS, 1956) and *The Adventures of Sir Lancelot* (NBC, 1957). ATV took over ITC in 1958, and bought British National Studios (renamed Elstree Studios) in 1961 as a production base (Osgerby and

Gough-Yates 2001: 18–19). By 1967, ITC had sold Gerry Anderson's filmed puppet series *Supercar*, *Fireball XL5*, *Stingray*, *Thunderbirds* and *Captain Scarlet and the Mysterons* to US networks. Each of these programmes was also networked by ITV, but the close association of Grade with US adventure series formats, the export drive to the US, and the Hollywood-like studio production system at ATV/ITC produced contradictory perceptions of Grade, his company, and ITV as a whole.

His skills in making such deals at opportune moments are among what Sendall (1982: 311) describes as 'those wiles which have made him something of a legend'. Official histories report attitudes to Grade that emphasize his personal sway over the direction that the strongest ITV companies took, and these histories tend to condense commercial and institutional negotiations into personal terms. For example, Sendall describes the reluctance of the smaller regional ITV companies to offend Grade by lobbying for programmes that would deflect accusations of poor quality, because Grade's ATV had a reputation for providing the ITV network with such 'low-brow' programmes as action-adventure series and their lobbying might offend him. Sendall (1983: 229) notes that Grade 'could be a formidable adversary just as readily as he could be a benevolent friend', and because ATV was one of the larger companies that provided the majority of nationally networked programmes his personal authority loomed large in the perception of fellow television executives. However, Grade's company offered not only financially successful programming but also defended ATV/ITC and ITV in general from accusations of triviality by making space for 'high-brow' series. Sendall (1982: 351) notes that persuading the former chairman of the ITA, Sir Kenneth Clark, to transform himself into the presenter of talks on art history for ATV in 1958, gaining audiences of up to 1.4 million homes by 1960, was 'not the least of the acts of showmanship performed by Parnell and Grade', again attributing this shrewd programming decision to personal flair. As Chapter 4 below on *Robin Hood* demonstrates, it was also the case that the adventure series associated with Grade were uncertainly poised in the perceptions of contemporaneous commentators as both high and low quality, as both British and American in character, so Grade's own role could be mobilized in conflicting and ambiguous ways. In summary, according to Sendall (1983: 237), 'for many people the image of Lew Grade seemed to personify all that ITV stood for', and thus he combined contradictory perceptions of independent television in a single persona.

This can be seen not only in written sources, but also in television's own retelling of its history. For example, images of Grade often appear in *The Showbiz Set* (Channel 4, 2002), a three-part series about light entertainment stars from the 1950s to the 1970s. It uses interviews, voice-over narration and brief extracts from programmes and actuality footage, to narrate a linear and developmental account of the evolution of the genre. The iconography of *The Showbiz Set*'s representation of Grade is interesting in itself. He appears in several sequences of contemporary news footage as an overweight, balding man, unsmiling and smoking a large cigar. The consonance between these images reinforces the sense of Grade as an icon who carries much more than a referential meaning: these are images not simply of what Grade looked like but what he meant to British television. His physical appearance crystallizes meanings that amount to a brand image, and constellate quirky individualism with a sense of presence and self-assurance based on his physical size and solidity, along with a variability of manner that includes avuncular familiarity and humour alongside a suggestion of hidden power and threat. Grade is posed as an executive, impresario, elder statesman of the television industry, and shadowy wielder of power and influence. In later decades the lack of this personalized authority was lamented by an anonymous industry insider who contributed to the Campaign for Quality Television's 1999 report, and said that there was 'no Lew Grade type character developing great pools of talent' anymore (Barmett and Seymour 1999: 69). For Jeremy Potter (1990: 34), in the 1960s Grade was 'Britain's nearest equivalent to a Hollywood showbiz mogul. A song-and-dance man at heart, he believed that television was, above all else, an extension of music hall and variety and that all television programmes should be classified as entertainment, whatever their subject-matter.' The tensions between populism and quality, personal power and institutional politics, and Britishness and Americanness have been articulated through discourses around Grade.

Grade and Americanization

The suggestion of parallels between Grade and US film or television executives is significant because of the divergent meanings of Americanness in the 1950s and 1960s. The fear of Amercanization in television was matched by fears about other cultural products such as jeans, rock-and-roll records and comics. As Dick Hebdige (1988: 9) shows:

> For critics pledged to defend 'authentic' British values, mass-produced commodities aimed at specific target groups begin to function as symbols of decadence. They are seen to pose a threat to native traditions of rugged self-reliance, self-discipline and the muscular puritanism of the stereotyped (male) workforce, thereby leading to a 'softening up' and 'feminization' of the national stock.

On the other hand, American products and the aura of Americanness in some ITV programmes attracted British consumers and enabled them 'to mark out aspirational differences in the social domain through the invocation of an exotic elsewhere' (Hebdige 1988: 9). America stood for commerce, and thus not only vigour, entrepreneurialism and progress, but also venality, greed and exploitation. It stood for modernity, youth and opportunity, but also disrespect for tradition, loss of national specificity and cultural colonization. These contradictory meanings were available to be mapped onto the aesthetics of the programmes that ATV/ITC made and onto Grade himself as their personification, providing grounds for both defences and attacks on commercial television. Sendall (1982: 371) reports the *Evening Standard*'s comment of 30 April 1960 that ITV was a 'dull routine of cowboys, crime, murders, pop singers and half-wit quiz games', demonstrating that although ITV was being regularly watched by some two-thirds of the British public, condemnation of ITV referred to programme genres associated with the US as evidence of the channel's poor quality.

Grade's apparent similarity to a Hollywood mogul and the attribution to him of the contradictory meanings of Americanness is crucially connected to attitudes to the television audience, and in particular the role of audience ratings. The issue of measuring ratings was an urgent problem for the ITV companies because reliable audience numbers were required to secure the commercial terms of their charges to advertisers (Sendall 1982: 133–7). Advertisers were charged according to both ratings and reach (the capacity of a programme to reach the eyes and ears of a demographic profile), so the need to compile accurate figures led to a fixation with numerical audience information. In this way, the much-vaunted and much-criticized populism of ITV, whose most obvious personification was Grade himself, was institutionalized by the ratings system. Referring to ATV's low-budget but widely-watched soap opera *Crossroads*, for example, Grade said 'I don't make programmes for critics – I make programmes for the viewers' (Potter 1990: 36). Inasmuch as Grade stands as the predominant representative of the conception of the audience as a market and a commodity for sale to advertisers, his discursive role is to act as a marker for anxieties about British television culture. In the debate about public service television, and the competition between BBC and ITV, Grade's function in accounts of television history is to crystallize the oppositional conceptualizations of audience as either a quantity or a citizenry.

Light entertainment was a key battleground on which both the perceived dominance of ITV over BBC and the concerns about Americanization were played out, for example in relation to *Sunday Night at the London Palladium*. Although the impresario Val Parnell was the name around which the programme was promoted, and its hosts were the anchors of its meanings aesthetically, Grade's business relationships with Parnell and the theatrical variety circuit lay behind its production and appeal. Lew and his brother Leslie Grade controlled the Palladium venue and were able to cherry-pick acts and performers who could be booked for *Palladium* shows. *Palladium*'s Britishness comprises its relationship with music hall and touring entertainment performances, and its British host and guests, for example. The stars of the period, such as Diana Dors, Gracie Fields, Bob Monkhouse and Alma Cogan appeared not only on this programme but also in theatrical shows and British films, and the variety format of *Palladium* allowed the touring stars of theatrical entertainment to be booked for individual broadcasts, so that each episode would showcase a line up of performers of much greater fame and attractiveness to audiences than at viewers' local music hall. Their image was moulded not only by Grade's theatrical agency and the television operation, but also by informal collaborations with the press, which at this time was compliant in running hagiographic celebrity stories.

On the other hand, *Palladium*'s format has much in common with US vaudeville, and some of its British performers were already associated with the emergent pop music industry and the connotations of 'trashiness' attributed by some commentators to radio stars (especially solo singers) appearing on both commercial and BBC radio. The presence of visiting US performers who featured at the top of the bill, and the use of game-show segments derived from US television formats, reinforced the potential ambivalence of *Palladium* as a mid-Atlantic hybrid. The programme both foregrounded its credentials as a popular form that was very much aware of its British audience's culture and modes of engagement with television and entertainment, and also exploited the negotiations being made in British culture with transnational entertainment forms that were already Americanized, such as the cinema industry, television quizzes and teen pop music culture. In these ways, *Palladium*'s ambivalences and negotiations parallel those in discourses about Grade himself. Each of them is a hybrid in which there is a perceived contamination or impurity in their Britishness and Americanness. This hybridity, however, opens a discursive space for questioning assumptions about the purity of each of the component terms from which the hybrid is composed. Neither Britishness nor Americanness are in themselves stable identities that exhibit the consistency against which contamination can be measured.

There is a similar point to be made about *Palladium* as television. In common with variety on stage as well as television, *Palladium* negotiated between a 'here' and 'there' of home and public spaces of entertainment, between ordinariness and spectacle, between 'us' and 'them' (Dyer 1973). Each of these terms, however, could blur into the other. The combination of star performers, the avuncular host, and the presence of 'ordinary' audience members on stage posed *Palladium* as both a recognition of the medium's domestic familiarity and ordinariness, and also as a means of access to a spectacular world of celebrity. Grade's close relationships with theatrical bookers and theatre owners facilitated this. The effect was to frame the programme as a mediating format between public entertainment space, signified by its liveness, auditorium setting and mix of turns, and on the other hand the regularity of broadcast, address to the home audience, and the multi-camera shooting techniques that characterized

Palladium as a programme and not just a relayed performance. In overseeing this programme, Grade and Parnell drew on an established television form (the relay or recreation of theatrical entertainment) but productively blurred the line between public and private entertainment, theatre and home, spectacle and intimacy. The role of *Palladium* as ITV's flagship supported ITV's self-proclaimed triumph in the new duopoly with BBC television in the 1950s, and the combination in Grade's persona of theatrical impresario, television mogul and *eminence grise* of commercial entertainment culture.

This question of Grade's and *Palladium*'s mid-Atlantic framing is also evident in relation to the different generic position of *Supercar*, *The Prisoner* and the many other filmed drama series he commissioned. Filmed drama was the most common programme form among US imports to the UK, partly because it was the most available because it comprised the majority of prime-time US network programming. Regulation and self-imposed quotas restricted US imports on BBC and ITV, but UK productions with export potential, like the US imports, had segmented episode forms allowing commercial breaks within programmes, and their production planning was normally based on US seasons of 26 episodes (or multiples thereof) for transmission in 9 months of weekly slots across a year, with repeats in summer. By adopting the medium of film for the series production of *Supercar* and *The Prisoner*, their producers aimed for US sales as well as broadcasts on British commercial television. In the production organization of programmes, and in some of their aesthetic choices (like casting American performers), hybrid components represent concrete instances of negotiation with Britishness and Americanness. Like Grade himself, ITC programmes mixed these national signifiers and thus provided ground for contemporary and subsequent commentators to question their meaning. In the case of *The Prisoner*, for example, the Britishness of its star and its pop art aesthetic were attractions to its US audiences, and drew on the cultural meaning of 'cool Britannia' as one of the period's invisible exports (see Chapman 2002).

Patron and publisher: Grade and programme creation

Grade did not write programmes, or author them in any conventional sense. He commissioned programmes, usually after personal meetings with the creative personnel responsible for them. The issue of creative origination has been an important point of debate in television studies. This is particularly noticeable in studies of television drama, where identifying a generative consciousness has led to competing modes of study that focus either on the individual writer or the collective production team behind programmes or, approaching the problem from the other direction, studies of how audiences decode programmes. The persistent desire to locate meaning in consciousness can be regarded as a general anxiety about the slipperiness of representation in general, for the search for a place in which meaning is located promises to arrest the infinite proliferation of interpretations. Origin stories about how television programmes came to be made, or look the way they do, are just one example of this desire to locate originary creation. The narrative form of the origin story has several particular attractions to people talking or writing about television history. It is usually brief and coloured by the conjunction of personality, accident and dramatic setting. In the examples discussed below, the origin story takes place in a moment of dialogue, a variant on the pitch meeting or the offer of a commission that commonly initiates a new television programme. Because of this conversational setting and its occurrence at a specific moment that its retellers can describe, the origin story has the rhetorical features of an anecdote. In stories about programme origins that include Grade as a key protagonist, his role oscillates between that of a patron and a publisher, terms that help to illuminate how a television executive like Grade can seem to take credit for the creative origination more often attributed to writers or directors.

Graham Murdoch (1980) discusses the question of authorship in television primarily in relation to the single play and the popular series. His analysis of authorship provides a historical framework that distinguishes between patronage and publishing as the predominant institutional systems on which authorship is dependent. His discussion of the shift between these modes in the post-Renaissance period is useful in disentangling the combined and sometimes contradictory roles of Grade described in the origin stories recounted next. As Murdoch (1980: 23) explains:

> In the traditional patronage relationship, artists were regarded as servants, skilled labourers whose job was to fulfil the briefs laid down by the patron. The new ideology of creativity shifted the balance of advantage, however, and patrons began to concede control over the productions they subsidized. Increasingly, artists and authors were supported for their talent or promise and left to decide on the subjects and forms of the work for themselves.

In television, and especially in commercial television, the commissioning and production of programmes are also dependent on market forces. Grade's role was therefore not only that of a patron but also of a publisher. Publishers, Murdoch (1980: 23) explains, 'acted as middlemen between writers and the marketplace, buying or commissioning works and selling them to the public'. In television as elsewhere in the cultural industries, the commercial success of any individual product is difficult to predict, so the publishing function is to seek work from authors that might result in a high volume of sales or viewers. But this demand coexists with a patronage function of commissioning work which may gain prestige but not necessarily commercial success. Thus a ‘primary’ sector in television production geared to anticipated market demand persists alongside a ‘secondary’ sector producing works of artistic prestige with limited appeal.

> This division between the ‘primary’ and ‘secondary’ sectors of production and the consequent tension between entrepreneurship and patronage, is common to all the major branches of the cultural industries, and it provides one of the keys to understanding the way in which authorship has become institutionalized within television drama production. (Murdoch 1980: 23–4)

In accounts of Grade’s role in the creation of programmes, his relationship with the authors and creators of programmes is uneasily poised between patron and publisher. While the publisher role often predominates, because commercial television is regarded primarily as a market operation, nevertheless the personal relationships that characterize patronage are also evident. For example, Gerry Anderson’s production of puppet drama series for Grade made so much money that Grade rewarded him with the gift of a brand-new Rolls Royce, and offered Anderson and his wife Sylvia the use of his holiday villa in Spain (Archer and Nicholls 1996: 72, 117–18). The economic relationships that may initially appear impersonal and institutional in the ‘primary’ sector of television production in the publishing model co-exist with the personal largesse and human interaction that are more redolent of patronage.

And the rest is history

In 1960, when his company AP Films was on the brink of financial collapse, Gerry Anderson attended a pitch meeting with Grade at which Anderson was given the go-ahead to produce the puppet series *Supercar*. *Supercar* ran for thirty-nine 30-minute episodes, and featured a car that could drive, fly and move under water. The car’s pilot and series protagonist was Mike Mercury, assisted by inventor Professor Popkiss, ten-year-old Jimmy, scientist Dr Beeker and Mitch the monkey. An account of the key meeting with Grade at which *Supercar* was commissioned is given in Anderson’s biography:

> Grade’s manner seemed somewhat impatient. He puffed at a large cigar and hurried on the petitioner. At the end of his presentation, Gerry was asked what the series budgeted out at and said £3000 an episode. Grade leapt out of his chair, slammed his fist down on the desk and barked, ‘That’s *ridiculous*! I can’t possibly afford that much for a programme of this sort. *No way*!’ Gerry was speechless ... But as quickly as it had arrived, the storm passed and Grade

returned to his original, more affable mood. He turned on what Gerry would later come to refer to as his Uncle Lew approach. 'I'll give you an immediate order for twenty-six thirty minute episodes provided you can cut the budget in half,' Grade decided. 'And I want you back here with an answer tomorrow morning at 7.30 a.m.' (Archer and Nicholls 1996: 48)

This origin story develops the construction of Grade as impresario in significant ways. He is attributed with the potential for sudden and dramatic exercises of power, and the iconography of the cigar and a physically imposing presence that were discussed above in relation to the caricature of the Hollywood producer is present. Here, however, Anderson is a 'petitioner' for Grade's almost regal largesse, and there is an emphasis on financial calculation that marries this patronage with the hard-headed deal making of the publishing model.

After the meeting with Grade, Anderson worked through the night and managed to reduce *Supercar*'s budget by one-third, and the subsequent meeting clinched the deal. 'Grade asked him to wait and rose from his desk. He walked over to a door, opened it and went through. Gerry heard faint mumblings of conversation. When Grade returned, he said, "Okay, you've got yourself a deal. But I want it on air within six months"' (Archer and Nicholls 1996: 48). Anderson later discovered that the door Grade entered was a clothes cupboard, and the mumbled conversation must have been a performance purely to unsettle Anderson. He asked Grade for a letter of intent to provide a financial guarantee for the production of *Supercar*. Grade replied, 'Just so long as you work for me, remember this: my word is better than any written contract or agreement. Got it? Now get out of here and make that series!' (Archer and Nicholls 1996: 49). Anderson made the series, which first aired in the UK on 28 January 1961. Grade also sold it to America, where it was broadcast in the autumn of 1962. According to Anderson, *Supercar* saved both his own company and also ITC, which had suffered reverses in its overseas sales success around this time (Archer and Nicholls 1996: 55). In relation to the rhetoric of the origin story, the promise of a verbal contract continues the patronage relationship of interpersonal trust that was signalled earlier, while the further details of time constraints and the suggestion of a corporate discussion with another unseen person marry this with commercial publishing culture. The detail in the story about the mysterious door that turned out to be a cupboard is also very significant in establishing Grade as a 'character' whose quirks and pretences suggest his power, unpredictability and also a kind of retrospective affection for him on Anderson's part.

A rather similar story recounts the discussions between Grade and the producer and actor Patrick McGoohan that led to the development of the spy-adventure series, *The Prisoner*. A brief account of the origin story for

The Prisoner appears both in Carrazé and Oswald's book on the series (1995: 7) and also in Chris Gregory's (1997: 29) study, each of whom extensively debate the issue of McGoohan's authorship of the series but have little to say about Grade's role. In each book, McGoohan is quoted as saying:

> I knew a man who backed hunches, and his decisions were his alone. Lew Grade, now Lord Grade, is such a man. He was behind my previous series. ... He didn't like reading scripts, but preferred to 'hear' the idea, to see it in his mind's eye. After listening to the bizarre concept, he took a few puffs on his cigar, walked around the office a couple of times and said 'It's so crazy it might work. Let's do it. Shake.' And we did. And he gave me carte blanche. I was very fortunate.

In a discussion of *The Prisoner* as postmodern narrative, Mark Bould (2005: 94) also gives a version of the origin story, referring to further recapitulations of it:

> Grade asked McGoohan 'to describe the project in his own words' and after listening to the pitch, 'Grade struck a deal there and then' (Davies 2002: 23), saying 'it's so crazy, it might work. When can you start?' (White and Ali 1988: 120). According to McGoohan, 'From the very moment that he said "go" and shook my hand, he never interfered with anything I did'. (Davies 2002: 23)

The respect for Grade that has been evident in the previous origin story recurs here as McGoohan notes Grade's decisiveness, trust in his own judgement, and a faith in McGoohan himself that seemed to launch *The Prisoner* in a matter of minutes. Again, the large cigar, exercise of power, and reliance on interpersonal relationships feature strongly. These are finely honed anecdotes that offer a glimpse behind the scenes where the personalities behind a programme reveal its birth in a few revealing turns of phrase and theatrical gestures. These origin stories are the kind of brief anecdotal narrative so fascinating to television fans, so useful in the early pages of academics studies, and in behind-the-scenes documentaries about the television industry. Grade's persona is ideally constructed to feature in them, and draw him into accounts of origination and authorship.

The relative autonomy of Grade and other television executives leading ITV regional companies and production outfits meant that ATV, for example, could commission programmes from ITC (or make its own), produce them, broadcast them in its own region and offer them to the national network. In this scenario of vertical integration where each level of the production process is linked to the others and under the control of the same executives, both patronage and publisher relationships could exist at the same time between Grade and the people who pitched ideas to him. Secondly, Grade was an impresario, and developed a persona as a quixotic and powerful individual. Although he did not author programmes in the usual sense, he cultivated relationships with such creators and had the power to make their ideas come to fruition. With the general concealment of the means of production that marks television as a commodity form, it is perverse to attribute authorship to Grade, a figure involved in executive decisions rather than directly in programmes, and thus apparently a publisher rather than a patron. On the other hand, programme-makers and performers were certainly aware of Grade's power and influence, would frequently meet him personally, and subsequently recount the colourful stories of these meetings. These factors reinforce the temptation in historiographic study to condense economic and institutional factors by personalizing them through narratives of personal agency and patronage. One final appraisal of Grade neatly demonstrates the collapsing of positive and negative attitudes to ITV into the language of personal responsibility and creation narratives:

> One of the first moguls of commercial television, Grade lived for work. He had three telephones in every room of his penthouse, including the sauna, and he arrived for work at 6.30 a.m. But he is chiefly legendary for founding a television dynasty and for his endless consumption of elephantine cigars. Unfortunately, he is also ultimately responsible for *Crossroads*. (Spence and Van Amerongen 1987: 44)

The difficulty for studies of television history is to disentangle the issue of agency from the biographical and anecdotal discourse that so readily becomes attached to it, but at the same time to allow space for the significance of Grade's specific persona rather than considering him as a conduit for impersonal forces. What television historiography needs, especially perhaps in Grade's case, is a non-Oedipal model of agency that can evade the twin temptations of desperately seeking paternity or rejecting a powerful father figure.

Acknowledgements

I gratefully acknowledge the support of the Arts and Humanities Research Board for the project 'Cultures of British Television Drama, 1960–82', based at the University of Reading. This chapter is one of the publications produced as part of the project.

Bibliography

Archer, S. and Nicholls, S. (1996) *Gerry Anderson: The Authorised Biography*. London: Legend.

Bakewell, J. and Garnham, N. (1970) *The New Priesthood: British Television Today*. London: Allen Lane.
Barnett, S. and Seymour, E. (1999) '*A Shrinking Iceberg Travelling South ...': Changing Trends in British Television: A Case Study of Drama and Current Affairs*. London: Campaign for Quality Television.
Bignell, J. (2005) Exemplarity, pedagogy and television history. *New Review of Film and Television Studies*, 3(1): 15–32.
Bould, M. (2005) This is the modern world: *The Prisoner*, authorship and allegory, in J. Bignell and Lacey, S. (eds) *Popular Television Drama: Critical Perspectives*. Manchester: Manchester University Press.
Carrazé, A. and Oswald, H. (1995) *The Prisoner: A Televisionary Masterpiece*. trans. C. Donougher. London: Virgin.
Chapman, J. (2002) *Saints and Avengers: British Adventure Series of the 1960s*. London: I.B. Tauris.
Davies, S. P. (2002) *The Prisoner Handbook*. London: Boxtree.
Dyer, R. (1973) *Light Entertainment*. London: BFI.
Grade, L. (1987) *Still Dancing: My Story*. London: Collins.
Hebdige, D. (1988) *Hiding in the Light: On Images and Things*. London: Routledge.
Murdoch, G. (1980) Authorship and organization. *Screen Education* 35: 19–34.
Osgerby, B. and Gough-Yates, A. (eds) (2001) *Action TV: Tough Guys, Smooth Operators and Foxy Chicks*. London, Routledge.
Potter, J. (1989) *Independent Television in Britain: Volume 3, Politics and Control, 1968–80*. London: Macmillan.
Potter, J. (1990) *Independent Television in Britain: Volume 4, Companies and Programmes, 1968–80*. London: Macmillan.
Sendall, B. (1982) *Independent Television in Britain: Volume 1, Origin and Foundation, 1946–62*. London: Macmillan.
Sendall, B. (1983) *Independent Television in Britain: Volume 2, Expansion and Change, 1958–68*. London: Macmillan.
Spence, R. and Van Amerongen, V. (1987) *Bluff Your Way in Television*. London: Ravette.
White, M. and Ali, J. (1988) *The Official Prisoner Companion*. London: Sidgwick and Jackson.

Note

1 Grade's autobiography (Grade 1987) tells his life story in detail, and there are many shorter accounts on web sites including www.transdiffusion.org/emc/TVHeroes/, and www.televisionheaven.co.uk/hisgrade.htm.

PART 2

INSTITUTIONS

4 TRANSATLANTIC VENTURES AND *ROBIN HOOD*

Steve Neale

Introduction

The Adventures of Robin Hood was one of the first programmes screened on ITV. Its opening episode, 'The Coming of Robin Hood', was initially broadcast in the London region in the UK on Sunday 25 September 1955 at 5.30 p.m., during the course of ITV's premiere weekend. Shot in black and white on 35 mm film at Nettlefold Studios in Surrey and on location in countryside nearby, 'The Coming of Robin Hood' starred Richard Greene as Robin Hood and Alan Wheatley as the Sheriff of Nottingham. Subsequent episodes introduced Archie Duncan as Little John, Alexander Guage as Friar Tuck, Bernadette O'Farrell as Maid Marian and Donald Pleasance as King John, with occasional alterations in casting due to injury, illness or the departure of actors from the series. Each episode pitted Robin, his outlaw band and his sympathizers against the unjust and tyrannical regime of King John, his allies and his agents.

There were eventually four seasons of *Robin Hood* comprising 143 26-minute episodes in all. These episodes were initially broadcast in the UK between 1955 and 1959, with repeats and reruns throughout this period and on into the early 1960s. As has now been well documented, many of them were scripted pseudonymously by American screenwriters who had been blacklisted by the US film and television industries on account of their real or alleged communist sympathies.[1] This is an important point of interest, one that still demands further investigation. But it has often obscured the nature and extent of other forms of American involvement in the production and distribution of *Robin Hood* and of other ITV series in the mid to late 1950s. Moreover, as I shall argue below, a lack of awareness of this involvement has distorted a number of accounts of *Robin Hood* both as an industrial and cultural product and as a commercial and critical success.

The commercial success of *Robin Hood*

The commercial success of *Robin Hood* was more or less instant. By November 1955, it was equal sixth in the Nielsen audience ratings in the UK.[2] By January 1956 it was second.[3] When ITV began broadcasting in the Midlands in 1956, it was second there too.[4] In January 1956, Dick James's recording of *Robin Hood*'s theme song became a top 20 hit. According to a clipping in 'The Robin Hood Collection' at the British Film Institute (Box 8, Folder 5), *Robin Hood* merchandising included bows and arrows, picture cards, wallets and watches. Its success led to two cinema spin-offs, *Son of Robin Hood* (1959) and *Sword of Sherwood Forest* (1960) (the latter starring Richard Greene and other cast members and directed by Terence Fisher, a regular director of *Robin Hood*'s episodes). It also helped cement a trend toward costume adventure on British television, giving rise directly or indirectly to subsequent series such as *The Adventures of Sir Lancelot* (1956–7), *The Buccaneers* (1956–7), *The Gay Cavalier* (1957), *The Adventures of William Tell* (1957–9), *Sword of Freedom* (1958–62), *Ivanhoe* (1958–9), *Richard the Lionheart* (1961–2) and *Sir Francis Drake* (1961–2).[5]

The Adventures of Robin Hood was a success in the US as well. Its opening episode was broadcast by CBS, one of the three US television networks, at 7.30 p.m. on Monday 26 September 1955. Sponsored on alternate weeks by Wildroot and Johnson & Johnson, the series ran for three seasons on CBS (1955–6, 1956–7 and 1957–8) before going into syndication on local and regional television stations entitled *The Adventures in Sherwood Forest* in 1958.[6] During its first two years on CBS, Nielsen's audience ratings placed it among the 20 most popular TV shows in the US, ahead of *The George Burns and Gracie Allen Show* (1950–58), *The Phil Silvers Show* (1955–9), *This is Your Life* (1952–61), *Lassie* (1954–71) and others (Brooks and Marsh 1999: 1245). According to an advertisement placed in *Variety* when the series went into syndication, *The Adventures of Robin Hood* had earned over $2 million in merchandising sales by 1958, with '33 licensed manufacturers offering Robin Hood products for previews, contests and give aways'.[7] By this time, it was in distribution worldwide, and was being shown in Canada, Australia, Syria, Japan, Iran and Puerto Rico as well.[8]

Appeal and identity

One of the reasons for *Robin Hood*'s success on both sides of the Atlantic was its ability to appeal to a crossover audience, to adults and families as well as to children. According to Miller (2000: 21), CBS regarded the 7.30 p.m. to 8.00 p.m. slot as 'a "children's hour"'. However, this slot in the 1950s was regarded as the start of prime-time. NBC broadcast *The Tony*

Martin Show (1954–56) at 7.30 p.m. on Mondays in 1955, *The Nat 'King' Cole Show* (1956–57) at 7.30 p.m. on Mondays in 1956 and *The Price is Right* (1956–86) at 7.30 p.m. on Mondays in 1957. ABC broadcast *Topper* (1953–56), *Bold Journey* (1956–59) and *American Bandstand* (1957) in this slot in these years respectively. While ABC's programmes in particular had definite juvenile appeal, the slot as a whole seems to have been regarded by all three networks as a family slot rather than as a slot for children alone. As if to confirm this, *Variety*'s review of 'The Coming of Robin Hood' noted its 'adult appeal'.[9] Its later review of 'The Salt King' (an episode in season three) placed it in what it called the 'kidult' category.[10]

In Britain, *Robin Hood*'s crossover appeal was marked by the nature of the initial and repeat screening slots of episodes in its first two seasons in particular. In season one, initial screenings at 5.30 p.m. on Sundays (a family viewing slot) came to be supplemented in 1956 by repeats at 7.05 p.m. on Tuesdays and 8.45 p.m. on Thursdays in February and March, at 10.00 p.m. on Fridays in April, May and early June, and at 7.00 p.m. or 7.05 p.m. on Fridays in June, July and August in the London region. Initial screenings of episodes in season two continued to be scheduled for Sundays at 5.30 p.m. from September 1956 on. Repeat screenings were scheduled for 10.00 p.m. on Thursdays from September 1956 to early February 1957, then at 6.30 p.m. on Fridays for the remainder of February through to the early summer. The sheer number of repeats is itself indicative of *Robin Hood*'s appeal. Repeats at 8.45 p.m. in the evening and 10.00 p.m. at night clearly suggest that that appeal was by no means restricted to children. As in the US, discussions of *Robin Hood* in Britain recognized its adult appeal. Indeed, as is often the case with cultural products, it was in many ways because of its 'adult' qualities that it was seen as particularly suitable for children. In this respect, and in addition, what were perceived as its 'English' or 'British' characteristics played a key role in the US and UK as well.

According to Jeffrey S. Miller, *The Adventures of Robin Hood* was one among a number of ITV programmes that received a warm welcome in the US in the mid-1950s. Drawing on a reputation for quality associated on US television with British feature films, with Alistair Cooke's role on the CBS magazine programme *Omnibus*, and with the BBC in the early 1950s, *Robin Hood* was promoted by the listings magazine *TV Guide* as 'a blessing compared to standard kids' fare' (Miller 2001: 21): '*Robin Hood* as produced in England, could very well be the answer to a mother's prayer about Westerns, as produced in Hollywood. Appealing to both children and adults, this CBS show . . . comes as a welcome relief from the "they-went-thataway" school of "childrens hour" programming' (*TV Guide*, 12 November 1955, cf Miller 2001: 21). A similar view was taken of *The Adventures of Sir Lancelot*, which was premiered on NBC in 1956. *TV Guide* praised it as 'a fine combination of charm, swashbuckling and literacy', adding that it was 'such a relief to hear proper English properly spoken' (17 November 1956, cf. Miller 2001: 22).

These themes were evident in the UK as well. Leslie Mallory, in an article in the *News Chronicle* (1956: 4), wrote that 'In thousands of homes from Manchester to Maine and Mannitoba today's youngsters have a new TV idol – Robin Hood. Davy Crockett and Superman have been ousted to the limbo of television while the kids clamour for English longbows and jerkins of Lincoln Green.' Hannah Weinstein, the executive producer of *Robin Hood* and *The Adventures of Sir Lancelot*, was quoted as saying that 'We have been highly praised by the schools in America, because the kind of English spoken in my films is infinitely more literate than the kind of stuff the kids hear around them at home' (Fenton 1955: 19). And Lindsay Anderson, who directed several episodes of *Robin Hood*, wrote in an article in *Sight and Sound* that 'many of the scripts originate in America, but are rewritten in Britain, without any attempt to Americanize speech or attitude' (Anderson 1956/7: 159).

I shall return to some of these points in a moment. Here, it is important to draw attention to some of the parallels between the discourse of contemporary commentators and the discourse of subsequent historians, and to the role played by both in the erasure – deliberate or otherwise – of *Robin Hood*'s American dimensions. Like Leslie Mallory, academic and journalistic historians of television in Britain have perceived and celebrated *Robin Hood*'s success in the US both in commercial and cultural terms. An insistence on its British origins, qualities, language and settings has accompanied an undisguised delight in its perceived status as a successful British export. Thus while Jeff Evans (2001: 7) characterizes *Robin Hood* as 'one of the pioneers of British television in America', James Chapman (2002: 7) argues that the 'most significant thing about *The Adventures of Robin Hood* was that it was sold to American television where it was successfully shown in syndication for many years'. Citing figures quoted from an article in *TV Times*[11] in John Caughie's book, *Television Drama* (an article Caughie himself suggests is a piece of 'blatant public relations' (2000: 54) at a time when ITV was particularly sensitive to accusations of Americanization), Chapman (2002: 7) goes on to note that 'It was reported in December 1955 that the sale of the ... series to America "has brought to England a million and a quarter dollars – nearly half a million pounds"'.

Bill Osgerby (2001) and Helen Wheatley (2003) also see *Robin Hood* as a British export. Like Chapman, Osgerby attributes *Robin Hood*'s success, and the success of subsequent ITV series, to ITV entrepreneur Lew Grade. Grade was a Managing Director of Associated Television (ATV), one of the first companies to hold a regional programming franchise at ITV. He was Managing Director, too, of the Incorporated Television Progamme Company (ITP), an ATV subsidiary that produced and subcontracted programmes. He later helped set up a partnership with a newly formed American group, the Independent Television Corporation (ITC), in 1958. ITP was then bought out by ATV, which went on to acquire ITC in 1960, thus providing ATV with an international distribution wing.[12] Writing about *The Saint* (1962–69) and its eventual success in the US in the 1960s, Osgerby (2001: 37) argues that

> British commercial broadcasters had already made forays into the American TV market in the 1950s. Lew Grade led the way, financing the production of historical adventure series such as *The Adventures of Robin Hood* ... and *The Adventures of Sir Lancelot* ... For American broadcasters and sponsors the savings offered by buying in pre-produced programming from Britain were very attractive – and for British producers the deal generated much-needed revenue for the finance [sic] of new ventures.

Helen Wheatley places *Robin Hood* and its success in the US within the context of the transatlantic trade in filmed series, especially those imported from the US by ITV. 'ITV took full advantage of the new possibility of broadcasting from film', she writes, 'and drew on the volume of filmed drama being made in the United States in the 1950s, filling the schedules in the early years of the channel with imported cop shows, such as *Dragnet* (NBC 1955–9, 1967–70) and *Highway Patrol* (Ziv/ UA TV, 1955–9) and Westerns, including *Gunsmoke* (CBS, 1955–75) and *Rawhide* (CBS, 1959–66)' (Wheatley 2003: 78). She adds, however, repeating the figure quoted for *Robin Hood*'s sales by Caughie and Chapman and citing Sapphire Films rather than ATV or ITP as the company responsible for its production, that

> British commercial television also produced a number of its own drama series which reflected this American 'cinematic' aesthetic and which could be readily exported to the United States ... The most successful of these filmed series were Sapphire Films' 'swashbucklers', such as *The Adventures of Robin Hood* (1955–9) (sold to the US for £500,000 before its first broadcast), and *The Buccaneers* (1956–7). (Wheatley 2003: 78)

There are several points worth picking up here. The first, an important if incidental point, is that the BBC, doubtless spurred on by ITV's example, imported filmed series from the US as well. In the period between 1954 and 1959, these included, in order of their appearance on the BBC's schedules, *The Burns and Allen Show*, *Hopalong Cassidy* (1949–51), *The Life of Riley* (1949–58), *Amos 'n' Andy* (1951–53), *The Cisco Kid* (1950–56), *The Jack Benny Programme* (also known as *The Jack Benny Show*) (1950–65), *Hey Jeannie* (1956–60), *Champion the Wonder Horse* (also known as *The Adventures of Champion*) (1955–56), *The Lone Ranger* (1956–62), *Circus Boy* (1956–58), *Wells Fargo* (also known as *Tales of Wells Fargo*) (1957–62), *Whirlybirds* (1956–59), *Boots and Saddles* (1957–59), *Union Pacific* (1958), *Frontier* (1955–56), *Bronco* (1958–62) and *Laramie* (1959–63). This list includes sitcoms as well as drama, and there is a distinct absence of cop shows. But it should be noted on the one hand that ITV imported US sitcoms too, most famously *I Love Lucy* (1951–61), and on the other that the BBC exported at least one of its own cop shows to the US, *Fabian of the Yard* (1954–56), which went into syndication as *Fabian of Scotland Yard* (also known as *Patrol Car*) in 1956.

ITV and the BBC imported filmed variety shows and one-off plays in addition to feature-length movies from the US as well.[13] But Wheatley's point about filmed drama series, an 'American "commercial" aesthetic', and the viability of *Robin Hood* in the US is an acute one, especially given *Robin Hood*'s general generic status as an action-oriented series, a series, therefore, with some similarities to the American Westerns with which it was otherwise contrasted, as Miller (2000: 22–23) points out.[14] Its specific status as a swashbuckler is even more important and will be discussed further below. In the meantime, whether conceived in terms of American influences or in terms of an accommodation to American tastes, there are signs that *Robin Hood*'s identity is not necessarily clear cut.

These signs emerge from time to time in 1950s discourse as well as in more recent scholarly accounts. *Variety*'s review of 'The Coming of Robin Hood' noted that Hannah Weinstein 'wisely eliminates British accents in her casting of subsidiary roles' and that 'this should overcome much of the alleged mid-Western resentment towards British-made pix'.[15] Peter Fenton's article on Weinstein in the *TV Times* pointed out that 'With a market on both sides of the world, she is the inventor of what she calls the Mid-Atlantic accent – a form of speech which might contain the odd American idiom, but which is also not-very-Oxford English' (Fenton 1955: 19). It is worth noting that among *Robin Hood*'s regular cast Bernadette O'Farrell was Irish, Archie Duncan, Scottish, and that Richard Greene, who was born in England, had worked in Hollywood for over a decade. It is also worth noting that *Robin Hood*'s script editor between 1955 and 1957 was an American journalist, Albert G. Ruben, who went on to edit and write scripts for *Richard Diamond, Private Detective* (1957–60), *Have Gun, Will Travel* (1957–63) and *The Defenders* (1961–65) among others, and that one of its script editors thereafter was Peggy Phillips, another American.

Sidney Cole, meanwhile, *Robin Hood*'s associate producer, was quoted by Lesley Mallory (1956) as saying that 'Robin Hood is an international symbol – he has an equivalent in virtually every language'. Referring to Weinstein, he goes on to argue that 'the secret of *Robin Hood*' was that 'Hannah supplied the American business drive and our own creative boys supplied the technical skill'. Finally, Bill Osgerby, Anna Gough-Yates and Marianne Wells (2001: 19) allude, as Wheatley does, to Sapphire Films and suggest that 'In an early instance of transatlantic economic co-operation, the series was made in conjunction with the American company, Sapphire Films, and purchased in America by the CBS network.' Sapphire Films was not an American company, as we shall see. But Hannah Weinstein was American and *Robin Hood* was indeed an instance of transatlantic economic co-operation. Hence its listing in *Variety* as one of many 'United States Telefilms in Display Around the Globe' as cited above. And hence the fact that Hal Hackett (1957: 103), president of a US television company called Official Films, discussed *Robin Hood* as an Official Films project in an article in *Variety* in 1957.[16]

Hannah Weinstein, Sapphire Films and transatlantic co-operation

Hannah Weinstein was born Hannah Dorner in New York in 1911. She worked as a journalist, publicist and campaigner for radical causes in the US in the 1930s and 1940s. She was a supporter of Roosevelt's New Deal and a campaigner for Henry Wallace as presidential candidate in 1948. In the wake of Wallace's defeat and the onset of the Cold War, and just prior to the second set of hearings by the House Committee on Un-American Activities into communism in Hollywood, she left America and went to France. Here she produced here first film, *Fait-divers à Paris* (1950), and renewed contact with a number of Hollywood exiles, among them blacklisted writers like Ben and Norma Barzman, Lee and Tammy Gold, and Abraham Polonsky. With Polonsky and Boris Karloff, in whose house in France she initially lived, she began planning a television police series, *Colonel March of Scotland Yard* (also known as *Colonel March*). She then went to London in 1952 and in an uncredited capacity produced three pilot episodes which were re-edited and released in 1953 as a feature film entitled *Colonel March Investigates*. On the basis of these pilots, a series was commissioned and distributed in the US by Official Films in 1954–55.[17]

Colonel March was a success, and with the advent of ITV now imminent, Weinstein set up a new production company, Sapphire Films, whose head office was in Cadogan Square in south-west London. Having discussed the idea for a new series, *The Adventures of Robin Hood*, with Ring Lardner Jr. and Ian McClellan Hunter (both blacklisted US writers based in New York), she began negotiations with Official Films in the US and with ATV and ITP in Britain for production funding and for distribution in the UK, the US, and elsewhere abroad. She also secured UK distribution for *Colonel March*, which was initially broadcast on ITV in the London region in the 1955–56 season.[18]

The Adventures of Robin Hood was thus produced by a British company for the British subsidiary of a British television franchise holder. But like Sapphire's subsequent swashbucklers, *The Adventures of Sir*

Lancelot, *The Buccaneers* and *Sword of Freedom*, it was also produced by an American in voluntary exile for an American television company, Official Films – a company that owned a 25 per cent stake in Nettlefold Studios and that contributed up to $5,000 in end-money towards what *Variety* estimated as *Robin Hood*'s $35,000 costs per episode.[19] In this way Hannah Weinstein and Sappire Films gained funding and distribution for their series, while Official Films, ATV and ITP were able to share production and distribution costs and gain access to each other's overseas markets. They were also able to circumvent the quota of foreign programming (no more than 7 hours a week) agreed by the ITV franchise holders and their regulator, the Independent Television Authority (ITA), in 1955. In these and in other ways – the appeal to authenticity in the use of foreign settings, locations and actors, reduced production costs when using foreign labour and foreign facilities, the ability, on occasion at least, to draw on foreign subsidies and to take advantage of foreign tax breaks – there are a number of parallels between these arrangements, conditions and practices and those associated with 'runaway' production – the production or co-production of films in foreign countries – in the 1950s (Guback 1969; Ryall 2001: 65–71; Lev 2003: 149–55).

Official Films, syndication, runaway television and costume adventure in the 1950s

Official Films was one of a number of US television companies involved in the production and distribution of ITV's costume adventure series in the 1950s. The others included Television Programmes of America (TPA), Screen Gems (a subsidiary of Columbia Pictures) and National Telefilm Associates (NTA). These were companies that specialized in syndication. They bought, produced, co-produced and sold programmes, series and films to sponsors, advertising agencies, local television stations and the national networks in the US. They also distributed programmes, films and series abroad. Among a relatively large group of companies specializing in syndication at this time (others included Flamingo Films, Ziv and Gross-Krasne), most of them were founded in the late 1940s and early 1950s.[20] They underwent a rapid period of expansion in the mid-1950s, following an announcement by the US Federal Communications Commission in April 1952 that it would lift its 3-year freeze on the licensing of new television stations and 'license up to 2053 stations in 1291 communities around the nation' (Von Schilling 2003: 181). Because they specialized in films and filmed programmes, companies like these found themselves in a position to supply a large and growing proportion of a rapidly expanding domestic market at a time when the networks alone were unable to meet the demand for syndicated programming and at a point prior to the involvement of most major Hollywood companies in the production of television programmes or in the distribution of films to television (Moore 1979: 24–34; Erickson 1989: 9; Kompare 2005: 51–6). They also helped feed an expanding market for television programmes abroad, especially in English-speaking countries.[21] The advent of ITV, in the year in which syndication became 'a $150million a year business' (Erickson 1989: 9), helped cement their position, extend the scope of their operations and increase their sources of income and profit.

The extent to which these companies were involved in ITV's series tended to vary. Official Films was by far the most prolific. In addition to *The Adventures of Robin Hood*, *The Adventures of Sir Lancelot*, *The Buccaneers* and *Sword of Freedom*, Official co-funded and co-distributed *The Four Just Men* (which was first broadcast in the UK in 1959–60 and initially syndicated in the US in 1959) and *The Adventures of the Scarlet Pimpernel* (which was first broadcast in the UK in 1955–6 and initially syndicated in the US in 1958). *The Four Just Men* was a Sapphire series with a contemporary international setting, *The Adventures of the Scarlet Pimpernel* a Towers of London swashbuckler produced by Harry Towers for ITP.

Harry Towers, like Lew Grade, was a member of the boards of ATV and ITP. He was also Managing Director of Towers of London. Like Grade and others involved in managing ATV and ITP he had been involved in discussions with Official Films since 1953.[22] But Official Films was not the only US company to deal with Towers, ATV and ITP. *The Count of Monte Cristo* (first syndicated in the US in 1955 and first broadcast in the UK in 1956–7) was initially produced in the US by TPA. Its stars were North American; its executive producers were North American; its producer was North American; its directors and writers were North American; and its first twelve episodes were shot at the Hal Roach studios in Hollywood. However, the remaining 27 episodes were produced in England through Towers of London. These episodes were initially co-produced by Sidney Marshall from the US and by Dennis Vance from the UK, then by Vance alone. They were all directed by British directors. *The Count of Monte Cristo* thus began as an American series, broadcast in Britain by ATV, but became a runaway British co-production, similar in status to a number of contemporary films.[23]

Ivanhoe provides a more straightforward example of runaway production. Aside from some exteriors in its opening episodes, it was produced and shot in Britain by Screen Gems. Using a British producer and British locations, directors and actors, it qualified for quota purposes as a British series and as such was able to take advantage of financing by the National Film Finance Corporation, an organization set up in the early 1950s to fund the production of British films.[24] *The Adventures of William Tell*, on the other hand, was initially planned as a British-German co-production prior to the involvement of NTA, who finally co-financed and co-distributed the series with ITP and ATV.[25]

Conclusion

In an article published in *Variety* in 1958, Harold Myers (1958: 93) argued that an 'Anglo-American partnership' that had taken 'half a century to mature in motion pictures' had 'been developed in the field of commercial television in just two years'. These years were coincident with what has been called the 'Golden Age' of syndication in the US (Moore 1979: 24). They were also coincident with a trend toward runaway production in the film and television industries and with a vogue for costume adventure on television prompted by a longer-term cycle in the cinema, a cycle that included films such as *Rogues of Sherwood Forest* (1950), *The Flame and the Arrow* (1950), *The Elusive Pimpernel* (1950), *Ivanhoe* (1952), *The Story of Robin Hood and His Merrie Men* (1952), *The Crimson Pirate* (1952), *Knights of the Round Table* (1953) and *The Thief of Venice* (1954) (Taves 1993: 72–80).[26] These are among the contexts in which the production, circulation and success of *The Adventures of Robin Hood* need to be placed in order fully to be understood. What cannot be emphasized enough, however, is the extent to which, like other ITV series, it was transnational in origin and appeal and in financial and institutional terms from the very outset.

Acknowledgements

I would like to thank the Arts and Humanities Research Board Centre for British Film and Television Studies for funding my research into *The Adventures of Robin Hood* and Sapphire's other series.

Bibliography

Anderson, L. (1955/6) Notes from Sherwood, *Sight and Sound*, 26(3): 159–60.

Barzman, N. (2003) *The Red and the Blacklist: The Intimate Memoir of a Hollywood Expatriate*. New York: Nation Books.

Bernstein, W. (1996) *Inside Out: A Memoir of the Blacklist*. New York: Knopf.

Brooks, T. and Marsh, E. (1999) *The Complete Directory to Prime Time Network and Cable TV Shows: 1946–Present*. New York: Ballantine.

Buhle, P. and Wagner, D. (2003) *Hide in Plain Sight: The Hollywood Blacklistees in Film and Television, 1950–2002*. New York: Palgrave.

Caughie, J. (2000) *Television Drama: Realism, Modernism, and British Culture*. Oxford: Oxford University Press.

Ceplair, L. and Englund, S. (1980) *The Inquisition in Hollywood: Politics in the Film Community, 1930–1960*. New York: Anchor Press.

Chapman, J. (2002) *Saints and Avengers: British Adventure Series in the 1960s*. London: I.B. Tauris.

Dick, B. (1989) *Radical Innocence: A Critical Study of the Hollywood Ten*. Lexington: University of Kentucky Press.

Erickson, H. (1989) *Syndicated Television: The First Forty Years, 1947–1987*. Jefferson: McFarland.

Evans, J. (2001) *The Penguin TV Companion*. London: Penguin.

Fenton, P. (1955) The Weinstein theory for brighter TV. *TV Times*, 6 June.

Gordon, B. (1999) *Hollywood Exile, or How I Learned to Love the Blacklist*. Austin: University of Texas Press.

Guback, T. (1969) *The International Film Industry: Western Europe and America Since 1945*. Bloomington: Indian University Press.

Hackett, H. (1957) When knighthood was in flower on TV film. *Variety*, 9 January.

Koch, H. (1979) *As Time Goes By*. New York: Harcourt Brace Jovanovich.

Kompare, D. (2005) *Rerun Nation: How Repeats Invented American Television*. New York: Routledge.

Laffin, P. (1955) The count has two 'teddy-boy' henchmen, *TV Times*, 9 December.

Lardner, R. Jr. (2000) *I'd Hate Myself in the Morning: A Memoir*. New York: Nation Books.

Lev, P. (2003) *The Fifties: Transforming the Screen, 1950–1959*. New York: Scribners.

Lewis, J.E. and Stempel, P. (1999) *The Ultimate TV Guide*. London: Orion.

McGilligan, P. and Buhle, P. (1997) *Tender Comrades: A Backstory of the Hollywood Blacklist*. New York: St. Martin's Press.

Mallory, L. (1956) Robin draws his longbow – and Davy bites the dust!, *News Chronicle*, 5 September.

Marks, L. (1990) Hood winked, *The Listener*, 18 January.

Miller, J.S. (2000) *Something Completely Different: British Television and American Culture*. Minneapolis: University of Minnesota Press.

Moore, B.A. (1979) Syndication of first-run television programming: its development and current status. Unpublished PhD thesis, Ohio University.

Myers, H. (1957) British com'l TV after 18 months has plenty to exhilarate about, *Variety*, 9 January.

Myers, H. (1958) Anglo-US television partnerships attain fullblown status in 2 years, *Variety*, 8 January.

Neale, S. (2003) Pseudonyms, Sapphire and Salt: 'un-american' contributions to television costume adventure, *Historical Journal of Film, Radio and Television*, 23(3): 245–57.

Osgerby, B. (2001) 'So you're the famous Simon Templar': *The Saint*, masculinity and consumption in the early 1960s, in Osgerby, B. and Gough-Yates, A. (eds) *Action TV: Tough Guys, Smooth Operators and Foxy Chicks*. London: Routledge.

Osgerby, B. and Gough-Yates, A. (eds) (2001) *Action TV: Tough Guys, Smooth Operators and Foxy Chicks*. London: Routledge.

Osgerby, B., Gough-Yates, A. and Wells, M. (2001) The business of action: television history and the development of the action TV series, in Osgerby, B. and Gough-Yates, A. (eds) *Action TV: Tough Guys, Smooth Operators and Foxy Chicks*. London: Routledge.

Parish, J. R. and Terrace, V. (1989) *The Complete Actors' Television Credits*, Vol 1. London: Scarecrow Press.

Phillips, P. (2002) *My Brother's Keeper*. San Jose: Writers Club Press.

Rapf, M. (1999) *Back Lot: Growing Up with the Movies*. London: Scarecrow Press.

Robb, D. (1996) Naming the right names: amending the Hollywood blacklist, *Cineaste*, 22(2): 24–9.

Rogers, D. and Gillis, S.J. (1997) *The Rogers and Gillis Guide to ITC*. Shrewsbury: SJG Communications Services.

Rouverol, J. (2000) *Refugees from Hollywood: A Journal of the Blacklist*. Albuquerque: University of New Mexico Press.

Ryall, T. (2001) *Britain and the American Cinema*. London: Sage.

Sendall, B. (1982) *Independent Television in Britain: Volume 1, Origin and Foundation, 1946–62*. London: Macmillan.

Street, S. (2001) *Transatlantic Crossings: British Feature Films in the USA*. New York: Continuum.

Taves, B. (1993) *The Romance of Adventure: The Genre of Historical Adventure Movies*. Jackson: University of Mississippi Press.

Von Schilling (2003) *The Magic Window: American Television, 1939–1953*. New York: The Haworth Press.

Wheatley, H. (2003) ITV: 1955–89: populism and experimentation, in M. Hilmes (ed.) *The Television History Book*. London: British Film Institute.

Notes

1 The literature on this topic is now quite extensive. It includes Bernstein (1996: 245–9), Barzman (2003: 260), Buhle and Wagner (2003: 42, 86, 87, 88, 246), Ceplair and Englund (1980: 405), Dick (1989: 177–8), Gordon (1999: 62, 87), Koch (1979: 201–2), Lardner Jr. (2000: 140–2), McGilligan and Buhle (1997: 16, 437, 459), Marks (1990), Neale (2003), Phillips (2002), Rapf (1999: 193), Robb (1996: 28) and Rouverol (2000: 203–4). In the context of the issues discussed in this article, I would want here to stress not their ideological views (views that undoubtedly made their mark on the series) but their

Hollywood training and hence their expertise in writing for audiences in the US as well as the UK and elsewhere abroad.

2 Palladium show no. 1 as Neilsen rates British com'l ITV entries, *Variety*, 23 November 1955: 25.

3 'Robin Hood' Brit. fave, *Variety*, 3 March 1956: 23.

4 Britain TV faves, *Variety*, 14 November 1956: 31.

5 These dates are for initial transmissions in the UK. *The Adventures of Sir Lancelot* was also broadcast on NBC in the US in 1956–57, *The Buccaneers* on CBS in 1956–57, *Sir Francis Drake* on NBC in 1963. *Sword of Freedom* was initially syndicated in the US in 1957 and *The Adventures of William Tell* and *Ivanhoe* in 1958. Precise transmission dates for all 39 episodes of *Sword of Freedom* in the UK are unclear. Listings in the *TV Times* indicate that transmission of the series in London began in January 1958. However, only 32 episodes appear to have been broadcast by the end of 1962.

6 It was probably the national advertising agencies responsible for securing sponsorship for *Robin Hood* in the US that negotiated its network screening and its network slot. According to Barbara Moore (1979: 13, 16, 28–9), it was standard practice at this time for advertising agencies rather than sponsors like Johnson & Johnson or syndication companies like Official Films (the company that, as we shall see, distributed *Robin Hood* in the US) to deal with the networks. Johnson & Johnson's agents were Young & Rubicam, Wildroot's were BBD&O.

7 *Variety*, 11 June 1958: 29.

8 United States telefilms in display around the globe, *Variety*, 4 June 1958: 36-7, 44.

9 The Coming of Robin Hood, *Variety*, 28 September 1955: 42.

10 *Variety*, 2 October 1957: 34.

11 Looking around, *TV Times*, 9 December 1955: 4.

12 Emmerson, A. A quick guide to ITC. Mainstay of ITV programming for thirty years, http://www.sigtel.com/tv_info_itc.htm; Marcus, L. and Hulse, S.R. The ITC story (the early years), http://freespace.-virgin.net/steve.hulse/itc.html; Sendall (1982: 66–79, 118–19); Britain, just like US, talks up mergers; ATV buys out ITP, *Variety*, 22 October 1958: 39; British ATV (a partner) buys out Wrather, Loeb's 50% of Biz, *Variety*, 10 February 1960: 31. There has been some confusion about ITP, ITC and *Robin Hood*, possibly because ITC was an acronym for the Independent Television Programme Corporation, an organization formed in 1954 to bid for a programming franchise from the Independent Television Authority (ITA), as well as for the later Independent Television Corporation. The ITA turned down ITC's bid, but suggested that it merge with ATV (or the Associated Broadcasting Development Company as it was then called) to bid for programming in the London and Midlands regions. The merger took

place and the bid was successful. The new company was called the Associated Broadcasting Company (ABC) before finally becoming ATV. When ATV acquired the American ITC in 1960, the new ITC became responsible for the overseas sales and distribution of series produced or commissioned by ATV. These included series previously commissioned, produced or co-produced by ITP, among them *Robin Hood*. Hence *Robin Hood*'s appearance, and the appearance of other 1950s series, in Rogers and Gillis (1997).

13 The BBC, in fact, broadcast more English-language feature films and imported more Hollywood movies than ITV in the mid-1950s, a policy it pursued, according to Myers (1957: 99), in response to ITV's programming initiatives.

14 As if to confirm this point, there is an American clipping on *Robin Hood* in 'The Robin Hood Collection' at the British Film Institute (Box 8, folder 5) simply entitled 'The British Hopalong'.

15 The Coming of Robin Hood, *Variety*, 28 September 1955: 42.

16 Hackett's claims are exaggerated, as we shall see, but it is worth pointing out that Official planned to distribute a series entitled *Tales of Robin Hood*, an adaptation of a Hal Roach feature film, as early as 1952 (Official 'Robin' release brings beef from Lippert, *Variety*, 16 April 1952: 22). The end credits on those video copies of episodes of *Robin Hood* distributed by Hollywood's Attic and derived from US distribution prints vary slightly in format, wording and layout but generally include phrases such as 'An Official Films presentation' or 'A Sapphire Films production for Official Films Inc. and The Incorporated Television Programme Co. Ltd' (see the credits on 'Tables Turned' and 'An Apple for the Archer' respectively).

17 There is some uncertainty as to the years in which *Colonel March* was shown in the US, and some uncertainty, too, as to when and even where it was filmed. According to Buhle and Wagner (2003: 85), *Colonel March* was shot in Paris. All other sources indicate that Weinsten was in England while the series being filmed and that it was shot at Southhall Studios in Middlesex (www.angelfire.com/retro/cta/UK/ColonelMarch.htm (accessed 24 March 2002); Fenton 1955: 19; and Weinstein obituaries in the *New York Times*, 11 March 1984: 136 and *Variety*, 14 March 1984: 46). *Colonel March* was syndicated in the US. Hal Erickson (1989: 23) gives its initial US transmission date as 1953, www.tvtome.com/tvtome/servlet/ShowManServlet/showid-9780/htm (accessed 31 January 2005) gives it as 1956, Lewis and Stempel (1999: 76) and Parish and Terrace (1989: 267) give it as 1957.

18 There is conflicting information about the initial transmission date of episodes of *Colonel March* in Britain as well. Chapman (2002: 6) and Lewis and Stempel (1999: 76) give an initial transmission date of 1955, Evans (2001: 130) an initial transmission date of 1956. According to the *TV Times* and the SIFT database on titles at the British Film

Institute, Chapman and Lewis and Stempel are correct and Evans is incorrect. Evans is also incorrect in attributing the production of *Colonel March* to Sapphire Films. Episodes 1 to 3 are credited to Criterion Films and episodes 4 to 26 to Fountain Films (copyright Panda Films Productions).

19 John Bullish on int'l Vidpix, *Variety*, 3 August 1955: 31; Estimated weekly network TV program costs, *Variety*, 16 November 1955: 26.

20 Who's who in TV-films, *Variety*, 15 February 1956: 37, 40.

21 See Brit. market for Vidpix, *Variety*, 15 April 1953: 27; Comm'l British TV would spark global Vidpix market, sez Towers, *Variety*, 30 September 1953: 26, 44; Telepix distribs eye O'seas, *Variety*, 10 February 1954: 27, 42.

22 John Bullish on int'l Vidpix, *Variety*, 3 August 1955: 31.

23 It is worth noting, *a propos* of the issues of accents and language discussed above, that according to Laffin (1955: 8) an American advisor called Rudi Flothow was assigned to the production team in the UK: 'I just want to keep a check on your accents. Your broad "A"s are OK for Broadway but way out West they don't know what you are saying.' For further discussion of these issues in the context of the reception of British films in the US at this time see Street (2001).

24 British TV writers ask ouster of Starr in protesting 'Ivanhoe' fees, *Variety*, 23 July 1958: 26.

25 British director in new German pix setup, *Variety*, 3 October 1956: 14.

26 In contrast to runaway cinema, runaway television has hardly been studied at all. See Moore, H. 'Foreign import shows', www.networks-plus.net/caseyguy/June01N.htm (accessed 10 May 2001). Helen Wheatley (2003: 78) gives examples of British runaway productions in Africa and James Chapman (2002: 6) discusses the Danziger Brothers, who produced a series of programmes in Britain in the 1950s and 1960s, initially for the US then for the US and Britain as well. The examples cited by Moore, Wheatley and Chapman, examples that include *Foreign Intrigue* (1951–55), *Mark Saber* (also known as *Mystery Theatre*, *Inspector Mark Saber – Homicide Squad*, *The Vise*, *Saber of London* and *Detective's Diary*) (1951–60), *Sherlock Holmes* (1954–55), *The Invisible Man* (1958–59), *White Hunter* (1958–60), *Glencannon* (1959) and *Interpol Calling* (1959–60), indicate that although costume adventure was prominent as a trend in runaway television in the 1950s, it was by no means the only one.

5 MAMMON'S TELEVISION? ITV IN WALES, 1959–63

Jamie Medhurst

Introduction

This chapter is a historical narrative and critical analysis of ITV in Wales between 1959 and 1963. It focuses on Wales (West and North) Television, or Teledu Cymru[1] as it was known in Welsh-speaking Wales (and the title which is used in this chapter), the only regional ITV company ever to fail on financial grounds. The evidence points to the fact that a range of internal factors (including the organization and management of the company) and external factors (including government broadcasting policy, technical issues, and institutional rivalry between the BBC and the ITA) influenced the creation, progress and ultimate failure of the initiative.

Those who have written on the history of broadcasting in Wales have tended to see the rise and fall of Teledu Cymru as being essentially a failed nationalist enterprise and stress the role of nationalist (political and cultural) pressure groups in the formation and demise of the company. Butt Philip (1975), Bevan (1984) and Evans (1997) all stress the nationalist pressure group influence on the project, although Evans is the only writer to provide any detail on the exact roles played. John Davies (1994: 230) points to the failings of this form of nationalism to encompass south Wales whilst Dai Smith (1999: 44, 46) underlines the failings of the rural language-based model, which excludes the industrial south-east. Sendall (1983: 76) also accounts for the failure of Teledu Cymru in terms of the 'impetuous excess of zeal ... common to men who are convinced of the rightness of their cause'. These writers, therefore, express the foundation and failure of the company in terms of the nationalist politics of the period but all, apart from Evans, fail to provide empirical support for their arguments.

The history of the demise of the company was not merely a heroic failure against all the odds, as Davies (1994: 228–30) suggests; neither can it be explained by gross incompetence on the part of the directors (especially Haydn Williams) driven by nationalistic zeal as Evans (1997:

28–30) argues. The notion of 'blame' is not one that adequately explains the reasons for the failure of Teledu Cymru; rather, a complex interweaving of events, circumstances and personalities led to the formation and failure of a television company that was founded on clear ideological principles. Teledu Cymru emerged and operated in a context characterized by internal and external divisions, financial difficulties and lack of internal financial control, external criticism, technical problems and shifting government policy. Arguably, those involved in the company were operating within a climate over which they had little control especially as the timing of the establishment of Teledu Cymru, coinciding as it did with Pilkington's review of broadcasting, was unfortunate.[2]

Indeed, the Pilkington Committee's role in the formation of Teledu Cymru has been one of the main omissions of the historiography relating to the company. The committee overshadowed much of the deliberation and decision-making in the early years of the 1960s at a time when demands were being made on the government from the Continuation Committee, the ITA and the BBC. The timing of the emergence of Teledu Cymru resulted in delayed decision-making and compromise from a government not only having to balance the demands that were being made on it, but from one which had to avoid pre-empting the Pilkington Committee's recommendations.

Criticisms could be made of the key players in the history of the company. The ITA could be criticized for not properly scrutinizing the company once it had been established. The government should have responded in a more active way, particularly after Pilkington, to remedy the situation in Wales. Clearly, the lack of commercial expertise and of financial management amongst the Teledu Cymru directors lays some responsibility on their shoulders. In this sense, there was no one person or organization entirely at fault. The failure of the company came about as a result of a combination of factors that worked to produce a difficult environment in which a commercial television company, founded as it was on clear ideological goals, found it impossible to operate.

Background

The roots of Teledu Cymru can be traced back over a decade before its inception. The activity surrounding the submissions and reaction to the 1949–51 Beveridge Committee, which considered the future of broadcasting in the UK, provides a framework for the study of the broadcasting politics in Wales in the early 1960s. What emerged from the submissions from Welsh political and cultural groups was a lack of consensus as to the best way forward for broadcasting in Wales. The BBC's Welsh Advisory Council, for example, put forward the suggestion of a Welsh unit within a wider British broadcasting framework, whereas the cultural group, Undeb

Cymru Fydd (The New Wales Union), called for an independent broadcasting corporation for Wales. This lack of agreement was to characterize the debates over Teledu Cymru 10 years later.

The key themes that emerged from the submissions to the Beveridge Committee and the wider debates were the threat to, and even disappearance of, a 'Welsh way of life' as characterized mainly by the Welsh language and culture. Another related theme was that of the alien influence of broadcasting, emanating as it did from London and – in the views of the Welsh groups that engaged with the broadcasting debate at the time – paying scant regard to the needs of Welsh listeners. At the same time, there was a recognition that broadcasting, in Welsh hands, could help revitalize the nation and keep the 'way of life' alive. One theme that did succeed in uniting the submitting groups was the rejection of the notion of commercial broadcasting on the grounds that such a service would not be able to answer the demands of the Welsh-language audience in particular.

Although the Committee decided to recommend the continuation of the broadcasting monopoly, it did so with what it termed 'safeguards' against the perceived dangers (Briggs 1979: 349–51). Allied to this was the suggestion that regional commissions be established in Wales, Scotland and Northern Ireland to oversee broadcasting developments in the respective nations and to 'secure their effective autonomy' (Beveridge 1951: 190). The Beveridge Committee did not see these commissions as leading to complete autonomy within (or without) the BBC, but it called for what it termed a 'federal delegation of powers' that would include a degree of financial independence (1951: 160). On 15 May 1952, the (now Conservative) government published its White Paper.[3] Contrary to the recommendations of the Beveridge Committee, the government made clear its intention of pursuing the notion of a commercially funded television service. It also recommended the creation of a Broadcasting Council for Wales, which would have an advisory role in relation to the new television service.

Television first came to Wales when the Postmaster-General, the Earl de la Warr, opened the Wenvoe transmitter on 15 August 1952. A degree of autonomy had been granted to Wales in 1937 with the establishment of the Welsh radio service, but this was brought to an abrupt halt with the outbreak of war in 1939. All services bar the Home Service were shut down and very little Welsh material (in Welsh or English) was heard until after 1945. When television arrived in Wales the BBC in Wales was tied to the West of England. The early 1950s saw the advent of the opt-out system whereby a 'national region' such as Wales could opt-out of the national (British) network and broadcast programmes of a 'regional' interest. However, in broadcasting Welsh language programmes during this opt-out period, the BBC would have deprived the English-language majority of programmes in English. Consequently, programmes in Welsh were broadcast at off-peak, often very unsociable hours, such as Sunday lunchtime.

The government's second White Paper on television in November 1953 proposed the establishment of a rival commercial television service.[4] The government had decided that the hitherto unused frequencies in Band III would be allocated to the new service and in doing so, they effectively negated the BBC's plans to create an all-Wales service that would serve the Welsh-speaking parts of west and north Wales (Davies 1994: 206). From that point on, Alun Oldfield-Davies, the Controller of the BBC in Wales, fought a running battle with the BBC in London to allow for additional resources in order to strengthen the Corporation's output in Wales.

On 9 December 1953, following a question from the Labour MP Raymond Gower, the Assistant Postmaster-General had confirmed that none of the initial ITV stations was likely to be in Wales (Hansard 1953a). The first ITV stations were to be established in the populous metropolitan areas of London, Birmingham and Manchester. Despite this, doubts were raised at this early stage with regard to the place of commercial television stations in Wales on two grounds: the commercial viability and general desirability. In a House of Commons debate on government television policy on 15 December 1953, Ness Edwards, the Labour MP for Caerphilly and former Postmaster-General, raised doubts over the general desirability of commercial television: 'Do they [the government] really think that education, religion and subjects of social importance will really be supported by beer, pools and pills?' (Hansard 1953b). He then turned his attention to Wales:

> Does the Minister for Welsh Affairs think that there will be a commercial programme in West Wales? Does he think that there will be one in North Wales? ... [A]ll the applications for commercial licences are in the best market areas – London, Manchester and Birmingham ... This Government of Tory businessmen at least ought to know that advertisers only advertise where it pays to advertise, and it will not pay to advertise in Montgomery or Meirioneth or West Wales or North Wales ... (Hansard 1953c)

The following year, during the debate on the Second Reading of the Television Bill on 25 March 1954, Eirene White, Labour MP for Flint East (north-east Wales) drew the House of Commons' attention to the scale of the objections to commercial television that she had received:

> Since the Government's proposals to have commercial television were first mooted, I have had a larger correspondence from outside my own constituency on this subject than I have had on any other subject since becoming connected with politics. I have had a number of constituency letters on the matter which is natural enough, but I

> have had from all over North Wales letters from educational bodies, from teachers, from associations such as the Workers' Educational Association, from religious bodies, from cultural bodies, and from Women's Institutes. Every single one without exception has implored me to oppose commercial television. (Hansard 1954)

She went on to state that she had not received any communication in support of commercial television from a Welsh source and that there was 'a very strong feeling indeed in Wales against this proposal for commercial television' (Hansard 1954). The reasons given for this were twofold: firstly that the Welsh people respected the 'cultural standards' established by the BBC and secondly that the Welsh-speaking population would not be considered a mass audience by advertisers and therefore would not be served by commercial interests: 'They feel they would be far better served by seeing the money to be devoted to commercial television interests devoted to the extension of the services of the BBC' (Hansard 1954). In this respect, the tone of the debate had changed from a sense that the BBC in Wales was 'bad' because of the perceived BBC-London bias and Anglicizing influence, to a sense that it was 'good' because it is better than any Welsh *commercial* broadcaster could ever be.

The parliamentary debate over ITV, from a Welsh perspective, focused on the perceived damage that would be inflicted on the language and culture of Wales from a market-driven service. The arguments, however, appear to be confined to Parliament, as, during the period 1952–56, there is little evidence to suggest that the population at large together with the main cultural organizations in Wales were overly concerned with developments. This was to change, however, with the advent of commercial television in September 1955 and the ITA's announcement of a licence area for south Wales and the west of England in 1956.

The main characteristic of the Independent Television service was its regional base and regional flavour, which was in stark contrast to the still London-centric BBC structure. By 1962, whilst the BBC produced around 33 per cent of its total output outside of London, ITV produced approximately 60 per cent (Independent Television Authority 1962: 7). After the launch of the new service in 1955, the network spread across the UK, with local consortia of mainly industrial, business and entertainment interests competing for the right to broadcast in a particular region.

The period between 1956 and 1959 highlighted a number of issues which are a key to understanding the history of Teledu Cymru. It is clear from the cultural, political and educational groups and institutions that engaged in broadcasting politics in the late 1950s that the shared assumption was that television was an influential medium. The main line of argument was that, in order for the Welsh language and culture to survive, a television service for Wales would be a prerequisite. Whilst this common assumption was held by the groups, at the same time there was a distinct lack of clarity over the best way forward and a number of different voices and opinions were put to the broadcasting authorities and the government. The main division amongst the groups concerned the nature of the service – commercial or public service. At the same time, both the ITA and the government came under increasing pressure to act to move towards a Welsh television service, not only from the aforementioned groups, but, in the case of the government, from the BBC. The Corporation was keenly aware of the nature of the competition from commercial television and during the period embarked upon an effort to secure its own service for Wales.

It is clear that a shift took place between 1954 and 1955, when the provision of a unified Welsh television service was not high on the agenda of either the ITA or the government, and late 1956, when, as a result of pressure, the ITA and the BBC were competing for control over a future service. The years following the announcement that commercial television had arrived in Wales (in October 1956), therefore, saw an intensification of political and institutional attention on the issue.

The genesis of Teledu Cymru

The Teledu Cymru initiative stemmed from the widespread view that the media influenced cultural life and as such needed to be harnessed to a nationalist agenda. The lack of consensus over what the agenda should be – public service, commercial, Welsh, English – led to a situation by 1959 (the first National Television Conference) where there were no unified proposals coming from Wales. The advent of commercial television in Wales in 1956, together with the fact that the BBC's television coverage of Wales was only partial, provided a platform for political intervention. From 1956 onwards, the level of activity amongst political and cultural pressure groups increased and the role of the ITA and the government became increasingly prominent. At this point, the complexity of Welsh politics meshed with the changing nature of television in Wales and engaged with Westminster politics. Added to this was a BBC under increasing pressure from ITV and a growth in the institutional rivalry between the two broadcasters. The environment from which the Teledu Cymru initiative emerged was one that fused Welsh politics with Westminster politics. Previous accounts have failed to pay regard to this complex interweaving of factors in their considerations of the origins of Teledu Cymru.

By April 1956, two groups had indicated an interest in applying for the south Wales and west of England area licence, but by the end of May, these groups had combined to form a consortium (ITA Minutes 1956a). An advert inviting applications for the licence area was published in the press in July 1956 and by September of that year ten applications had been received (including those from existing broadcasters such as ATV and Granada) (ITA Minutes 1956b). The Authority decided to interview four groups, all of which were interviewed on 16 October 1956. The ITA agreed to give the licence to Television Wales and West Ltd (TWW) on the understanding that NBC and RCA (the company's American shareholders) would not be involved in the company. The applicant agreed to this condition.

The ITA, in creating a new licence area for this part of the UK, was driven by technical and economic considerations. As Sendall (1982: 210) notes:

> It was a hybrid area determined in part by what was considered the necessary population coverage to sustain a viable independent company and in part by the ineluctable fact that no transmitter located near the Bristol Channel and, as technical factors dictated, near the Wenvoe transmitter of the BBC, could throw a signal to the north and west of the estuary without also reaching south and east.

At a later date, Charles Hill, former Postmaster-General and later Chairman of the ITA, referred to Wales as an 'awkward area' in his broadcasting memoirs (1974: 48). The reason for this, as he outlined, was that TWW had to serve Wales and England in both the Welsh and English languages. He tells the story of the Welsh Parliamentary Group urging him to establish a purely Welsh company on the grounds that Wales was a country in its own right. However, several days later, one of the MPs saw Hill privately and told him to ignore what his fellow MPs had said. As Hill (1974: 48) wrote:

> Wales needed the English 'rump', for without it and the advertising income derived from it a Welsh company would be too poor to put on an acceptable service. This, indeed, was the snag. The English part of the area supplied the larger share of the income, although its population was but a minority of the population of the whole area. Wales would have to pay for its nationalism and the price would be high.

Referring to the St Hilary transmitter in the Vale of Glamorgan, John Davies (1994: 214) wrote in a somewhat sardonic manner:

> The area it served was roughly the same as that served by Wenvoe, for the Authority had decided that south Wales and south-western England should constitute a single franchise territory, presumably on the grounds that, as the mistake had been made twice, there was no reason why it should not be made a third time.

Following a period of delay (mainly due to the issue of the location of the ITA transmitter in south Wales following concerns that the height would interfere with the flight path of air traffic), TWW went on the air for the first time on 14 January 1958. As the 1958 edition of the *Television Annual* noted: 'Independent television . . . grows like a lusty adolescent, rapidly increasing its frame. The network is now spreading to . . . South Wales and the South-West. Its "flesh", the audience within reach of the network, waxes fatter each month' (Bailey 1958: 11).

The period between 1959 and 1961 witnessed a heightened level of activity in the demand for a television service which would cover the whole of Wales. Driven by Plaid Cymru,[5] and subsequently by Undeb Cymru Fydd,[6] a National Television Conference was called and held in Cardiff on 18 September 1959. A complex web of cultural nationalism, institutional rivalry, lack of consensus amongst Welsh groups and government policy on television ensured that the conference would not be an easy one. A representative gathering from all walks of Welsh life debated the future of television in Wales and agreed on a resolution that charged a small group to continue with the work of pressing the government and broadcasting bodies for a separate television service for Wales. The conference highlighted divisions or, at least, a lack of agreement on the best way to proceed with this goal. The parameters were left relatively open to definition and interpretation.

The committee that emerged from the first conference, calling itself the Continuation Committee, met for the first time on 13 November 1959.[7] By the time it met for the second time on 11 December, Haydn Williams, the chair of the committee, had prepared a technical memorandum that came to the conclusion that, given technical restraints, the best way forward for a television service for the whole of Wales would be via the ITA. At the same time Williams mapped out the clear cultural aims of any company that would be charged with providing a service to the west and north of Wales and, ultimately, to the whole of the country. The Continuation Committee then met with Robert Fraser at the ITA on 7 January 1960 and with the BBC on 22 January, a sign that the ITA route was not the only option available. A third Continuation Committee meeting, this time with government ministers, took place on 22 January 1960.

The Continuation Committee continued to produce memoranda suggesting ways of overcoming the technical problems, whilst at the same time the BBC went on the offensive with a meeting on 3 May with government ministers to put their case for a television service for Wales. On 6 August 1960, during a visit to the National Eisteddfod in Cardiff, Sir Robert Fraser announced that the ITA would soon be inviting applications from companies to operate an ITV service in the west Wales area. The BBC's reaction to the announcement began a flurry of memoranda and correspondence, which reached the highest levels of the Corporation and of the ITA.

On 12 September 1960, Haydn Williams invited a group of people who he thought might act as sponsors of a new ITV company for west Wales. The aims of the proposed company were made clear:

> [T]he prime purpose of the company would be presented to the public and those in authority as a desire on behalf of the Promoters to contribute towards the safeguarding of the language and culture of Wales through this potent instrument of culture and entertainment. (NLW 1960)

Those present were Cennydd Traherne, Lady Olwen Carey Evans (the daughter of the former Liberal Prime Minister David Lloyd George), Gwynfor Evans, Sir T. H. Parry-Williams (former Professor of Welsh at Aberystwyth) and Tom Jones. Work began on eliciting financial backing for the company and in forming clear ideals for the new service.

At the same time, the Continuation Committee was still active in pressing the government for the third transmitter to provide a west and north Wales service. The BBC fought back at the ITA again on 4 October when Hugh Carleton Greene, the Director-General, launched an attack on the Authority's plans for Wales (BBC WAC 1960). As a result a fierce volley of letters went back and forth between the two institutions.

In the meantime, the Wales Television Association (which was established as a result of the meeting called by Haydn Williams in September 1960) was developing its structures and plans. Shareholders continued to come forward, mobilized not only by Haydn Williams but also by Plaid Cymru. On 7 April 1961, the invitation to apply for the west and north Wales licence was released by the ITA (ITA Press Notice 1961) and on 15 May, the Wales Television Association submitted its application.[8] Interviews took place on 30 May in Cardiff, and on 6 June 1961 the licence was awarded to the Wales Television Association. A second National Conference was called by Undeb Cymru Fydd on 7 July 1961 at which concerns were expressed regarding the way in which the Continuation Committee had operated, in the sense that three members of the Committee (Williams, Traherne and Ellis) were also directors of a company applying for an ITV licence. It was strongly suggested that the three had taken advantage of their position on the Continuation Committee in pushing for the licence.

On 20 June 1961, the Wales Television Association met to hear the news that the Postmaster-General had given the go-ahead for the ITA to build a transmitter in the Flint-Denbigh area of north-east Wales, thus extending coverage to the whole of west and north Wales. However, there were certain conditions attached to this that were seen by the company and the ITA as onerous, including the suggestion that 50 per cent of the company's material should be original material. The ITA negotiated these conditions with the Postmaster-General and secured an agreement of an eventual 10 hours of originated programming per week, still a figure far higher than any other regional company of a similar size. This compromise position was put to the Board and accepted, though not without discussion over the financial implications of such a deal. The financial concerns were to emerge at directors' meetings throughout the year.

The period after January 1962 witnessed increased criticism of the new company. Internally, divisions were rife over the financial situation; technically, the roll-out of transmitters proved to be slow for a variety of reasons and resulted in Teledu Cymru going on air in September 1962 with only the Preseli transmitter in operation. Within this context of debate and uncertainty about the way forward for television in Wales, if Welsh-speaking Wales was looking for fireworks to celebrate the New Year in 1962, they were given them in the form of the pamphlet *Teledu Mamon* (Mammon's Television). In early January 1962 the Welsh Radical Group's Radical Publications of Carmarthen published a provocative 15-page pamphlet in Welsh entitled *Teledu Mamon*. It was written under the pseudonym of 'Sodlau Prysur'.[9] The pamphlet appeared at a time when there were widespread doubts about the company's viability. The pamphlet is best understood in this climate of doubt about the project (a Welsh commercial television station), and of quite fierce divisions within Welsh elites over issues of principle and viability of the project. These doubts and divisions stemmed from political affiliations, an ideological stance opposed to commercialism and reservations about competition.

Teledu Mamon's argument was that, by its very nature, commercial television was at the mercy of the London-based advertisers. This would dictate the timing of programmes and that Welsh programming that had been promised at good viewing hours would again be shunted into the inconvenient off-peak hours. 'The fact that there are a good number of Welsh people who have invested in this company will not impress the advertisers. They have only one measure – the size of the audience. This is the foundation of their ungodly profits over the last few years' (Sodlau Prysur 1962: 9). *Teledu Mamon* is a complex document. On one level it was an angry outburst against commercial television by a BBC employee (for it was written by Aneirin Talfan Davies, at that time Assistant Head of Programmes at the BBC in Cardiff). However, although the pamphlet may have ruffled a few feathers, there is no evidence to suggest that the attack damaged the reputation of the company or its directors. In his personal diary, T.I. Ellis merely referred to the fact that '[i]t would appear that there is an attack on a number of us in a pamphlet from Sodlau Prysur, and that is A.T.D.' (T.I. Ellis Diary 1962). At the same time, however, the pamphlet did hit a number of targets that reflected the underlying concerns about the project amongst Welsh political and cultural groups.

On the air

Teledu Cymru went on the air for the first time on 14 September 1962. The programmes were carried by the Preseli transmitter alone as the other transmitters in Arfon and Moel-y-Parc (the Flint-Denbigh transmitter) were not ready.[10] After speeches by the Lord Mayor of Cardiff, Haydn Williams and Sir Ivone Kirkpatrick (the ITA Chairman), Kirkpatrick pressed the master control button to begin the transmissions (NLW 1962a). Writing in the first edition of the programme television listings journal, *Teledu Cymru* (1962: 3), Haydn Williams stated that,

> The aim of Teledu Cymru is to introduce on your screen the rich heritage and entertainment which exists in Wales. We will try to offer patronage to the Welsh language, but we will also have to offer programmes which will be of interest to those of us who do not speak Welsh ... I hope that the programmes will be interesting and edifying to the people of Wales, and that they will be a way of uniting north and south by allowing one to better understand the other.

The *Western Mail* gave the company a cautious welcome. Its editorial of 14 September posed the question 'A quiet start – and then?' It noted the company's rather inauspicious start but stated that the output would increase as time went on and the other transmitters were opened. The editorial ended by juxtaposing what it saw as two ends of the spectrum, namely Welsh culture and entertainment. The difficult task facing Teledu Cymru, it argued, was to create a satisfactory balance of the two: 'We are still speculating on how much of this network's output would be cultural and Welsh and how much entertainment?' (Teledu Cymru 1962: 3).

At the Board of Directors on 12 October 1962, it was reported that the Television Audience Measurement (TAM) service had estimated that 46,000 homes were receiving the Teledu Cymru signal from the Preseli transmitter (NLW 1962b). When the directors next met on 10 November, Gwynfor Evans proposed that a fourth transmitter (in addition to the ones at Preseli, Arfon and Moel-y-Parc) be erected in Montgomeryshire so as to increase the set count. The directors agreed to put this proposal into abeyance for the time being (although no reason was given), however it could be said to demonstrate a certain amount of confidence on behalf of the Board that they should already be thinking in terms of a fourth station (NLW 1962c). However, it could also suggest that Evans was concerned at the likely slow growth in the overall set count and that his suggestion, in the eyes of the Board, complicated an already complex situation. The implications of an increased set count was one of the main items for discussion at the Board meeting on 23 November. The Sales Director, Philip Thomas, estimated that a count of 100,000 with three transmitters and an average TAM rating of 45 would result in a net income of £400,000 (NLW 1962d).[11]

At a meeting of the Independent Television Authority on 18 December 1962, the financial situation of Teledu Cymru was a topic of discussion, the outcome of which was an agreement on the part of the ITA to a moratorium on the balance of the rental due for the first year of the company's operation (ITA Minutes 1962). The Teledu Cymru Board meeting on 21 December 1962 received a report from the Chairman, Haydn Williams, which predicted a set count of 124,000 by the time the Moel-y-Parc transmitter would begin transmitting. At the same meeting, concerns were raised as to the late hours at which Welsh-language programmes were broadcast. This practice was defended by Williams and Nathan Hughes on the grounds that the company had to transmit network programmes that attracted high TAM ratings as these resulted in large advertising revenues (NLW 1962e).

The first Board meeting of 1963 on 25 January highlighted the growing tensions between the directors and Nathan Hughes, the company's General Manager. On a more positive note, the Moel-y-Parc transmitter, covering the Flint-Denbigh region, began transmitting on 28 January. This fact was welcomed in the first meeting of the ITA's Advisory Committee for Wales on 1 February 1963 which also noted the ITA's sympathy for the 'cultural aspirations' of Wales (ITA CW 1963a). Despite the addition of a third transmitter, the financial situation of Teledu Cymru grew worse. On 25 February, Nathan Hughes wrote to all directors alerting them to his concern that the quantity of original programming being produced was in excess of the company's facilities and resources. The meeting of the Board of Directors on 1 March underlined this fact. Pre-air losses were confirmed as being £160,000 and the set count had only reached 83,000 (NLW 1963a). On 7 March, the Teledu Cymru directors met with the ITA. The annual rate of loss was estimated at £100,000 and Fraser raised the key question as to whether or not the ITA was right to expect the company to become a viable proposition even with three transmitters (NLW 1963b). A two-day directors' meeting on 28 and 29 March called for reductions in expenditure, noting that whilst the weekly expenditure in March 1963 was £8,000, income was only £6,500 (NLW 1963c).

Meeting on 3 May 1963, the ITA's Advisory Committee for Wales noted a chronic lack of income for Teledu Cymru, which was hampering the effective running of the company. The key issue for the Authority was the need to ensure the conversion of sets and to ensure that relay companies (which relayed television signals, often via cable, to communities that did not fall under the immediate area covered by a transmitter) carried Teledu Cymru programmes (ITA CW 1963b). By the time of the meeting of the full Authority on 9 May, however, it became apparent that there was no possibility of Teledu Cymru continuing as viable programme company. The idea was raised of TWW transmitting its programmes from Teledu Cymru's three transmitters and this was put to a meeting between a group of Teledu Cymru directors (Haydn Williams, Emrys Roberts, Cennydd Traherne, Eric Thomas and P. O. Williams) and ITA senior officers on 14 May 1963 (ITA Minutes 1963; NLW 1963d). At a meeting of the Board of Directors on 17 May 1963, the decision was taken (unanimously) that all original programme production would cease.

The company failed because it was never a viable financial proposition. The directors could be blamed for being blinded by their nationalistic zeal, Haydn Williams being fingered as the main culprit. The directors, it could be argued, were interpreting the cultural mission too loosely, at the expense of sound financial management (Evans 1997: 28). Whilst acknowledging this argument – based on the evidence, there is no doubt that the controversial figure of Haydn Williams created numerous problems for Teledu Cymru – it does not reflect the complexity of the reasons for failure. The company did not plan properly or have realistic forecasts of finance. Neither did it have a united Board of Directors or exercise clear financial control. It was also blighted by internal staffing problems. The ITA and the Post Office could be accused of being responsible for burdening the company with a high number of hours of original programming, an issue that Bernard Sendall describes as 'breathtakingly unrealistic' (Evans 1997: 14). Blame could also be apportioned to the south Wales relay companies who refused to carry Teledu Cymru programmes, insisting instead on relaying the programming of the neighbouring Westward Television.

For the remainder of 1963, Teledu Cymru operated as a relay company, transmitting the Welsh-language and Welsh-interest programmes of TWW together with the ITV network programmes. On 16 October, Teledu Cymru shareholders voted in favour of the TWW takeover bid (*The Times* 1963: 7). In a memorandum to the ITA on 30 October 1963, Lyn Evans, the ITA's officer for Wales, reported that thanks to Eric Thomas a good deal 'has been salvaged from the WWN wreck' (ITC 1963). On 4 December 1963, Lord Derby, Alfred Francis, Huw T. Edwards, John Baxter and Alfred Goodman from TWW were interviewed for the new Wales and West franchise area. The contract was offered to the company on condition that they avoided clashing with the BBC on Welsh and Welsh-interest programmes (ITC 1963). However, the same day, Derby wrote to Charles Hill, the ITA's Chairman, and noted that he was unwilling to let any Teledu Cymru director join the 'new' TWW board as they had let Wales down and would be a 'disaster' (ITC 1963). At the final Teledu Cymru Board meeting, the directors were to learn that TWW would not be requiring the services of any of their staff. On 27 January 1964, Teledu Cymru as a company was officially taken over by TWW and ceased to exist.

Programming

Teledu Cymru's programming policy can be split into two distinct periods: that prior to January 1963 and that after the first week of

January 1963. From 14 September 1962 until the end of the year, Welsh-language and Welsh-interest programmes were transmitted between 6.06 p.m. and 7.00 p.m. and between 10.30 p.m./10.45 p.m. until 11.00 p.m./ 11.15 p.m. on weekdays. Only occasionally were Welsh-language or Welsh-interest programmes broadcast at the weekend. It can be seen from this that although such programmes were broadcast during 'good evening hours' (between 6.00 p.m. and 7.00 p.m.), the programmes broadcast later were considered to be on the periphery of the schedule. In general, the programmes during the early evening period tended to be those originating from Teledu Cymru whilst the late programmes were those from TWW (such as the magazine programme *Amser Te* or the quiz show *Taro Deg*). It should also be noted that the government's regulations allowed for a total average of around eight hours broadcasting per day.

During the first period (September to December 1962), Teledu Cymru originated approximately 4 hours 30 minutes of its own programming per week, with approximately 3 hours per week coming from TWW. The remainder came from the network companies such as Associated-Rediffusion, ATV and Granada.[12]

During the last week of November 1962, Teledu Cymru announced that it would be increasing its original output and transmitting around 10 hours per week of Welsh-language and Welsh-interest programmes from January 1963 onwards, thus Teledu Cymru entered the second period which was heralded by the company as 'quite an achievement and a challenge . . .' At the same time, it reassured its viewers that they would not be missing out on the popular network programmes such as *Coronation Street* or *Emergency Ward 10*, thereby underlining the popularity of such programmes amongst the Teledu Cymru audience (Teledu Cymru 1962b). By extending the early evening hours from 6.06 p.m. to 7.30 p.m., Teledu Cymru was able to boast that it offered Welsh-language or Welsh-interest programming during the peak hour period (7.00 p.m.–7.30 p.m.). It also offered viewers the chance to watch programming from Wales on a Sunday. For example, on Sunday 6 January 1963, viewers could watch *Myfyr a Mawl* (a religious programme) from 5.00 p.m. to 5.30 p.m. and TWW's *Amser Te* between 5.30 p.m. and 6.05 p.m. The monthly networked *Land of Song* (a TWW production) was transmitted from 6.15 p.m. to 6.55 p.m. and at 10.35 p.m. a programme on Welsh museums, *Trysorau Cymru* (another TWW production) was broadcast (Teledu Cymru 1963a).

As a result of the increased broadcasting hours, and the opening of the Moel-y-Parc transmitter, Teledu Cymru maintained an average of 10 hours and 51 minutes of Welsh-language or Welsh-interest programmes per week (the balance between the two languages averaging out as being 50:50), thereby fulfilling the requirements as set out by the Postmaster-General (Sendall 1983: 79). There was, therefore, a concerted effort on the part of the company to reach its target, albeit with the help of programming from TWW.

Teledu Cymru's strengths in Welsh language programmes were in the factual area. TWW had pioneered with quiz shows and these were retransmitted to the Teledu Cymru area. Teledu Cymru soon developed a strong news output and used expertise of John Roberts Williams and the ex-BBC journalist T. Glynne Davies. The company pioneered in this area and the team headed by Williams provided peak-time Welsh-language television news for the first time ever. One reason for the strength of the service was the fact that Williams had been editor of *Y Cymro*, the Welsh-language weekly newspaper, for 16 years before joining Teledu Cymru and had built up an impressive base of contacts. The news team also depended on stringers[13] to report from various parts of the area who were willing to contribute to the venture for very little money.[14] Sport was also seen as an important part of the output and *Cip ar Chwarae* and its English-language counterpart, *Welsh Spotlight*, featured regularly in the schedule.

The more general Welsh programming tended to focus on the history, politics and literary traditions of Wales an example being, *Golwg ar Gymru*, produced by Havard Gregory, the company's Senior Producer. Other programmes such as *Pawb a'i Bethau* was presented by John Roberts Williams and profiled Welsh 'characters'. Although no footage exists of this programme, the billing suggests that the aim of the programme was to capture a way of life that was rapidly changing or disappearing, which is important given the nature of Teledu Cymru itself and its cultural aim (Teledu Cymru 1963b).

At the same time, concerns about the location of Welsh-language programming in the schedule were prevalent and were discussed in the Board meeting on 21 December 1962. It was minuted that '[m]embers of the Board were perturbed at the late hour in which Welsh language programmes were being transmitted' (NLW 1962e). Haydn Williams and Nathan Hughes defended the schedule, pointing out that locating such programmes was very difficult 'in view of the necessity of the company to transmit Network programmes which commanded a very high TAM rating' (NLW 1962e). Already, the realities of commercial television were hitting home, and the meeting signalled a turning point in the fortunes of the company.

The issue was raised again on New Years Day 1963 when Nathan Hughes wrote a memorandum entitled 'Local origination and TWW programmes' to the company's Programme Committee. He outlined the company's policy on transmitting Welsh and Welsh-interest programming during the period 6.00 p.m. to 7.00 p.m. and drew attention to the fact that most of the Teledu Cymru originated programmes were of a magazine style because the company had no formal agreement with the artists union and could not, therefore produce music programmes.

Hughes also highlighted the fact that light entertainment programmes such as *Discs a Gogo* and *Taro Deg* were already being supplied by TWW. Hughes' suggestion was for the company to consider presenting Welsh-language programmes in the 7.00 p.m. to 7.30 p.m. slot on certain week nights. Whilst acknowledging that this would be a risk in commercial terms, he argued that Teledu Cymru and the ITA could be exposed to serious criticism should no attempt be made to transmit Welsh-language programmes between 7.00 p.m. and 10.30 p.m. He ended by arguing that it was essential that a policy decision be made as soon as possible on the notion of transmitting such programmes between 7.00 p.m. and 10.30 p.m. (NLW 1963e). As noted in section 7.4.3.1, the company had already taken the decision to broadcast a Welsh-language programme between 7.00 p.m. and 7.30 p.m. and had announced its decision at the end of November 1962 in the programme journal.

Criticism of Teledu Cymru's Welsh-language programming also became an issue following the announcement of the cessation of original production. On 23 May 1963, the radio and television critic of the Welsh-language weekly newspaper, *Baner ac Amserau Cymru*, reported on the motion passed at the Undeb Cymru Fydd Women's Conference criticizing Teledu Cymru programmes for not being at peak-time hours. The lack of Welsh-language programming was noted as being disappointing: 'We were promised more than was possible to achieve' (*Baner ac Amserau Cymru* 1963: 5).

Conclusions

The debates surrounding the establishment and eventual collapse of Teledu Cymru resonate with other areas of Welsh life – education, publishing, cultural activities. That is, a community that sees itself as being under threat from an increasing tide of Anglo-American culture (in all its forms), resisting and creating structures whereby the tide can be stemmed. However, there also exists a sense of ownership and control from within the community itself (Hechter 1975). Ironically, the fact that Wales is a stateless nation creates a situation where the British state has ultimate control and it is as a result of support from the British state that these new structures emerge (as was the case with Teledu Cymru). Colin Williams (1980: 229) raises this crucial point and it resonates with the Teledu Cymru venture:

> The enigma of Welsh cultural promotion is that it has consistently been portrayed as a reactive response to the intrusion of the British state, and the imposition of a uniform Anglophone culture. Yet it appears, given the increased demands made by Welsh organizations upon the state, that the vitality and the future of Welsh may depend

> to a greater extent than ever before, on the capacity of central and local government to establish the conditions within which the language may flourish.

The Teledu Cymru directors had to 'work the system' in terms of the British state and make the system work to their best advantage.

One of the key issues that explains the demise was the cultural basis of the company and, in this respect, Evans (1997: 28) is broadly correct. The Board lacked the requisite business and financial acumen required for any television company operating within the commercial sector. Added to this, the evidence shows that the organization and management of the company was poorly executed, particularly in the area of finance. At the same time, however, the geographical (overlapping areas) and technical complexities (transmitter delays and the demands for Channel 13 in Band III) created a situation that made the day-to-day operation difficult. The growing institutional rivalry between the BBC and the ITA was bound up with the technical issues as both broadcasters demanded Channel 13 in Band III to provide a service for Wales. This debate, taking place as it did in the shadow of Pilkington, exacerbated delays which in turn created financial difficulties for Teledu Cymru. The timing of the project is also a crucial factor in assessing the company's history. The willingness of the ITA to advertise the contract and the Wales Television Association to apply for it were badly timed. Haydn Williams and the Wales Television Association were seeking a speedy solution to a problem that had been in existence for a number of years and the ITA was keen to appear in a good light to both Pilkington and the government. Had both parties waited until after the Pilkington Report, the venture might have been more fruitful.

Teledu Cymru gave an intimation of what *could* be achieved if economic and technical circumstances had been more favourable. Although BBC Wales was established in 1964 and a separate ITV network began to transmit in 1965, it took another 18 years and another Conservative government for a separate Welsh company to emerge and for a new chapter in Welsh broadcasting history to begin.

Bibliography

Bailey, K. (ed.) (1958) *The Television Annual for 1958*. London: Odhams Press.

Baner ac Amserau Cymru (1963), 23 May.

BBC W[ritten] A[rchive] C[entre] (1960) R34/1144. Cardiff Business Club. 4 October. Address by H. Carleton Greene, Director-General of the B.B.C.

Bevan, D. (1984) The mobilization of cultural minorities: the case of Sianel Pedwar Cymru, *Media, Culture and Society*, 6: 103–17.

Beveridge, Lord (Chair) (1951) *Report of the Broadcasting Committee, 1949*, Cmd 8117. London: HMSO.
Briggs, A. (1979 [2000 reprint]) *The History of British Broadcasting in the United Kingdom. Volume IV. Sound and Vision.* Oxford: Oxford University Press.
Butt Philip, A. (1975) *The Welsh Question: Nationalism and Welsh Politics 1945–1970.* Cardiff: University of Wales Press.
Davies, J. (1994) *Broadcasting and the BBC in Wales.* Cardiff: University of Wales Press.
Evans, I.G. (1997) Teledu Cymru: an independent television service for Wales? (1959–1963). Unpublished MA dissertation, University of Wales.
Hansard (1953a) Vol. 521, col. 242. London: HMSO.
Hansard (1953b) Vol. 522, col. 240. London: HMSO.
Hansard (1953c) Vol. 522, col. 241. London: HMSO.
Hansard (1954) Vol. 525, col. 1505. London: HMSO.
Hechter, M. (1975) *Internal Colonialism: the Celtic Fringe in British National Development, 1536–1966.* London: Routledge & Kegan Paul.
Hill, C. (1974) *Behind the Screen: the Broadcasting Memoirs of Lord Hill of Luton.* London: Sidgwick & Jackson.
Independent Television Authority (1962) *Annual Report and Accounts.* London: Independent Television Authority.
ITA C[ommittee for] W[ales] (1963a) 1 (63), 1 February.
ITA CW 3 (1963b) (63), 3 May.
ITA Minutes (1956a) 55 (56), 29 May.
ITA Minutes (1956b) 62 (56), 18 September.
ITA Minutes (1956c) 64 (56), 16 October.
ITA Minutes (1962) 169 (62), 18 December.
ITA Minutes (1963) 176 (63), 9 May.
ITA Press Notice 141 (1961) 'Programme Contracting Arrangements for West and North Wales', 7 April.
Independent Television Comission (ITC) (1963) A/S/0038/8. 1964 Contract – Applications – J – TWW.
National Library of Wales (NLW) (1960) Elwyn Roberts Papers 20. 'Television for Wales, Meeting of Sponsors' minutes, 12 September.
NLW (1962a) Sir T.H. Parry-Williams and Lady Amy Parry-Williams Papers. LL58. Programme for the Official Opening, 14 September.
NLW (1962b) Emrys Roberts Papers 20. Minutes of the Executive Committee of Teledu Cymru, 12 October.
NLW (1962c) Emrys Roberts Papers 20. Minutes of the Executive Committee of Teledu Cymru, 10 November.
NLW (1962d) Emrys Roberts Papers 20. Minutes of the Executive Committee of Teledu Cymru, 23 November.
NLW (1962e) Emrys Roberts Papers 20. Minutes of the Board of Directors of Teledu Cymru, 21 December.

NLW (1963a) Emrys Roberts Papers 20. Minutes of the Board of Directors of Teledu Cymru, 1 March.

NLW (1963b) Emrys Roberts Papers 20. Minutes of a meeting between Teledu Cymru and the ITA, 7 March.

NLW (1963c) Emrys Roberts Papers 20. Minutes of the Board of Directors of Teledu Cymru, 28 & 29 March.

NLW (1963d) Emrys Roberts Papers 20. Minutes of the Board of Directors of Teledu Cymru, 14 May.

NLW (1963e) T.I. Ellis Papers. C59. Memorandum from the General Manager to the Programme Committee, 1 January.

Sendall, B. (1982) *Independent Television in Britain. Volume 1. Origin and Foundation, 1946–62*. London: Macmillan.

Sendall, B. (1983) *Independent Television in Britain. Volume 2. Expansion and Change, 1958–68*. London: Macmillan.

Smith, D. (1999) *Wales: a Question for History*. Bridgend: Seren.

Sodlau Prysur (1962) *Teledu Mamon*. Carmarthen: Radical Publications.

Teledu Cymru (1962a) 14–22 September.

Teledu Cymru (1962b) 25 November–1 December.

Teledu Cymru (1963a) 6–12 January.

Teledu Cymru (1963b) 31 March–5 April.

T.I. Ellis Diary (1962) 6 January.

The Times (1963) 17 October.

Williams, C.H. (1980) Language contact and language change in Wales, 1901–1971: a study in historical geolinguistics, *Welsh History Review*, 10(2): 207–38.

Notes

1 Translates literally as 'Wales Television'.

2 On 13 July 1960, the Conservative government announced its decision to establish a Committee of Inquiry into broadcasting in the UK, to be chaired by Sir Harry Pilkington. The Pilkington Committee reported in 1962.

3 *Memorandum on the Report of the Broadcasting Committee, 1949* (1952), Cmd. 8550. London: HMSO.

4 *Broadcasting: Memorandum on Television Policy* (1953), Cmd. 9005. London: HMSO.

5 The Welsh Nationalist Party.

6 The New Wales Union, a cross-party cultural nationalist society.

7 The members of the Continuation Committee were Cennydd Traherne, Haydn Williams, T.I. Ellis and Jac L. Williams.

8 Four groups were interviewed by the ITA on 30 May: Television Wales Norwest led by Lord Tenby, Gwilym Lloyd George; the Wales Television Association led by Haydn Williams and Traherne;

Cambrian (North and West Wales) Television under the leadership of the Marquess of Bute and Cambrian Television led by Lord Ogmore.

9 This translates as 'Hasty Heels', a play on words, for 'Sodlau Segur' ('Idle Heels') was a regular columnist in the literary journal *Y Genhinen*.

10 The Executive Committee of Teledu Cymru were aware of the fact that only one transmitter would be operational at the end of July, but decided to go ahead with the launch as planned on 14 September (see NLW. Emrys Roberts Papers 20. Minutes of the Executive Committee of Teledu Cymru, 20 July 1962).

11 The set count was an index based on the total number of all those homes whose aerials were set up in such a way so as to receive the transmissions of a particular mast. The TAM rating was applied to individual programmes, the figure relating to the estimated number of people watching at a given time. The higher the figure in both indexes, the better in terms of advertising revenue.

12 These figures are derived from copies of the programme journal, *Teledu Cymru*. Granada, however, had ceased production of its Welsh programme, *Dewch i Mewn*, when Teledu Cymru began broadcasting in September 1962.

13 Journalists who regularly filed copy from a particular location.

14 Author's interview with John Roberts Williams, 28 February 1998. The programme budget for individual news programmes was often as little as £45, this often coming from the pockets of the staff themselves.

6 LONDON WEEKEND TELEVISION IN THE 1980s: PROGRAMMES, PUBLIC SERVICE OBLIGATIONS, FINANCIAL INCENTIVES

Rod Allen

In the 1970s and the early 1980s, the producer was at the centre of British independent television. Each programme company worked to provide an environment in which the producer could perform at his or her best, and management was careful not to burden producers with such commercial matters as ratings or efficiency of production. The goal of the programme departments of ITV companies was to produce excellent programming, measured on the whole by peer approval rather than ratings. The fact that this objective aligned with the commercial objectives of the companies as well was the reason why producers were allowed to pursue excellence rather than ratings; and it also enabled companies to claim (see, for example, IBA 1975) that they were fulfilling their public service obligations.

In support of these arguments, this chapter looks mainly at activity in the programme-making departments of London Weekend Television (LWT) in the period from approximately 1978 to 1986, when John Birt was head of current affairs and features, and subsequently director of programmes, at LWT. It draws on the personal experience of the author, who was a senior producer and then head of development at LWT over this period, and who thus had the good fortune to share not only the experience of the producer but also the commercial objectives and decision-making of the company over time.

There has always been substantial difficulty in defining precisely what public service means in broadcasting; some would hold, for example, that a public service broadcaster provides an electronic version of Habermas' (1971) public sphere, in which enlightened discussion can be shared by the populace; others argue that universal availability of a broadcasting service containing information, education and entertainment represents public service. The theoretical framework proposed by Tracey (1998) suggests an eight-point list of 'Principles' for a public broadcasting service, grounded in the work of the Pilkington Committee (1962) and with some roots in Steiner's (1985) humanistic approach.[1]

It is possible to find within Tracey's principles much support for the provision of public service broadcasting by a commercial company, such as an ITV programme company, although the sixth principle, which says that public broadcasting should be distanced from vested interests, argues strongly against the provision of public service broadcasting supported by advertising. Many would argue that public service and advertising support are entirely incompatible because the existence of advertising income means that programme scheduling decisions have to be made on commercial grounds alone; but it is certainly true that the system operated by the Independent Broadcasting Authority (IBA) in the period from 1955 to about 1986, under which the Authority approved broadcasting schedules in advance (and often caused them to be changed in a pro-active fashion), meant that a form of public service broadcasting, bounded by the vision of a number of more-or-less enlightened bureaucrats, could be imposed on the ITV companies. Even so, Potter reveals the contempt with which senior LWT executives, notably its highly respected chairman, John Freeman, felt for the IBA and the vision of public service that it imposed on the companies, which he thought consisted of a 'stultifying proportion of its airtime and network access being devoted to worthy but audience-repellant programming' (Potter 1990: 80).[2]

London Weekend Television occupied a unique position in the ITV network: unlike any other programme contractor, it was only on the air, as its name suggested, at the weekend. Together with Thames, Granada, ATV/Central and Yorkshire, it counted as an ITV 'major', and as such it was both entitled and required to supply its proportional share of the network schedule. The companies carved up the network among them according to each one's share of net advertising revenue after levy (NARAL), thus allowing smaller companies like Southern or HTV to produce a few network programmes each year, but effectively excluding the smallest, such as Border, from more than token network exposure. It is important to remember that the company's NARAL share *entitled* it to network access: it was not a matter (as it is today) of a network controller choosing the best programmes from those on offer.

Like every ITV company, LWT was obliged by its contract with the IBA to provide a wide range of programmes across the weekend, which for the purposes of that contract began at 5.00 p.m. on Friday and ended at closedown on Sunday night or Monday morning. In that period, the company had to put on entertainment, drama, current affairs, factual, sports, religious, news, children's and documentary programmes in approximately the proportions it had promised to do in its application for the contract. Carrying a balanced schedule of this kind was itself considered to be a function of public service broadcasting, and broadcasters were particularly valued by the IBA if they could manage to include high-cost, prestigious programming of all kinds. Industry awards, such as BAFTAs and the Prix Italia, were seen as particular identifiers of quality: ratings were not so highly considered.

Under the network tariff system, a programme company was only able to earn from its colleagues on the ITV network a fixed sum of money for each category of programming, no matter what it cost to produce. In the early 1980s, the tariff for *Coronation Street* (Granada, 1960),[3] for example, was £90,000, which Granada received (in a complex mixture of cash and 'points', or credits representing programme exchange value) from the rest of the network for each half-hour episode; by contrast, a major network drama could only command around £400,000 per hour of programme exchange value, while actual production costs were already running upwards to £900,000 or £1 million per hour. So it was difficult to produce prestigious drama without seeking funding from outside the ITV network. Yet once that funding had been found, the financial advantages that became available were substantial; so LWT, along with other programme contractors, developed a taste for overseas sales and co-production.

London Weekend Television was well known for its entertainment and fiction programming, including such shows as *Saturday Live* (1985), *Two's Company* (1976), *Dempsey and Makepeace* (1985), *The Professionals* (1978) and *Philip Marlowe* (1979); Johnny Hawkesworth and John Whitney's *Upstairs Downstairs* (1971) had come to an end in 1976. Some of these programmes were already the subject of complex international co-production agreements, and it is important to understand that at the time the fiscal arrangements surrounding international sales and co-production were such that it was possible to offset a very large amount of the production costs of a programme that was successful in world markets against the programme company's tax – or, more precisely, levy – liabilities. The levy was an excess profits tax that obsessed ITV's managers during the period under review: companies were taxed at the extraordinary rate of 66.7 per cent of net domestic profits, as well as paying the usual corporation tax. But overseas sales revenue could be offset against levy. Thus doing well in export markets not only won hard currency and public relations kudos for the company, but it also created funding to produce or enhance programmes almost literally out of thin air. In this process, the most important strategy was to find an international co-production partner or sales end-user who would commit in advance to the programme. *Philip Marlowe* is a good example: the mini-series about Chandler's famous private eye, played by Powers Booth, was shot in the UK, with the streets of Teddington doubling for the streets of Los Angeles in the 1930s, and LWT's client for the show was Home Box Office (HBO) of the US, whose production chief Jane Deknatel had recently discovered the efficiencies of overseas co-production with the Indian epic *The Far Pavilions* (HBO, 1978).

The effect of the financial regulations was that the income received from HBO for its share of the costs of the programme was not subject to the 66.7 per cent levy, which was only calculated on the basis of domestic profits. So not only did LWT receive the money, but it also received an effective tax credit of 66.7 per cent as well – and in some analyses, it was possible to say that every £1 of overseas income received by the company was actually worth £1.67 in value. The *Philip Marlowe* deal, negotiated by the then head of drama Nick Elliott and by Sydney Perry, the deputy director of programmes, served as a model for the financial advantages obtainable from the levy; by the time it came to negotiating the long-running series *Dempsey and Makepeace* with the Chicago Tribune's broadcast stations, Perry and I had the formula worked out to the company's very best advantage.

By using what came to be known as the levy trick, LWT was able to pursue a policy of producing high-production-value, highly prestigious drama programming that enhanced the company's reputation in terms of public service. Other programmes which used this formula to enhance LWT's profile included Richard Drewett's *The Trial of Lee Harvey Oswald* (1985), for Showtime, the US cable channel, which was based on a formula originally created by Drewett and Jeremy Potter for a reasonably modest domestic production called *The Trial of Richard III* (1984). *Lee Harvey Oswald* was anything but modest: LWT built a replica of the Dallas, Texas, Federal Courthouse in its South Bank studios and imported judge, jury and prosecution and defence teams from the US to populate it for a 5-hour-long programme; and for the first time ever one of the items of intellectual property negotiated for the programme were the telephone rights – US viewers were to phone in whether they thought Oswald was part of a conspiracy or acted on his own, and LWT and Showtime shared a cut of the premium telephone charges for this viewer vote. LWT's share was, of course, set against levy. Under similar financial circumstances the company also made a version of Evelyn Waugh's *Scoop* (1987), adapted by Will Boyd and directed by Gavin Millar, for Mobil Masterpiece Theatre, for which the overseas broadcaster was WGBH-TV in Boston. Another project, an adaptation of E.F. Benson's *Mapp and Lucia* (1985), was partially funded by a group of E.F. Benson fans in New York.

So in the field of drama and entertainment, LWT was able to pursue the perception that it fulfilled its obligation to provide a public service with high-cost and prestigious programming, while at the same time enjoying quite remarkable financial returns from following this policy. In the area of factual programmes, co-production and overseas sales income were not so readily available. Yet in this area there was even less pressure on producers and executives to deliver audiences, and John Birt was free to exercise his theories about factual programme production – with funding provided by shareholders and advertisers. In 1975, John Birt and his LWT colleague Peter Jay (who was to be the first presenter of LWT's *Weekend World* (1972)) published a series of articles in *The Times* (1975) setting out a new and controversial approach to television news and current affairs. Briefly, the articles, under the heading 'Bias against understanding', criticized the contemporary approach to current affairs for moving from the particular to the general; starting, for example, with what was generally thought to be a 'human interest' story about an unemployed person and moving to generalizations about employment policy, said Birt and Jay, was not an effective way of discussing employment policy on television. The use of expert witnesses and the graphic presentation of relevant facts was said by Birt and Jay to be a more efficient way of approaching the problem. Birt and Jay also attacked the practice, prevalent throughout television at the time, of 'researching on film'. The approach then followed widely was to go out and film interviews with relevant people and to try to assemble a story from the material that had been amassed, on the whole finding out what each person had to say during the interview itself. Birt and Jay believed it would be more efficient if the nature of each contribution were to be ascertained in advance, and the filming portion of the exercise limited merely to getting the contributor to say his or her piece in front of the camera, for incorporation into a programme the approximate order of which had been predetermined in advance. This idea came in for a great deal of criticism from contemporary programme makers, who saw it as an encroachment upon their freedom and, worse, as dishonest. They thought that having a predetermined script for a programme meant somehow putting words into the mouths of the interviewees. Actually, all it meant was knowing what the interviewee had to say, which could be achieved by interviewing him or her in advance over the inexpensive telephone, rather than in front of an expensive 16 mm film camera.[4]

Birt and Jay's approach actually made it possible to make programmes with more financial efficiency; it eliminated a great deal of waste in filming interviews that ended up on the cutting room floor, and made the process of interviewing the participants who were essential to the programme shorter. It was, however, open to abuse, and a producer who had already conceived of the ideological thrust of the programme could easily restrict his or her choice of interviewees to those who agreed with it – or, at least, load the argument with articulate individuals on one side against less able proponents on the other. This abuse could be avoided by having managers or executive producers of great probity controlling the output – and if those executives were John Birt or his trusted lieutenants Barry Cox, head of current affairs, or Nick Elliott, head of features, then the theory was likely to hold good. Lesser executives were able to exert less rigorous control.

Although the Birt-Jay theories commanded a good deal of intellectual respect, they could be regarded as a highly risky prospect by a television company that depended on attracting audiences to make its money. The implication of Birt-Jay was the production of programmes that were inherently less attractive to audiences, even if they were more rigorous and addressed issues that were difficult to cover on television.[5]

Perhaps this was unimportant for programmes like *Weekend World,* which appeared at noon on a Sunday, when the available audience was relatively small. And it was *Weekend World* that carried the main burden of promoting Birt-Jay in public, fronted at first by the co-proposer of the theory, Peter Jay, and then (after Jay's appointment as British ambassador to the US) presented by a formidable former Labour MP, Brian Walden. But once he was in charge of LWT's current affairs output, Birt made sure that his theory was applied, to a lesser or greater extent, to the whole of the department's output, much of which was played in vulnerable slots throughout the weekend. David Cox, editor of *Weekend World* from 1977, is quoted in David Docherty's history of LWT as saying 'John's solution to the new areas . . . was to do a *Weekend World* about religion, a *Weekend World* for children, a *Weekend World* for the arts, and a *Weekend World* for broadcasting policy' (Docherty 1990: 140). What is important to understand is that at this time, paradoxically, low ratings positively benefited the company in general terms, and in particular general sales manager Craig Pearman and director of sales Ron Miller had developed a sales story for LWT that generated a 'weekend premium' for the high-quality demographics that were alleged to be delivered by low-rated but high-quality factual programmes (Docherty 1990: 88). The theory under which it was thought low ratings delivered a benefit was based on the absolute monopoly that ITV had over television advertising at the time; in order to reach their own audience targets, so the thinking went, advertisers had to buy more time in order to accumulate sufficient audience impacts. Today, of course, advertisers have much more control over the prices they pay for airtime, and they tend to pay a uniform amount per thousand impacts regardless of the broadcaster's revenue targets. In those days, however, because of the monopoly, ITV companies had considerable power to charge what they wanted for each particular slot; the main control exercised by advertisers took the form of late booking, a practice to which LWT was particularly vulnerable, as its salespeople sold off time for low prices towards the end of each Friday evening. This practice could be compared to the selling of standby seats by airlines; once the aircraft has taken off there is no hope of selling an empty seat, so any price that can be obtained for it is better than none. Equally, once the airtime slot is transmitted, there is no hope of filling it, so any income it can generate is better than none. The gamble the advertiser takes is on whether there is any airtime left, and in times of high demand the late buyer was given short shrift.

So no pressure to win audiences, particularly in off-peak, filtered through to the programme-makers. High quality rather than popular programmes not only allowed LWT's salespeople to tout effectively for the weekend premium, because of the perceived 'quality' demographic, but of course they also pleased the regulators at the IBA (and, it was thought, the 'opinion-formers') and enhanced the perception of public service broadcasting that it was thought benefited the company. (As has been pointed out, LWT chairman John Freeman rather thought that it was the IBA's fault that LWT made all these unpopular shows (Potter 1990: 80)). Other companies' prestige factual programming, such as *This Week* (Associated-Rediffusion/Thames, 1956) and *World in Action* (Granada, 1963), occupied protected peak-time slots that allowed those companies to collect brownie points without genuinely having to create programmes that stood up on their own to win audiences; for many years, for example, *World in Action* played exactly against *Panorama* (BBC, 1957) at 8.00 p.m. on Mondays, leaving the mainstream audience no option but to watch current affairs at that time (BBC2 did not exactly offer a populist alternative). There is absolutely no evidence that the BBC and ITV openly colluded over this arrangement, which greatly benefited both organizations' factual programme-makers, although the IBA defended the practice in public (Potter 1990: 290). Of course, as soon as multi-channel competition was under way the practice was no longer sustainable, with the result that ITV's only factual-in-peak programme is now Granada's sensationalist *Tonight with Trevor Macdonald* (1999), which does not bear scrutiny as a successor to *World in Action*. London Weekend Television's protective strategy towards its factual programme makers was more sophisticated, but no less effective.

John Birt's theory of factual programme-making extended into all corners of his programme empire of the time, and most of the output was executive-produced in a highly hands-on fashion by Birt himself. *Weekend World*, with its (often rather accusatory) film package followed by a major live interview by Jay or Walden of a top politician occupying seventy minutes of Sunday lunchtime, was the flagship for this policy, but it extended into a substantial group of minority and mainstream programmes, some of which were undoubtedly groundbreaking in one way or another. Among the mainstream programmes that benefited from Birt-Jay rigour were Andy Mayer's teen-oriented *London Weekend Show* (LWT, 1977), which established Janet Street-Porter as a television presenter and played in an early evening slot (6.00 or 6:30 p.m.) that would be coveted by entertainment programmes, and *Credo* (LWT, 1974), a programme about religious, moral and ethical issues (to give it its full and deliberate internal description) on which many distinguished journalists, like David Tereshchuk and Cresta Norris, cut their teeth, and which played in the then-mandated religious slot occupied today by the *Antiques Roadshow* (BBC, 1982) and *Emmerdale* (Yorkshire

Television, 1972); this slot, at 6:30 p.m. on Sunday, falls at the time when the second largest audience of the whole week is available to view, yet *Credo* remained an uncompromisingly serious programme.[6]

With the advent of Channel 4 in the early 1980s it became possible for LWT to earn the IBA's approval without having to transmit all of the approval-seeking programmes itself. The London Minorities Unit, which had made *Skin* (LWT, 1978) for the ITV schedule, developed its expertise in making programmes for ethnic minority audiences on Channel 4 with the series *Eastern Eye* (LWT for Channel 4, 1982) and *Black on Black* (LWT for Channel 4, 1982), the executive producer of the latter programme, for Afro-Caribbean viewers, being Trevor Phillips, who went on to present *The London Programme* (LWT, 1975) and is today a London politician and chair of the Equal Opportunities Commission. It would be unfair to attribute these programmes solely to the seeking of brownie points, as they were developed from a deeply held belief among executives and programme-makers alike that television was failing the minority communities; yet it took the opening of Channel 4, with its specific remit to address unserved audiences, to make it possible to show these programmes. Just prior to the start of these programmes, LWT mounted a survey among London's minority communities to find out what kind of programmes they liked; unsurprisingly, the response came back that they liked the same kind of programmes that everyone else liked – Elaine Stritch and Donald Sinden in the LWT sitcom *Two's Company* (1976) was top of the list.

In a similar vein, producer Michael Atwell was encouraged to develop output that appealed to a different minority with his remarkable series *Gay Life* (LWT, 1980). This managed to occupy a relatively mainstream slot on ITV without attracting a great deal of complaint to the IBA or the company, at least partly because it was absolutely honest about its intentions and its target audience. Again, the programme was grounded in its producer's (and his bosses') belief that the minority was generally ill-served by television; but yet it did no harm whatsoever to the company in the all-important eyes of the IBA, who were unstinting in their praise of the company for such output (see, for example, IBA, 1980).

The author's own *Look Here* (LWT, 1978), presented by Andrew Neil, was in some ways a more complex offering. It was the first ITV series about television itself, and it followed the Birt-Jay precepts in providing a rigorous analysis of the issues confronting television every month. Many shows in the series looked forward to the multi-channel future (and at least one to the enormous spread of high-quality home video equipment that lay 15 years ahead), and applied standard media studies analysis (not to mention media studies experts in interviews) to the issues. This won the approval of the IBA (Potter 1990: 80), although not always of LWT's executives themselves – the director of programmes Michael Grade expressed great anger, for example, about an edition which attacked his

Saturday night entertainment strategy. Outside LWT, management attitudes to it were mixed: Paul Fox, of Yorkshire Television, said that he thought it was 'a funny way to promote ITV' (Docherty 1990: 213).

One edition managed at the same time to provoke and to impress the IBA. It was subtitled 'The Question of Television Coverage of Northern Ireland', and it told the story of the documented clashes between regulators and programme-makers over this sticky topic. Much of what went on resulted in accusations of censorship against the Authority by programme-makers. Of course, the programme's script had to be sent for approval in advance to the IBA, and in due time the Authority's then head of television, David Glencross, telephoned the author to read out the list of changes that the Authority would be requiring. In a moment of reckless inspiration, I said to Glencross that I would, of course, make the changes, but I would also be announcing on the air that the IBA, in a clear act of censorship, had required us to make them. Within the hour, he had called back to withdraw the changes. I was extremely worried about this episode, on the grounds that it would alienate the IBA; but I was reassured by John Birt, who was acting as executive producer on this edition, that acting in this somewhat macho fashion would do us no harm in the eyes of the Authority; and in fact it so turned out, with further praise for the series emerging from IBA executives.[7]

Birt's insistence on the seriousness and rigour of his current affairs output came at a considerable financial cost. Although the Birt-Jay theory implied a reduction, in particular, in shooting ratios and hence a reduction in production costs, other practices, such as the somewhat bizarre one of shooting interviews in suites in the great hotels of London, drove up production costs (several *Look Here* interviews took place in a £300-a-day suite in the Hyde Park Hotel in London, complete with room service lunch). No producer at LWT could really complain that the company was mean with its budgets; the cash was always there, within reason, to put into a show and to show quality on the screen. Yet although the quality of financial control within LWT was reasonably high, maintained in the hands of people who are now (in 2005), for the most part, in financial control of ITV spending on behalf of the unified ITV plc at the Network Centre, there is no doubt that budgetary control was not the most important consideration for producers in the monopoly days of ITV.

It was not until the revenue crisis of the early 1980s dawned that John Birt decided to find out how much it really cost to make programmes – and even then the true intention was not to control internal costs but to find ways of encouraging the rest of ITV to support LWT more effectively in the weekend schedule (Docherty 1990: 161–4). Birt commissioned Colin Freeman and others in the finance division to look again at the true cost of production in such a way that the capital and overhead costs associated with programme production were taken into account; until then, only the marginal costs of production were recognized, which made programmes seem to be extremely inexpensive. But once the charges for maintaining the studios and the central London office accommodation, the salaries of the security and canteen staff and the overheads of running the sales department were taken into account, the costs clearly soared. Both inside and outside LWT, the theoretical underpinning for what came to be known as total costing was challenged. Critics of the scheme argued that the studio costs had to be paid whether programmes were made or not, as did the wages of catering and security staff. Most importantly, the scheme made a total nonsense of the programme exchange tariff between the ITV majors, as tariff prices bore no resemblance at all to total programme costs. The main argument that could not properly be answered by the critics was based in the fact that total costing made no difference at all to the company's profit-and-loss statement or balance sheet – the same amount of money was expended, and the same amount taken in; it was simply that the sums were on different lines in the accounts. Although many die-hards in ITV took a great deal of time to accept the argument, and Birt at times wanted to give up the fight to get them to understand it (Docherty 1990: 175), today (in 2005) total costing is a standard throughout the television industry, and it also formed the basis for the development by Birt at the BBC of the so-called Producer's Choice scheme for introducing market competition into the supply of production services at the BBC. With the advent of the market for independent production, of course, it became essential for both commissioners and programme makers to know the real cost of making programmes.

At LWT, some producers resented being charged overhead costs in their budgets, but it soon dawned on them that production budgets themselves – in terms of the direct expenditures to be incurred – in fact hardly changed at all, and the movement of overheads to programme budgets had little effect on programme output. Of course, because of the insistence on identifying individual costs, it did go some way to making internal cost control easier, and made considerable inroads into such industrial practices as allocating line-up time prior to a studio session. This practice dated from the times when valve-filled studio cameras were inherently unstable, and had to be wrestled into submission prior to every transmission; an hour was allowed in each studio day for the vision controllers to adjust the cameras in order to make them safe to go on the air. By the time LWT's Kent House studio complex was opened, cameras were transistorized, modular and stable, and the hour's line-up time, which was insisted upon by the unions with the approval of the production department, simply gave everyone on the studio crew time for a cup of tea and a smoke as the studio emptied for an hour each day, and the actors or participants kicked their heels trying to maintain their energy levels for an unproductive hour. Much of the internal effect of total costing addressed industrial practices of this kind before it started to affect real production budgets.

Anecdotally, the financial abandon which characterized ITV's production practices is said to have come to the attention of the then prime minister, Margaret Thatcher, when LWT sent two OB vans and 50 technicians to Number 10 to cover a two-handed interview with the prime minister. But the real cause of the end of ITV's profligacy was the beginning of competition for television advertising sales, with the advent of what was then a very a small threat from Sky Television, operated in its early days by an entrepreneur-engineer named Brian Haynes from a communications satellite over Europe. It turned out that the Astra communications satellites proposed by SES, of Luxembourg, were actually powerful enough to be used as direct broadcasting satellites, and with the acquisition of Sky Television by Rupert Murdoch's News International, the rest, so to speak, was history. The decline of the monopoly took time, but it was greatly hastened by the Broadcasting Act 1990, which formalized the entry of competition into the field of television; and today, ITV is regularly outrated in multi-channel households by a combination of non-terrestrial channels.[8]

It is argued, though increasingly forlornly, that regulation and a finite amount of airtime resources had a positive effect on ITV's output in the 1970s and 1980s, allowing the regulators to specify what should and should not be broadcast. The arguments against this position are powerful; to entrust the nation's culture to a small number of enlightened metropolitan bureaucrats is certainly undemocratic and at worst dangerous; the accepted wisdom today is that the market is the correct arbiter of what should be broadcast. Yet looking back at the late 1970s and early 1980s in ITV, it is hard to deny that some remarkable programming was made possible by the fiscal effects of the levy and the monopoly – programming that almost certainly would not have a chance of getting on the air today.

Bibliography

Birt, J. and Jay, P. (1975) The bias against understanding, *The Times*, 28 February.

Docherty, D. (1990) *Running the Show: 21 Years of London Weekend Television*. London: Boxtree.

Franklin, B. (ed.) (2001) *British Television Policy: A Reader*. London: Routledge.

Habermas, J. (1971) *Knowledge and Human Interests*. London: Heinemann.

IBA (1975) *ITV 1975*. London: Independent Broadcasting Authority.

IBA (1980) *ITV 1980*. London: Independent Broadcasting Authority.

Pilkington, H. (Chair) (1962) *Report of the Committee on Broadcasting, 1960*, Cmd 1753. London: HMSO.

Potter, J. (1990) *Independent Television in Britain: Volume 4, Companies and Programmes, 1968–80*. London: Macmillan.
Steiner, G. (1985) *Language and Silence*. London: Faber & Faber.
Tracey, M. (1998) *The Decline and Fall of Public Service Broadcasting*. Oxford: Oxford University Press.

Notes

1 Tracey's (1998: 26–31) full list is as follows: (1) universality of availability; (2) universality of appeal; (3) provision for minorities, especially those disadvantaged by physical or social circumstance; (4) serving the public sphere; (5) commitment to the education of the public; (6) distance from all vested interests; (7) structured so as to encourage competition in good programming rather than competition for numbers; (8) rules should liberate rather than restrict the programme-maker.
2 For further attempts at definitions of public service broadcasting, see the selection offered in Franklin (2001: 19–43).
3 The date given in parentheses after each programme title throughout is the year of its first transmission.
4 At this time, the cost of one 10-minute roll of reversal colour film, which was the normal medium on which interviews were recorded, was £100 in stock and processing, and a lot more in crew time. Today, acquisition of material on videotape is very much cheaper.
5 Former staff on *Weekend World* still remember with awe an edition that attempted to explain the European Common Agricultural Policy.
6 Apart from the IBA-mandated live Sunday morning church services, for which LWT's outside broadcasting department developed a handy expertise, ITV's other main religious offering was Sir Harry Secombe in *Highway* (1983), produced by a consortium of regional programme companies, which was not much liked by the IBA although it was loved by its large and loyal audience.
7 This story is completely unsupported by documentation because the key exchanges took place on the telephone. The details, of course, remain engraved on my heart to this day.
8 For more details, see BARB's web site, www.barb.co.uk (free registration required).

7 FROM NEWSREELS TO A THEATRE OF NEWS: THE GROWTH AND DEVELOPMENT OF INDEPENDENT TELEVISION NEWS

Jackie Harrison

Introduction

From the start the development of Independent Television News (ITN) has been characterized by its hybrid nature. It has a history and immediate future played out against the contradictions forced upon it by its desire to be pioneering and innovative in its approach to telling the news (and more recently managing archive material and mobile phone content) and the constraints placed upon it by the various organizational arrangements within which it has had to operate. This chapter focuses on the relationship between ITN and independent television (ITV), and the way ITN's core news remit has had to exist within a television distribution system that, in spite of an ambiguous public service broadcasting (PSB) role imposed upon it, is entirely commercial and dependent on winning advertising revenues.

Before ITN

In Britain fears about the negative effects of broadcasting have coexisted alongside the belief that television has an important role to play in a democracy in its direct relationship to the information or knowledge content of the 'public sphere' of rational critical debate (Habermas 1989). This is particularly true of television news (Harrison 2005). In response to concerns about the best way to manage broadcasting, public service commitments were developed that would define the British Broadcasting Corporation (BBC) and influence the ITV system particularly through its relationship with its news provider ITN. These public service commitments can be summarized as the responsibility broadcasters have 'to inform, educate and entertain'. Or expressed in more grandiloquent terms, PSB should adopt and work according to the principles of universality, inclusivity, sustaining and informing the electorate, and providing cultural and educational enrichment. These principles were inculcated into the establishment of the BBC and more or less provide its rationale to this day.

However, by the early 1950s many in postwar Britain were critical of the BBC's monopoly and its elitist and paternalistic approach to broadcasting which was still based on the strict moral and religious values of its founding Director General, John Reith. It was argued that the BBC produced television that appeared old fashioned, condescending and prudish (Briggs 1961). As far as television news was concerned the BBC seemed to be struggling with reconciling traditional radio news practices with the new skills required to manage and present news in a televisual way. There was a distrust of the televisual at BBC news, which was associated with cinema and music halls and the Movietone reels that had provided newsreels to cinemas since the 1920s. Moving news pictures and their association with entertainment media were seen as a phenomenon that would trivialize the high values of the Corporation (Crisell 1997). What the viewer saw was little more than radio news presented by an anonymous reader over a picture of Big Ben. Where pictures were used the BBC simply copied the cinema format of the newsreel with a voice-over. Using pictures for news was 'disdainfully permitted' (Cox 1995: 21) 'if they [were] thought developing' (Cox 1995: 34). As for news itself this was subject to the traditional radio news policy of 'scrupulous accuracy, with facts checked and double-checked [which] should go hand in hand with equally scrupulous impartiality and objectivity' (Cox 1995: 35). Unfortunately, in those days, this laudable policy resulted in television news that was both long-winded and dull (Cox 1995). It was to be the introduction of independent television and its own ITN that would revolutionize the way in which television news would be selected and presented whilst maintaining public service commitments.

The emergence of ITN

The Independent Television Authority (ITA) was established by the Television Act 1954. The ITA's role was to supervise and regulate the new ITV companies by ensuring that the priorities of revenue raising (from advertising) did not override the need for quality programmes. The ITV system had a regional structure comprised of several ITV companies and was accompanied by the formation of one separate news provider, ITN, to provide them with national and international news. All the ITV companies shared the cost of ITN's news service. Indeed, the fact that news was only provided by one company meant that the requirement for accuracy and impartiality demanded in the Television Act could be upheld by all the ITV companies more easily than if there had been more than one news provider.[1] Also, as Lindley (2005a) notes, these arrangements ensured that ITN would not be put under pressure by a single owner. ITN's values were 'shaped' and 'constrained' by the demands placed upon the ITV companies by the Television Act to conform to the PSB requirement to inform, educate and entertain. Both ITV and ITN were circumscribed by clearly stated (if ambiguous) PSB requirements. For ITN this was to prove to be (at the time) a godsend.

Independent Television News' own mission was to 'make significant news more interesting, more comprehensive and more acceptable' (Crisell 1997: 92). From the start it interpreted its PSB obligations in a different way from the BBC: it exhibited much less deference to the establishment and government; it understood the relationship between words and pictures more coherently; it valued, promoted and defended interviews that probed for answers; it treated its audience as capable of understanding complex and ambiguous issues, and it exhibited greater flair. A point that Conboy (2004: 199) refers to, somewhat misleadingly, as the 'beginning of a popularization of broadcast journalism in terms of its content and the audience it was aimed at'. Independent Television News certainly aimed to be popular but was not at the beginning popularist.[2] Overall ITN was using the television medium intuitively and imaginatively. There was no surrender to tabloid news values, but an understanding of the postwar *zeitgeist* that contemporary events required accurate reporting and interpretation. Official views were to be offset by the news journalists' own disposition and requirement to probe, investigate and interrogate in order to provide accurate accounts of contemporary events (Harrison 2005). This was well understood by ITN, which supported its journalists in this endeavour as they sought to become the benchmark for television news journalism.

The first editor of ITN, Aiden Crawley, had 6 months to get his team together, train it and go on air. ITN's opening night began at 10.00 p.m. on 22 September 1955. Staff had been recruited from the BBC and from cinema newsreel companies, and foreign coverage was provided via a deal with CBS and the use of a network of freelance string camera crews (Cox 1995). The broadcast went without a hitch – setting high technical standards, which were to be the pride of ITN for many years to come. Crawley had promised that ITN would 'report the idiosyncrasies – harmful or harmless – of individuals as well as the great news of nations' (Cox 1995: 46) although the first bulletin (like so many after it) covered many of the same stories as the BBC. Between ITN and the BBC (and without collusion) common news agendas were arrived at simply because what constituted news was well understood by both in similar regard. Priorities were by and large common to both and have remained so.

However, style and a willingness to extend the boundaries of television news were not.

By borrowing certain techniques and styles from the US, ITN set about using new and unorthodox techniques to distinguish itself from the BBC (Cox 1995). It encouraged the personalities of the newsreaders and their correspondents to be revealed. It used new informal vox pops and was less cautious than the BBC about breaking stories and broadcasting scoops, and from the first, ITN broadcasters wrote their own news script. The news programmes opened with a fast moving title sequence showing film being shot and rushed to the studio and a jaunty signature tune that, according to Cox (1995: 46) set a note of 'professionalism allied to informality'. ITN's slogan was 'see it happen on ITN' (Cox 1995: 65) and in accordance with that maxim, it founded and used a probing style of interviewing (getting people to reveal more and thereby display something newsworthy) and pioneered live news broadcasting in a bid to bring the news to the audience in a more effective way. In these ways it challenged the deferential approach of the BBC to politicians and the establishment, and challenged restrictions on the coverage of controversial issues and elections (Rudin and Ibbotson 2002). It exploited the aridity and ambiguity of its public service broadcasting requirements to manipulate the television medium itself, to accept and facilitate changing communications technology and capacity, to develop a greater understanding of the role of television news journalism and to achieve a greater understanding of its real and potential audiences. However, such an auspicious start belies the commercial reality that surrounded ITN. ITN was after all a hybrid organization – with a public service broadcasting remit within a television distribution system that was commercial and dependent on advertising revenues.

ITN: a hybrid

The hybrid nature of ITN is manifest in its relationship to ITV, which can be expressed in formal policy terms as a public provision delivered through the vectors of private competition. Or, as Lindley (2005a: 1) writes: 'the big issue for ITN has always been this: what is it for? Is it a news service provider, essentially owned by its most important customer, ITV, or is it an independent company, competing with others to sell television news and associated services worldwide?'

In Britain, in the 1950s television news was not seen as a commodity to be sold overseas, nor, despite the fact that ITN had entered into overseas commercial relationships (for example with CBS), was there a perceived market for international news relationships of any commercial significance. Independent Television News had its ambiguously defined public service news remit in the parochial setting of the ITV franchise companies. And, at that time, parochialism describes those companies best of all. The contradictory nature of a dominant private ethos across the ITV system and dominant public ethos within ITN produced a relationship in which an international and national news service was located within companies that were run according to the exigencies of securing advertising revenue and fulfilling regional or local sales remits. Such a mix was bound to produce unworkable relationships.

So it was hardly surprising when in December 1955 the Managing Director of ABC Television – the ITV franchise contractor for weekend programmes in the north and the Midlands – called for shorter ITN bulletins. During the first year of broadcasting, the ITV companies faced a financial crisis and the first thing they wanted to cut was the ITN news service. Aiden Crawley resigned in protest but stayed when the ITA ruled that there must be a minimum of 20 minutes of news a day and that this must contain a reasonable amount of film. As Cox (1995: 48) reports, this figure was 'plucked out of the air' although 'the ruling was to be the Magna Carta of ITN, giving it secure foundations upon which to build'. As to how secure those foundations proved to be is something that is frequently overstated. Indeed as foundations go ITN was not (as we shall see ahead) built on secure footings at all. The internal dynamics of ITN and ITV's relationship were now set, they were 'divided and undivided'.[3] Both were free but not free of each other; both could behave as if they were supportive of each other and both were free to pursue contradictory policies. Thus, ITV could behave, quite properly, as a commercial system with some public service broadcasting obligations, whilst ITN could pursue its public service news ideals. With regard to this first skirmish it defined the real relationship between the two – economics and ownership. Crawley and the ITA had won a temporary respite but of course the ITV companies attacked ITN where they knew it would hurt and in an area 'where they were absolute masters' (Cox 1995: 48): finance. The ITV companies refused to accept Crawley's budget for the required 20 minutes of news, demanding drastic cuts from £350,000 per year to £200,000 per year (Cox 1995: 48). The companies also wanted to establish a sub-committee of the ITA Board to examine the operational remit and costs of ITN and to make subsequent recommendations. Crawley resigned again, this time permanently, there was uproar in Parliament and there were suggestions that the ITA should take over ITN and produce the news itself. In 1956 Geoffrey Cox was appointed Editor and Chief Executive of ITN. Cox had 15 years' experience with national newspapers and had worked for BBC television.

Cox like Crawley understood the televisual nature of news. He understood that ITN must continue to differentiate itself from the BBC and (of course) the newspapers, although when describing ITN Cox would frequently resort to the use of newspaper analogies (Cox 1995). Cox, and more importantly ITN, had to satisfy two critical agendas –

fulfil a PSB remit and more importantly and pressingly, satisfy ITV that their services could attract viewers. Independent Television News settled for a strategy of 'market differentiation'; that is, they challenged the orthodoxy of reporting the news by the BBC. And like all who settle for a heterodoxical approach they sought to establish new conventions and new ways of doing things. These they pursued with gusto. They continued to develop and use probing interviews, 'slice of life' stories (for example using the camera more and more to bring the news to the public), portraying news in human terms by bringing onto the screen ordinary people in vox pops that sought to display gaps between classes by allowing ordinary people with accents to speak (Cox 1995: 57). All in all, ITN was patronizing and radical at the same time. But those who challenge an orthodoxy (even where such a thing is imagined) run this risk. Cox (1995: 57), sounding like an apologist and evangelist at the same time, describes how ITN valued the camera and conveyed life with an attempted honesty and without condescension, adding interest and humanity to the bulletins in a way unique to the new medium. Of course the ambition to portray life honestly and without condescension is admirable (and taken for granted now) but camouflages the fact that ITN bulletins were not perceived by the ITV franchise contractors as serving their commercial needs. To put it simply but accurately ITN and ITV did not get on.

The hybrid nature of ITN was what most rankled the ITV franchise directors. Why should they be constrained to take a service with which they did not have a genuine supplier relationship? Why should they pay for a service over which they had no ultimate control? This was shown in 1967 when the ITA, supported by ITN, told ITV that their schedules should compulsorily provide a half-hour slot for a news programme at 10.00 p.m. For the ITV companies such peremptory intervention was a restriction on their commercial activity and an impediment to scheduling. Again this led them to question why they should be forced to pay for and accommodate a public service news provider. This question today usually combines both an economic argument with an attack on the BBC and can be paraphrased as – 'why shouldn't other public service news providers have some of the BBC's licence fee?'[4] These questions have a compelling logic just as much as Cox's (and before him Crawley's) aspirations are admirable and worthwhile. Combined, they describe the contradictory character and setting within which ITN's radical and innovative approach to television news occurred. Overall ITN provided a product to ITV, which in hindsight was high quality, innovative and changed the way things were done, and one would think a recipe for commercial success. But without a news market of the kind we have today, hampered by the lack of channels and outlets, constrained by the parochial nature of those outlets and the commercial imperatives dominating those outlets, ITN was in fact a subsidized service. Only this time the subsidy was not from the public purse as is the case with the BBC but from the ITV franchise companies. Expressed in ideological terms, a public utility (or more accurately a public good) was being paid for by a compulsory requirement placed upon private companies. In short: a tax by any other name. Independent Television News did what it did because it neither existed in a real market place nor in a proper commercial relationship with a purchaser(s) of its services. In fact the ITV companies, who after all were forced to buy ITN's services, did not at first greatly value it or necessarily want it. The economics were absurd. And ITN's foundations were anything but secure, although this fact was not apparent until much later.

If the economics were absurd, ITN's news services were not. Crisell (1997: 92) observes that 'independent television's greatest contribution to the history of broadcasting was to make TV news into something truly telegenic.' ITN effectively challenged the BBC's established news practices and inevitably the BBC began to adopt some of the techniques introduced by ITN.[5] By the 1960s an era known as the 'benign duopoly' emerged. This was to last more or less untroubled until the Peacock Report in 1986. ITV and the BBC settled down into an era characterized by competition for audiences but not for revenue. Although competition between the BBC and ITV had been criticized because it would inevitably lead to a decline in standards it would, until the era of multi-channel competition, be rationalized as being entirely consistent with public service principles, because the revenue sources (advertising for ITV and licence fee for the BBC) were different (Seymour-Ure 1991). As for ITN, it flourished in a television news environment that, to viewers, must have seemed to consist of a single public news service. During this period the unstable foundations of ITN were masked, for all practical purposes, by the appearance of a successful relationship with the ITV companies. The premise of this success was nothing other than the lack of competition for advertising revenues, which the ITV companies enjoyed during this period. Even the introduction of BBC2 in 1964 and Channel 4 in 1982 (the latter's news service was supplied by ITN) did not disturb what appeared to be a stable broadcasting environment. As for the introduction of Rupert Murdoch's Sky Channel in 1984, ITV saw little at that time to concern itself with. Free market fundamentalism and technology were about to change all of that.

The Peacock Report and after

F.A. Hayek (1979: 84) wrote: 'quite generally it can probably be said that what is harmful is not the existence of monopolies that are due to greater efficiency or to the control of particular limited resources, but the ability of some monopolies to protect and preserve their monopolistic position after the original cause of their superiority has disappeared.' Such was the real nature of the Prime Minister Margaret Thatcher's judgement on the BBC. In 1984 the BBC announced that it wished to see an increase in the television licence fee. This poorly timed announcement resulted in the BBC being granted a compromise figure but also drew attention to the issue of BBC funding. A Committee of Inquiry into BBC finances led by the economist Professor Alan Peacock was set up (which reported in 1986). The intention of Margaret Thatcher was to introduce advertising to the BBC. Or to put it another way, to ask the question why should the BBC receive a licence fee when ITV did not? While Peacock did call for a fundamental rethink of the long-term funding of the BBC and discussed the sell-off of Radios 1 and 2, advertising on the BBC was rejected. The licence fee remained and was to be pegged to the Retail Price Index (RPI). However, the Peacock Report also had the effect of placing ITV under scrutiny, as the publication of a Broadcasting White Paper in 1988 was to reveal. The White Paper proposed replacing the Independent Broadcasting Authority (IBA) with a lighter touch Independent Television Commission (ITC), and the award of ITV franchises by competitive tender.

The White Paper of 1988 was followed by the Broadcasting Act 1990, which created an auction for ITV licences. At first, the White Paper did not require, through the use of a must-carry clause, any requirement for ITV to take a news service at all. Independent Television News was threatened with extinction. Paradoxically it was the support of Margaret Thatcher who saw in ITN an alternative voice to BBC news, which she disliked more than ITN's protected status as a news supplier to ITV, that ensured that ITV would have to provide news using a nominated supplier.[6] At the same time, the ITV companies were lobbying government to ensure that franchises were not simply sold to the highest bidder. They did this with the potentially disingenuous argument that quality safeguards should be introduced into the forthcoming Act. Bizarrely, Mrs Thatcher appeared to militate against a free-market proposal concerning ITV's freedom to manage its own news services, whilst the ITV franchise companies appeared to support quality thresholds and public service broadcasting. The former was undertaken due to distrust of the BBC, the latter to protect commercial interests (after all, the quality threshold was minimal and the public service broadcasting commitments largely rhetorical).[7] By the time the Broadcasting Act came into effect on 1 January 1991 it was made clear 'that "news programmes of high quality" would be required from a "nominated news provider" and would have to be carried by all the ITV . . . licensees at the same time, including peak viewing times' (Lindley 2005a: 292). Under the terms of the Act, ITN's nominated sole news supplier status was protected for another 10 years, although this was subject to a periodic review after 5 years. This was a situation that meant that ITN's continued sole supplier status was contingent on whether the ITV companies were satisfied with their news services, if not, another news provider could be licensed and ITN replaced. However, ITN's position was protected to an extent by its reputation and familiarity as well as the ITC's uncertainty about ITN's major rival, Sky News. In 1993 ITN was awarded a £57 million a year contract to supply ITV's news (this was a figure that ITV regarded as too high), subject to review at the end of 1997. Although the ITV network was obliged to take and broadcast three news programmes a day, from 1993 it could, under the terms of the Act demand more flexible scheduling arrangements from ITN. At this point ITN's core business was simply providing news services to ITV and Channel 4. It was utterly dependent for its revenue on these two contracts, each of which was looking increasingly too demanding to operate, and for the future more difficult to secure. The Broadcasting Act 1990 had allowed Channel 4 to be self-financing, giving it 'a much greater incentive to "shop around" for a good deal on its news' (McNair 1996: 102) and ITV was demanding a cheaper and more flexible supply of news for its network. The issue facing ITN was (and still is) the possibility and viability of expansion beyond the dependency on Channel 4 and ITV.

In April 1993 ITN ceased to be solely owned by the ITV companies. Instead its new owners were members of a business consortium comprising Carlton Communications, Daily Mail & General Trust, Granada Group, Reuters and United Business Media – all were restricted to owning no more than 20 per cent. Above all they acted like shareholders rather than sponsors and insisted on a profitable return for their investment, further affecting the relationship between ITV and ITN. Independent Television News was now required to make a profit rather than be funded solely to provide a good quality news service irrespective and regardless of the costs. A new commercially aggressive ITV system, a profit orientated ITN and the post-1990 Broadcasting Act environment ensured that the original public service orientated ethos of the ITV system was diluted. And if that was not all, the consequences of the rethinking of Conservative governments' broadcasting policy in relationship to the market meant that ITV had to face increasing competition from other companies and the consequences of deregulation. As Tambini and Cowling (2003) note, many argue that Peacock was ahead of its time, because the 1986 Peacock Report foresaw an age of digital plenty and consumer sovereignty in media markets. Peacock argued that with many of the original justifications, such as spectrum scarcity, for public service broadcasting removed, traditional models of public service broadcasting were no longer sustainable. The truth of this observation is to be found in the subsequent history of ITN and not, as many believed it would be, at the BBC.

ITN: the consequences of deregulation

From the 1980s onward communications technology was evolving rapidly and with dramatic effect on television. Satellites were launched, fibre optic cables were laid and the public increasingly accepted digital broadband. Spectrum scarcity became a thing of the past and the multi-channel universe was upon us. The broadcasting market was changing and the old ITV and BBC duopoly was shattered by the development of new competitors: Channel 5 (now known as Five), cable, satellite and later digital terrestrial services. Accompanying the proliferation of cable and satellite channels was a debate about the implications for the future of quality television in this country and the appropriate levels of regulation. Cable and satellite channels were exempt from some of the regulatory programme requirements that the terrestrial companies have to meet. They only had to adhere to consumer protection requirements such as taste and decency and rules on due impartiality.[8]

Within this environment, ITN had to become both efficient and competitive to secure its position as news supplier to the ITV network. The Broadcasting Act 1990 had transferred ITN 'from a "cost–centre" which it had been for thirty-five years into a profit-making business' (McNair 1996: 102) no longer run by an ITV system willing to pour money into it. Independent Television News was to become the subject of constant financial restraints and cost cutting and had to make 400 staff redundant in 1991–2, in an effort to claw back a deficit of £10 million. Indeed, ITN was forced to make cuts to its number of international bureaux. Despite all the cutbacks, in 1993 ITN made an annual pre-tax profit of £5.6 million on an £83 million turnover (Peak 1994: 104) rising to £8 million in 1994 (McNair 1996: 108), and some considered the time was right for ITN to be floated on the stock exchange. Although the ITC favourably reviewed ITN in December 1995, ITN was told that it could not maintain the current rate it charged the ITV companies for its product. In September 1996, the ITV companies managed to get a £15 million further reduction to the £55 million ITN charged for its news services. Significantly all of this was conducted against a background of emerging changes in the ownership of the ITV system and the relationships between the various ITV companies. Smoke and mirrors dominated this period for ITN in its business dealings with ITV because what was emerging was quite simply that Carlton and Granada were moving closer together in their ambition to run the ITV system and for these two companies all else was subordinate to that interest, and that by extension meant ITN.

As if to illustrate the precarious position of ITN in relation to an increasingly commercially aggressive ITV and a regulatory environment that was relaxing, the ITN flagship programme *News at Ten* became the subject of a dispute between the two as to its impact on ITV's peak-time schedule: ITV claimed it lost audiences whilst ITN argued it maintained audiences. This disagreement lasted several years, but in March 1999 ITV was allowed to move *News at Ten* from 10.00 p.m. After 30 years *News at Ten* was no longer to be ITV's flagship news programme. This title was adopted by the 6.30 p.m. news and the late evening news was shown at different times after 10.30 p.m.[9] Michael Grade, writing some years later, was to describe the move of *News at Ten* as signalling the end of public service broadcasting on ITV (Lindley 2005a: 349). However, the subordination of news to a more entertainment orientated evening schedule was justified by the then head of ITV Network Centre as a vital one, which would reinvigorate ITV's broadcasting service (Eyre 1999). In short: justification based upon the need to attract advertising revenue. For several years ITV moved ITN's late evening news around the evening schedule, but the damage to ITN was profound and ITV's viewing figures fell.[10]

But if ITN was subject to constant cost cutting, efficiency savings and imposed changes, what of the quality of its overall news service provided for the ITV network? Richard Tait, former editor-in-chief of ITN, argues that in the decade 1991–2001 ITN's news programmes for ITV remained successful and competitive. 'In that period', he says, 'ITN won twenty-five Royal Television Society news awards, as against BBC 1's twenty-four, and of the other major prizes – from BAFTA, Monte Carlo and the American Emmys – ITN's news on ITV won twelve awards while BBC 1's news won five' (cf. Lindley 2005a: 363). In 2004 ITN won six Royal Television Society awards. In short ITN consistently produced a high quality news service that rivalled the BBC, a point that is largely uncontested by news journalists and is remarkable given the circumstances. However such illustrious achievements as ITN could muster could not, against a background of falling audiences, fail to coincide with a further reduction in ITN's budget. And so it was that between 2001 and 2004 ITN received £35 million a year for its news services to the ITV network.[11] If we compare this with the BBC's news budget of around £400 million per annum for the same period, it becomes clear that ITN's resources are considerably inferior to the BBC's, a problem recognized by the ITC in its 2003 Annual Report. Again this puts the quality of ITN's services into further relief. The former editor-in-chief of ITN (1995–2002) observed recently that ITV news depends on the size and organization of ITV, and the amount that the Office of Communications (Ofcom) tells ITV to pay its news supplier (Tait 2004). And Ofcom is not as keen on a subsidized ITN as its predecessors.

Inevitably, further changes were in store for ITN. In 2000 the Department for Trade and Industry (DTI) and Department for Culture, Media and Sport (DCMS) recognized the likelihood that the necessity for there to be a single nominated news provider, previously recognized in the Broadcasting Act 1990, would diminish as further news providers emerged in a competitive news market. They subsequently inserted a clause into the Communications Act 2003 that would allow the government to revoke the nominated status of news provider on the advice of Ofcom if the latter believed the marketplace provided the conditions for a diversity of news suppliers to flourish. However, there still appears to remain the requirement that all the ITV companies as a single body corporate share the same news provider.[12] The Communications Act also relaxed the ITV ownership rules still further allowing for consolidation of the English and Welsh regional franchises, owned by Granada and Carlton, into one company – ITV plc. Since March 2004 ITV plc has owned all of the regional ITV licences in England and Wales – excluding Scottish, Grampian, Ulster and Channel. ITV plc now controls over 90 per cent of ITV's advertising revenues, as well as owning a 40 per cent share of ITN.[13] ITV plc's relationship to ITN can be characterized as simultaneously both main customer and dominant shareholder. These two contradictory roles serve to highlight, yet again, the hybrid nature of ITN. Indeed, when the contract to supply news to ITV was advertised in 2003, Sky News bid against ITN for the contract: a competition which succeeded in making ITN lower its price. This represented both a loss for ITN's shareholders and a win for the contractors – the same people in both cases. Whatever ITN's future is, it will be one defined by bidding wars, competitive tendering for its services, as well as any new commercial strategies which exploit their resources.

ITN's current position

In spite of all the turmoil surrounding it, and the difficult relationship it has with the ITV network, ITN still remains one of the largest news organizations in the world, producing news and factual programmes both in Britain and overseas. It has demonstrated an ability to diversify its news coverage over a range of platforms and outlets. ITN's 24-hour news channel was launched on 1 August 2000, offering a similar format to Sky News and BBC News-24, with a round-up of news every 15 minutes and an interactive service. Independent Television News continues to broaden its news for television services. It currently provides the news for the ITV network (for the *Lunchtime News*, the *Evening News, News at 10.30 p.m., Early Morning News*, regular news headlines during the day and night and three programmes a day at weekends); an ITV London News service; news for the 24-hour ITV News Channel;[14] Channel 4 and Five (until 31 December 2004 when Five's news contract was taken over by Sky News) and radio news for Independent Radio News (IRN). Independent Television News's Archive is now the world's biggest commercial television-based video news archive (at the time of writing, 680,000 hours) and includes all ITN's material, the Reuters television archive, the Channel 4 clips archive, the whole of Granada's programme clip catalogue, the British Pathe news archive and Fox News. It also provides material for 3G phones and other platforms and undertakes broadcast news consultancy as well as providing programmes through its own programme-making division, ITN Factual. What is apparent is that it is becoming a content company and is expanding its content services. The chief executive of ITN, when asked if he could imagine an ITN without its core news supply business replied: 'No. A lot of the business is reusing content brought in for the main news bulletins. It's a model that fits together well and you wouldn't want to pull it apart' (Wood 2005: 27). A more commercially orientated and profit-making ITN has emerged, one that understands that it has to fight to retain and win contracts to supply television news. And, which understands that the use and exploitation of its own content ranges from video Valentines for mobile phones to the educational value of historical archives (Wood 2005: 27). The culture of ITN has changed from one dominated by journalists, where it considered itself to be a centre of journalistic excellence run by journalists for journalists, to one dominated by commercial calculations or, perhaps more fairly, one that is more businesslike. Cuts in resources, staff and international bureaux has led to concerns over the quality of ITN news coverage, and the loss of its own ITN brand has led some to say it has lost its identity as a news provider (although its corporate identity lives on in its archives, its web site and some of its content provision ventures). Today all news programmes shown on the ITV channel (currently called ITV1 and previously known as Channel 3) and the 24-hour news channel must now carry the prefix 'ITV', accompanied by the ITV logo in the colours of blue and yellow. All of this is an attempt to give 'ITV News a recognisable and consistent style and look' (Lindley 2005a: 363) and to make news congruent with the rest of the channel; thereby demonstrating that ITV is taking an increasingly interventionist role in the management of the identity of its own services to the detriment of ITN's own brand.[15]

Today the ITV network is bullish and vocal about how it regards the public service broadcasting obligations imposed upon its terrestrial channel ITV1. It has argued successfully that these obligations cause a financial drain on the network, raising questions about their sustainability in the digital age.[16] Ofcom's recent reduction of ITV1's public service obligations[17] seems to have responded to the 'feeling around ITV's more commercially minded people that until Ofcom starts dropping some of ITV1's public service requirements, the growth of ITV1 will be difficult' (Revoir 2004b: 13). As the number of channels increases in the digital television environment and the use of the Internet grows, it is likely that ITV1's share of viewing will continue to decline, reducing its revenue from advertisers (predicted to drop from 52 per cent to 42 per cent by 2012).[18] Under these circumstances it is not surprising that ITV is lobbying government to have its public service broadcasting commitments, licence fees and advertising taxes reduced. And yet at the same time Ofcom has been awarded increased powers to ensure that ITN receives the resources it needs[19] – a move that could thwart ITV's plans to further reduce news costs – although it would not prevent them turning to, for example, Sky News as their news supplier in the future. It is difficult to see the powers of Ofcom as anything other than a defensive strategy designed to protect ITN from further cuts in the short to medium term. Stuart Purvis, a former chief executive of ITN argues, accordingly, 'at present the regulator, Ofcom, has powers to intervene to protect the quality and range of ITV News's service ... it acknowledges that this right will probably not last after analogue switch-off' (Purvis 2005: 16–17). Whatever else it does, Ofcom's right to intervene buys ITN some time to expand its operations other than those to supply news to ITV1. Overall, an economic reality is emerging in which ITV1 will not be able to afford to pay for its PSB obligations and at the same time retain a competitive position against other channels. The future of ITN as a public service news provider for ITV1 is therefore uncertain.

As for the news ITN provides, a 'creeping London centralisation of network programming' is reported to be part of ITV plc's strategy (Revoir 2003: 9). Those ITV companies remaining outside ITV plc, in particular the Scottish Media Group (SMG), are reported to be uneasy about the way in which the new ITV sector is developing (Revoir 2003: 9). ITV plc has already moved control of news from the ITV Network Centre, operated on behalf of all ITV companies, to the ITV News Group, which is wholly owned by Carlton and Granada (Revoir 2004a: 3): a move the SMG argues will result in domination of the news by England and Wales. This criticism is rejected by the ITV News Group chief executive who argues that 'editorial control remains, where it always has been, in the individual newsroom [although] good practice is being shared' (Jones 2004: 18-19).

Today television news providers have to ensure their news competes and succeeds in an increasingly dynamic news marketplace. The volume of national news on the five main channels has increased by 80 per cent since 1994 (mainly due to more daytime and weekend news). Viewers also now have far greater choice not only about which news programme to watch, but when they watch it, thanks to the advent and increasing availability of the 24-hour news channels: Sky News, BBC News 24, ITV News Channel as well as other news channels such as Al-Jazeera, Fox News, CNN and the Internet. These fundamental changes in the television news market have had an impact upon competition between broadcasters for news audiences, the approach they take to telling news stories, and the ways in which audiences consume news (Harrison 2005). As Hargreaves and Thomas (2002: 44) recently noted, we are now in a world of 'ambient news' in which news is available from many different sources throughout the day. Over the five-year period 1998 to 2002, the volume of news in the schedules of the five main channels rose steadily from 15.2 to 18.0 hours a week in peaktime (Hargreaves and Thomas 2002).

Within this changing news environment, ITN is still attempting to innovate and differentiate itself from its competitors, particularly the BBC and Sky News. In 2004 it undertook a £1.3 million revamp of the ITV news set and now presents its news through what it calls a 'theatre of news'. Independent Television News is becoming increasingly visual (returning to a familiar *leitmotif*) and sees the 'theatre of news' as a way of bringing pictures into a studio environment so that their presenters and correspondents can react and inter-react with the news story. The reason for this approach was summarized by Clive Jones, the chief executive of the ITV News Group, as an attempt 'to try and break the gap that has always existed between the formal atmosphere of a traditional studio and the pictures gathered in the field and the computer generated graphics deployed to explain and analyse the news' (Jones 2004: 18). For example, a science correspondent no longer needs to describe the surface of Titan, he can walk on a mock-up of it in the studio. Similarly a presenter's walk across the arc of the studio is described as 'a compelling illustrated walk into the story of the day' (Jones 2004: 19). Today it is recognized that appointment news programmes must work much harder and deliver added value if viewers are to continue to feel that watching them is worth their time. Independent Television News has returned to its tradition of pioneering and innovating different styles and approaches to news presentation. And whether it combines style with substance, as it has done in the past, or sees the two diverge, is an open question. It has also exhibited a remarkable ability to diversify its news provision for a number of different and diverse outlets, programmes and commercial contractors; a skill that still singles it out from the crowd. Although even here it must now compete with Sky News, which exhibits similar skills, as was demonstrated when it recently won the contract to supply news for Five from ITN.

Overall, though, the future of ITN is very uncertain (despite the respite provided by Ofcom) and its relationship to ITV plc is parlous. The facts are simple: ITV plc owns 40 per cent of ITN and is its biggest customer. The chief executive of ITV plc told journalist and author Richard Lindley that, 'either, in the remaining years of the contract, I will be able to buy the other 60 per cent and then will own the company in its entirety or, at the end of the licence we will not contract our news with ITN. We will undertake to produce our news in-house' (Lindley 2005b: 7). With such thinking it is obvious that ITV plc recognizes that ITN is not independent and is in all but name an in-house supplier. Quite how ITN sees it is another matter. Lindley cites Stewart Purvis (2005b: 7), a former chief executive of ITN, who assesses the situation accordingly:

> I suspect the race between survival and oblivion [for ITN] will be a close-run thing. The key factor is that the existing ITN national news contract runs until the end of 2008. As that date approaches, ITV plc ... will regularly point out to the three non-ITV shareholders, Reuters, United Business Media and the Daily Mail Group, each with 20 per cent, that ITV has the power to make ITN relatively worthless by not renewing the contract. ITV's alternative, it will emphasise, is to provide its own news output, having already brought the expertise of ITV's and ITN's key news managers in-house with the creation of the ITV News Group, covering both national and regional news

The projected scenario for Lindley and others is that ITN is inevitably going to be 'folded' into ITV and that comparisons with the US are more appropriate. Lindley (2005b: 7) notes that every major broadcaster in the world owns its own news and that in America 'CBS NBC and ABC would find it bizarre if they had to take their news programmes from some independent company'. Yet in business terms 2008 is a long way off, projected scenarios are invariably risky and the commercial variables manifold. Indeed the question might just as well be put: 'what of ITV's future?' Or what is to stop someone else buying ITN? It is by no means certain that ITN will sell to ITV plc or that ITV plc will be in a position to buy ITN (Wood 2005: 27). If, for example, ITN's diversified news services, content services, consultancy and programme making activities expand and grow, and as such make a greater and greater contribution to ITV plc's revenues, the balance of need and dependency between the two shifts yet again. The only thing certain is yet more change for ITN.

Bibliography

Allan, S. (1999) *News Culture*. Buckingham: Open University Press.

Briggs, A. (1961) *The Birth of Broadcasting: the History of Broadcasting in the United Kingdom*. Oxford: Oxford University Press.

Briggs, A. (1995) *The History of Broadcasting in the United Kingdom: Competition 1955–1974*. Oxford: Oxford University Press.

Carter, S. (2005) Voice of the Listener and Viewer Conference, http://www.ofcom.org.uk/media_office/speeches_presentations/carter_voice_20040429 (accessed 12 January 2005).

Conboy, M. (2004) *Journalism: a Critical History*. London: Sage.

Cox, G. (1995) *Pioneering Television News*. London: John Libbey.

Crisell, A. (1986) *Understanding Radio*. London: Methuen.

Crisell, A. (1997) *An Introductory History of British Broadcasting*. London: Routledge.

Davies, N. (1996) *Europe: A History*. Oxford: Oxford University Press.

Department of Trade and Industry and Department of Culture, Media and Sport (2000) *A New Future for Communications*, Cmd 5010. London: HMSO.

Eyre, R. (1999) 'Public interest broadcasting'. MacTaggart Memorial Lecture, Edinburgh International Television Festival, 27 August.

Graham, A., Kobaldt, C., Hogg, S. *et al.* (1999) *Public Purposes in Broadcasting*. Luton: University of Luton Press.

Habermas, J. (1989) The structural transformation of the public sphere, in O. Boyd-Barrett and C. Newbold (eds.) (1995) *Approaches to Media*. London: Arnold.

Hargreaves, I. and Thomas, J. (2002) *New News, Old News*. London: ITC and BSC.

Harrison, J. (2005) *News*. London: Routledge.

Hayek, F.A. (1979) *Law, Legislation and Liberty*. London and Henley: Routledge & Kegan Paul.

Home Office (1988) *Broadcasting in the '90s: Competition, Choice and Quality*, Cmd 517. *White Paper*, 7 November.

Independent Television Commission (1993) *Report and Accounts*. London: ITC.

Independent Television Commission (1994) *Report and Accounts*. London: ITC.

Independent Television Commission (2003) *Report and Accounts*. London: ITC.

Jones, C. (2004) Back on Form, *Broadcast*, 9 July.

Lindley, R. (2005a) *And Finally ...? The News from ITN*. London: Politico's Publishing.

Lindley, R. (2005b) And finally ... the end, *The Observer*, 23 January.

McNair, B. (1996) *News and Journalism in the UK*. London: Routledge.

Peak, S. (1994) (ed.) *The Media Guide 1995*. London: Fourth Estate.

Purvis, S. (2005) A fight to the finish, *Television*, February 2005.

Revoir, P. (2003) ITV's £100m savings plans, *Broadcast*, 5 December.

Revoir, P. (2004a) SMG fears news agenda change, *Broadcast*, 23 January.

Revoir, P. (2004b) Welcome to ITV's world, *Broadcast*, 2 July.

Rudin, R. and Ibbotson, T. (2002) *An Introduction to Journalism: Essential Techniques and Background Knowledge*. Oxford: Focal Press.

Seymour-Ure, C. (1991) *The British Press and Broadcasting since 1945*. London: Basil Blackwell.

Tait, R. (2004) Why can't the market decide? Should competition law regulate television and radio? *Oxford Media Convention*, 13 January.

Tambini, D. and Cowling, J. (2003) Living in cloud Peacock land, *Financial Times, Creative Business,* 11 March.

Wood, D. (2005) More than news, *Broadcast*, 18 February.

Notes

1 The formation of a single national and international news service for all the regional companies also meant that a serious competitor to the BBC was established.
2 The original intention of popular journalism was to provide information in a fashion that did not bore the reader, by presenting stories in an accessible way, or by concentrating on elements of the story which would interest the audience. A distinction can be made between popular journalism and journalism that is popularist and only seeks to entertain or enthral the audience (see Bertstein cf Allan 1999: 185).
3 I have borrowed this phrase from the title of Chapter XII, 'Divisa et Indivisa: Europe Divided and Undivided, 1945–1991' (Davies 1996: 1057).
4 See the Ofcom Review of Public Service Broadcasting, www.ofcom.org.uk/ (accessed 20 February 2005).
5 In June 1955, 3 months before ITV began broadcasting, the BBC changed the title of its main news from 'News and Newsreel' to 'TV News Bulletin' and placed their newsreaders before the cameras. When ITN overtook the BBC's viewing figures in 1957, the BBC undertook an audience survey (BBC, 1957: 5–10, cited in Briggs 1995: 71–2), which showed that 'one seventh of the items broadcast in a sample of ten 6 p.m. news bulletins in February and March 1957 had been voted "rather dull" and "very dull" by sizable minorities'. Although the BBC had showed some concern about the competition from ITN, the Corporation was still rather complacent about its relationship with the audience. The BBC's view was that the lower viewing figures were not a result of the audience's dislike of the BBC's programmes, but were due simply to 'audience inertia' (Brigs 1995: 72), by which they meant viewers stayed with the same channel all night. The BBC continued to argue that it enjoyed 'greater respect than ITN' (Briggs 1995: 72).
6 See Lindley's (2005a: 286–95) fascinating account of this.
7 As can be illustrated by the first attempt by the ITV companies in 1993 to move *News at Ten*.
8 Indeed the notion of quality was absent from cable licence requirements and the Broadcasting Act 1996 contains no 'quality' requirement in respect of the new terrestrial multiplex agreements for digital terrestrial broadcasting (except those channels that have public service obligations and are simulcast on analogue television, namely BBC1, BBC2, ITV1, Channel 4 and Five).
9 This move sparked a flurry of activity on other channels, which moved their own news bulletins around the evening schedules to try to ensure that the new ITV schedule did not damage their own ratings. In

January 2001 ITV moved its late news back to 10.00 p.m., but only for three nights a week. On other days it had no fixed slot. In some parts of the press it became known as 'News at When?.' In February 2004 the ITV network finally moved its late news back to a fixed time of 10.30 p.m. for five nights a week.

10 In 2005 ITN appears to have permanently lost part of its late evening audience. Its 10.30 p.m. news averages around 3 million viewers, which is 'one million fewer than ITV chiefs had hoped for' (Wood 2005: 27).

11 Independent Television News was awarded £20 million per annum to provide news for Channel 4's lunchtime programme and the evening Channel 4 News at 7 p.m. until 31 December 2006. It now makes 8 hours of news per week for C4.

12 See Section 280(10) of the 2003 Communications Act, which revokes Section 32 of the 1990 Broadcasting Act and states that '(nomination of bodies eligible for appointment as news providers) shall cease to have effect'. However, Section 280(2) specifies that it is a condition of the Channel 3 licence that the ITV companies must do all they can to ensure 'that arrangements for the appointment of a single body corporate as the appointed news provider are maintained between all holders of regional Channel 3 licences'. This seems to be aimed at ensuring that all the ITV companies have the same news service. The obligation in 280(2)(a) is backed up by 280(5) which says that there can be no news from other providers.

13 Carlton and Granada each had 20 per cent shareholding of ITN; now combined they have 40 per cent and the others remain each with 20 per cent.

14 The ITV News Channel was originally launched as the ITN News Channel and was a joint venture with NTL. It remained a lossmaking company and the ITV network bought out the majority share in June 2002. The ITN News Channel was then relaunched as the ITV News Channel.

15 However, ITN still makes day-to-day editorial decisions and it would be ITN, not the ITV News Group, which made decisions about purchasing a particular piece of news footage of Sky News or other news suppliers.

16 It was recently reported that 33 per cent of ITV1's schedule is taken up with public service broadcasting requirements, which costs about £250 million on top of the £200 million licence payment it has to make for all its regional licensees (Revoir 2004b: 13).

17 Detailed in its Phase 3 Report, www.ofcom.org.uk/media_office/latest_news/nr_20050208 (accessed 19 February 2005), see also Johnson and Turnock in this volume.

18 Figures reported in *Broadcast*, 11 July 2003: 11.

19 Stephen Carter, chief executive of Ofcom said on 29 April 2004 that

'Ofcom will hold ITV to its output obligations – in news, regional investment and production, originated quality network television.' However, this statement was balanced against the caveat that 'provided it [ITV] meets its output obligations, management should be free to manage, within the overall rules Parliament has given to us and ITV' (speech made to the Voice of the Listener and Viewer). (www.ofcom.org.uk/media_office/speeches_presentations/carter_voice_20040429, accessed 12 January 2005).

PART 3

TEXTS AND INTERTEXTS

8 ROOMS WITHIN ROOMS: *UPSTAIRS DOWNSTAIRS* AND THE STUDIO COSTUME DRAMA OF THE 1970s

Helen Wheatley

Upstairs Downstairs and the critical canon

Upstairs Downstairs holds an unusual place in the history of television drama in Britain. Whilst the series remains ever present in the public consciousness, fuelled by the commercial availability of the series on DVD and video and its current re-broadcasting on the digital satellite channel UKTV Drama, it continues to be broadly absent or under-explored in critical histories of the costume drama and the historical or classical serial. Discussing a more general lack of critical writing on the costume drama, John Caughie (2000: 207) has argued that this absence is partially explained by a masculinist turn in the historical study of television drama, which, in his opinion, has led to a sidelining of genres more traditionally associated with women and, particularly, women's tastes and pleasures. However, whilst analyses of the 'heritage genres' (costume drama, literary adaptation, historical drama and docudrama, the classic serial, and so on) have begun to circulate, *Upstairs Downstairs* remains broadly absent as an object of study, as do many of other studio-based costume dramas[1] made for independent television in the UK during the 1970s.[2] Whilst attending to the question of *Upstairs Downstairs*' place within the critical histories of British television drama, the following analysis seeks to explore the ways in which it might be inserted into current debates surrounding the costume drama and the historical serial of the 1970s. Beginning with the issue of the visual pleasures offered by *Upstairs Downstairs*, this chapter will offer an examination of the small pleasures in heritage detail presented by the studio based costume drama. Leading on from this analysis, *Upstairs Downstairs*' position as heritage drama will then be reassessed, re-reading the programme from a feminist perspective in relation to the notion of 'working through', or rather 'worrying at', women's position in society at the beginning of the 1970s.

Upstairs Downstairs was a long-running costume drama made by London Weekend Television between 1971 and 1975, which interweaved the stories of the Bellamy family (upstairs) and their servants (downstairs) from the Edwardian era to the late 1920s. Created by actresses Jean Marsh and Eileen Atkins, the series was produced by John Hawkesworth and script edited by Alfred Shaughnessy. It employed a number of prominent and upcoming television writers and directors including Fay Weldon, Rosemary Anne Sisson, Joan Kemp-Welch, Bill Bain, Cyril Coke and Derek Bennett. *Upstairs Downstairs* played a key role in the changes to London Weekend Television in 1971, following Rupert Murdoch's purchase of shares at the end of 1970 (the company had initially miscalculated its focus on current affairs and the arts, losing lucrative metropolitan viewers to a more entertainment-focused BBC). Initially produced during LWT's fight back in 1971, *Upstairs Downstairs* offered a more clearly populist address to a mass audience, whilst arguably still producing intelligent drama that drew a series of key parallels between British society at the turn of the century and at the beginning of the 1970s. First broadcast in the autumn of 1971, according to Jeremy Potter (1990: 75) the programme 'attracted an audience of 15 million in its second week . . . By 1977 it had won 26 national and international awards.' Exported to 40 countries and seen by an estimated billion viewers in the 1970s alone, *Upstairs Downstairs* had made £1 million in export sales by 1973 and was the first LWT programme sold to the US, alongside export to countries as diverse as Hong Kong, Sierra Leone and Yugoslavia. It also became an important brand beyond the initial success of the series, with spin-off novels, a film, a magazine, a spin-off television serial (*Thomas and Sarah*, LWT 1979), and even an *Upstairs Downstairs* cookbook.

It is not the intention of this chapter to produce a business history of the *Upstairs Downstairs* brand, or to write a detailed account of the production of the series; indeed, two of the most sustained discussions of the series already offer precisely this kind of account, written at the moment of production/broadcast and, significantly, before the formation of television studies as a discipline. Catherine Itzin's article '*Upstairs Downstairs*: a London Weekend drama series', published in *Theatre Quarterly* in 1972 and written during the first season of the show, and Charles Barr, Jim Hillier, and V.F. Perkins' 'The making of *Upstairs Downstairs*: a television series', published in *Movie* in 1975 at the end of the series' fifth and final run, offer analyses of the commissioning process and the conditions and processes of production respectively. Interestingly, neither of these articles offers close textual analyses of the programme itself, perhaps because they were written before the development of a vocabulary for analysing television, and before the technology was widely available for the repeat viewing of television necessary for close analysis.[3]

Both articles are united by the sentiment that *Upstairs Downstairs* was a purely industrial object of study, made under financially and temporally restricted conditions of production, and that close textual analysis of the programme might therefore prove rather unrewarding. However, the current availability of the series (both through commercial sales and rebroadcasting) enables us to revisit *Upstairs Downstairs* and to examine the studio costume drama *textually* as well as *industrially*.[4]

Rooms within rooms: the possibilities of studio space

Recent research into the early period of television drama production in the UK has shown the studio to be a dynamic space in which drama was produced. For example, John Caughie's (2000: 77) notion of the studio as 'performative space – a space for acting – rather than narrative space – a space for action' has gone a good deal of the way towards describing the function and possibilities of the studio as a dramatic space during the 1950s and 1960s, refusing to disregard it as either theatrical space transposed to another medium or a primitive precursor to location filming. However, when histories of television drama reach the 1970s, the studio is often conceptualized differently, as a problem or a handicap, with studio drama identified as being produced within a compromised dramatic space. It is tempting, looking at dramas from this period with hindsight, to read the studio-based drama as being clumsy, dated, and inexpressive; however, avoiding this approach, we might begin to think about the meaningful and expressive uses of studio-based *mise en scène* in the 1970s, and in the case of *Upstairs Downstairs* we can do this by looking at the representation of domestic life.

Speaking at the University of Cambridge in 1974, Raymond Williams described a continuity from the great naturalist dramatists, beginning with Ibsen, to the present state of television and television viewing, by focusing on the concept of the room. In this speech, Williams (1989: 12) proposed,

> the room is there, not as one scenic convention among all the possible others, but because it is an actively shaping environment – the particular structure within which we live ... the solid form, the conventional declaration, of how we are living and what we value. This room on the stage ... [is] a set that defines us and can trap us: the alienated object that now represents us in the world.

This makes a great deal of sense if we understand the television studio as a room in which another room is created (the dramatic room), only to be broadcast into a third (the room of the viewer at home); the room in this sense is television's definitive space. According to Williams' description, the room is an eloquent and expressive space that is permeated with meaning; as a structure it is declamatory and active. Thus, in the context of *Upstairs Downstairs*, the room asks to be read and understood as a meaningful space, as a space which is more than a neutral backdrop, but which acts as a shaping and defining structure within the dramas in hand.

In addition to discussing the studio in *Upstairs Downstairs* as an expressive and coherent dramatic space (an idea that will be explored toward the end of this chapter), we might also reconsider its role as a space of visual pleasure. Recent examinations of the costume drama have taken for granted that the visual pleasure specific to this genre is located in the sweeping vistas and location shooting of *filmed* costume drama, where stately homes glide onto our screen in the long-take long shot that is seen as emblematic of the genre. This version of heritage visual pleasure stems directly from Andrew Higson's (1993, 1996) work on the heritage spectacle, in which he acknowledges the continuities between heritage film and heritage television of the early 1980s (specifically the Granada productions *Brideshead Revisited* (1981) and *Jewel in the Crown* (1984)), and lays out the terms by which filmed heritage drama can be seen as visually pleasurable. However, John Caughie's recent revisitation of this debate points towards a sense of visual pleasure that is more clearly specific to television and that does not exclude earlier incarnations of the costume drama which were neither shot on location nor with 'cinematic' production values. In Caughie's (2000: 213) terms, 'detail [is] part of a poetics which is specific to television' and he therefore locates the visual pleasure of the televisual costume drama in the small, ornamental, everyday, and, importantly, feminine pleasures of the genre, pleasures 'which the academy, and academic film and television theory, has not regarded as manly, noble or dignified' (Caughie: 2000: 215).

With Caughie's description of the generic pleasures of the costume drama in mind, it is easier to see how the studio-rooms of *Upstairs Downstairs* might be written into the costume drama/visual pleasure debate. By offering the viewer the sumptuous detail of period set dressing within the studio space (the 'antiqued' rooms of the Bellamy household in particular), the programme explicitly offered viewers an achievable 'look' for their own homes that corresponded with a burgeoning trend for Victorian and Edwardian fashion and interior design in the early 1970s. This relationship between studio setting and home decoration was noted in March 1977 in Lord Annan's *Report of the Committee on the Future of Broadcasting* when, towards the end of a long section on the potentially negative effects of violence and sex on television for the 'vulnerable viewer', the report noted that '[s]ometimes programmes influence people in comparatively trivial ways. The furnishing of studio sets can influence the way people furnish their homes' (Annan 1977: 259). However, an examination of a selection of lifestyle magazines from this period (for example, *Ideal Home*, *Vogue*, *Woman*) shows that rather than directly *influencing* the way viewers dressed themselves and their homes in a simple and easily defined way, the costume drama of the 1970s tapped into a existing trend, offering the viewer the visual pleasure of *familiar* antique detail within the rooms of the studio-based drama. This trend, exemplified by the ultra-fashionable Biba shops selling Victorian and Edwardian inspired clothes and homeware (see Dobbin 1970), or by the 'Edwardian Lady' photographs taken for *Vogue* of Princess Anne on her twenty-first birthday (Parkinson 1971), meant that before, during and after the transmission of *Upstairs Downstairs*, antiques were very much in fashion and part of the quotidian detail of many viewers' lives.[5] Lifestyle magazines such as *Ideal Home* and *Woman*, as well as ITV's listings guide, the *TV Times,* were full of advice during the early 1970s about buying and selling antiques, how to transform your 1930s semi into an Edwardian town house, how to dress like a Victorian in bed, and so on, suggesting an appreciative audience for what Caughie terms the pleasure in the ornamental and the everyday within television costume drama, particularly those set in and around *fin de siècle* Britain.

In *Upstairs Downstairs* there are moments where the visual pleasure of the Edwardian everyday is put firmly on display, and where the studio-room operates as a structuring space for the exhibition of quotidian antiques. It is these antique knick-knacks, gadgets and garments that are the studio costume drama's equivalent of the long-take, long shot of the stately home on the hill in filmed versions of the genre. In the series we frequently see characters dressing and undressing, stressing the every-dayness of period detail; in a sense, underwear and night clothes are as important as pieces of costume as dresses and suits are here. Episodes also feature domestic antiques, the role and prominence of these objects in individual scenes often extending far beyond their narrative function. In a first season episode entitled 'Why is her door locked?', which focuses on the cook's 'theft' of a baby from outside a local shop, two of the maids are depicted operating an early vacuum cleaner whilst discussing the crime. The scene, which begins with a slow zoom out from the front of the machine and is shot in a single long take, serves little narrative function within the episode other than to reiterate what the viewer has been told previously through the servants' gossip. Here there is no connection between the action taking place on screen (the operation of the vacuum cleaner) and the dialogue being delivered (the servants' gossip); the entire scene serves simply to put the vacuum cleaner on display within the heritage setting, offering a quotidian visual pleasure that is tied to the representation of the everyday detail of the historic household and domestic life.

The representation of food and cooking is also significant in understanding the visual pleasure offered by the studio-based heritage drama, with the camera lingering over shots of fully laden tables and kitchen pantries. For example, in the first half of the *Upstairs Downstairs* episode 'Guest of Honour', in which the household is shown preparing for the arrival of King Edward, the narrative is punctuated by empty scenes without dialogue where nothing else takes place but the display of food, with extreme close-ups and close-up zooms of jellied salmons and cascades of prawns rendered an integral part of the heritage spectacle, the silence emphasizing the pleasure that we might take in *looking* at this food. These sequences are also underscored by the fact that an article published in the *TV Times* to accompany this episode (Anon. 1972a) recreates the dinner menu ('Caviar au Blinis, Royal Natives, Consommé de Volaille, Sauce Medoc, Pate de Perdix'), as if inviting the viewer to dine alongside the Bellamy's guests. As mentioned in the introduction to this chapter, this extra-textual emphasis on food and cooking was also later extended to a cookbook entitled *Mrs Bridges' Upstairs Downstairs Cookbook* (Macmillan), published by LWT before the end of the final series in 1975. Here then, both text and intertext clearly promote a sense of pleasure to be taken in the preparation and display of food and therefore in the spectacle of the everyday. This is clearly a special meal prepared according to the upper-class tastes of the early twentieth century, but the fact that it is food rather than property that is put on display in the studio-based costume drama is indeed significant. This quotidian visual pleasure is an appeal to what Caughie (2000: 215) calls 'pleasures in detail, our engagement held not by the drive of the narrative but by the observation of everyday manners and the ornamental'; it is pointedly *not* the spectacular visual pleasure of filmed-on-location heritage drama, though it employs the same formal techniques (such as the long-take tracking shot) to place everyday heritage artefacts on display.

As well as being excluded from discussions of the classic serial and the costume drama, *Upstairs Downstairs* has also been compared unfavourably to the more obviously radical or progressive historical dramas made by the BBC in the 1970s, and thus extended discussion of this programme as historical drama has been replaced by far more lively debate about progressive dramas such as *The Cheviot, the Stag and the Black, Black Oil* (BBC1, 1974) and *Days of Hope* (BBC1, 1975). For example, Lez Cooke, discussing an argument proposed by Colin McArthur (1978), suggests that,

> In some cases there were lessons to be learned from history – in the cases of progressive dramas ... this was part of the agenda. In most cases, however, this was not the main motivation – the attraction for the TV companies in producing multi-episode historical drama series residing more in their potential for maximising and retaining audiences. (Cooke 2003: 113)

This argument, that the production of long-running historical dramas produced financial profit for the (mainly commercial) television companies rather than producing a discourse on the 'lessons to be learned from history', has prohibited extended critical discussion of *Upstairs Downstairs* as historical drama. However, the notion that commercial success and a critical engagement with history were incompatible can be reconsidered through close examination of *Upstairs Downstairs* as one of the most popular and successful examples of the historical drama. Adapting Newcomb and Hirsch's (1987) notion of television as 'cultural forum', the concluding part of this chapter looks at how *Upstairs Downstairs* participated in a kind of public thinking and significantly worked through some of the 'lessons to be learned from history', particularly in relation to the discursive contexts of the women's liberation movement in the 1970s. As Newcomb and Hirsch (1987: 461) argue:

> in popular culture generally, in television specifically, the raising of questions is as important as the answering of them ... Indeed it would be startling to think that mainstream texts in mass society would overtly challenge dominant ideas. But this hardly prevents oppositional ideas from appearing ... [W]e argue that television does not present firm ideological conclusions – despite its formal conclusions – so much as it *comments on* ideological problems ... for the most part the rhetoric of television drama is a rhetoric of discussion.

Television's role in the process of 'working through' events and issues has recently been explored by John Ellis in relation to what he terms the 'eras of availability and uncertainty' (Ellis 2000: 78–9), although the term is useful beyond this particular historical context. However, in relation to *Upstairs Downstairs*' engagement with the discourse of women's rights in the early 1970s, the term 'worrying at' rather than 'working through' might be more appropriate, given that 'working through' suggests a sense of conclusion or 'exhaustion' (Ellis 2000: 79) which the series does not produce.

'I suppose some sort of movement is necessary': *Upstairs Downstairs* and second-wave feminism

It has become critically orthodox in the context of the heritage/costume drama to argue that at times of social upheaval the genre offers the viewer an image of a 'golden age' in which life was easier and more settled. Initiating this critical trend, Colin McArthur (1980: 40) speculated that,

> it seems reasonable to suppose that a society going through a period of historical transition and finding it immensely painful and disorienting will therefore tend to recreate, in some at least of its art, images of more (apparently) settled times, especially times in

which the self-image of the society as a whole was buoyant and optimistic.

The argument that at moments of social unrest or disenfranchisement we turn towards images of a more settled past was made by McArthur in relation to *Upstairs Downstairs*, and has been reiterated by a number of others in the programme's critical history (for example, Giddings and Selby 2001: 28–9; Cooke 2003: 113). This critical orthodoxy therefore arises out of discussions of *Upstairs Downstairs* that focus on the issue of class representation, reading the heritage drama as restorative, conservative and potentially ameliorative of feelings of alienation and class inequity within the viewer. However, when we read this series from a feminist perspective we might begin to question McArthur's thesis, or indeed Mary Douglas's and Karen Wollaeger's (1982: 11) notion that the series is a 'drama of social harmony'. On the contrary, it is possible to argue that *Upstairs Downstairs* is a series in which characters *worry at* their place in society, and in which dramatic conflict is produced by characters serially challenging, rejecting, or speaking up against the status quo. Second-wave feminism was clearly an important context in the early 1970s for a series written, in part, about women's domestic life and work. Charlotte Brunsdon, discussing the women's film of the same decade, has argued that second-wave feminism provided a set of discursive contexts for popular culture during the 1970s, which she identifies as 'changing patterns of women's employment and education; increasingly effective and available contraception; the fall in the birth rate, with changing patterns of marriage and divorce; [and] the impact of the women's liberation movement itself' (Brunsdon 1997: 54). These contexts can, perhaps, be seen even more clearly in the serial episodic narrative of *Upstairs Downstairs*, which provided a weekly return to storylines encompassing all of the above issues. Indeed, one need only look at the commercial television listings guide, the *TV Times*, to see how prevalent these discursive contexts were within television *in general* in this period: in the early 1970s the magazine is full of feature articles discussing women's role in society and celebrity interviews that focus on a famous woman's struggle to achieve a home/work balance.[6] As media historians we might read the television listings guide as a microcosm of television's broader cultural forum, in which the 'rhetoric of discussion', to borrow Newcomb and Hirsch's phrase, dominates. Like television itself, the *TV Times* explicitly set out to present contradictory material that raised questions about women's role in society without providing a singular or coherent set of answers: one columnist might argue for the right for equal pay for female performers, another might set out to denigrate the working mother. It might therefore also be argued that the *TV Times* helped to shape a set of potential positions in which programmes like *Upstairs Downstairs* were to be viewed.

The *TV Times* also explicitly connected these debates to *Upstairs Downstairs*. For example, half way into the first season, an interview with Jean Marsh, one of the series co-creators and lead actress (playing Rose, the house parlour maid), discusses her position in relation to feminism:

> Jean isn't a staunch female liberator. 'But I suppose some sort of movement is necessary because women aren't paid equally ... I can go out to work, keep myself and keep my parents, run this house in Oxfordshire and a flat in Knightsbridge. I can cook, sew, drive. I am totally self-reliant and still manage to look like a girl ... It is very difficult for any man to accept this.' (Anon. 1972b: 5)

Marsh's position here reflects the position of her character in the series – as moderate believer in 'basic equality', which nevertheless does not extend towards an extreme position either for or against feminist principles. However, what is significant about this interview is that it acknowledges the centrality of these issues in relation to the series, whilst furthering the *TV Times* dialogue on 'women's lib'. *Upstairs Downstairs*, as a long-running serial drama, has a complex kind of authorship, with a number of key creative personnel shaping the series and its concerns, from the programme's creators (Marsh and Atkins) to its director and script editor (Hawkesworth and Shaughnessy respectively), with a large team of writers and directors also moulding the identity of the series. For example, Fay Weldon, as scriptwriter of the first episode and a number of other episodes during the programme's run, certainly played an important role in establishing *Upstairs Downstairs*' 'feminist' concerns, particularly in its first two seasons. In a interview with Weldon, Sarah Gristwood argues that '[t]here was then ... no voice for the feminist movement. In [Weldon] it found one' (Gristwood 1985: 13); Weldon goes on to state that 'I thought that if I worked out the problems and thoughts in a fictional way it would cause no offence to anyone' (ibid.), suggesting that she used the popular serial drama to 'work through' or worry at feminist issues in a covert way, voicing her own political stance in the guise of mass entertainment. From the outset, there is evidence that Weldon's writing for *Upstairs Downstairs* was at odds with the programme's key producers, Hawkesworth and Shaughnessy. For example, the following description was edited out of the first draft of her script by Shaughnessy:

> Clemence walks bravely towards her future home. She carries a carpet bag. She walks perhaps too freely and boldly for someone in her position – which is one of the underlings of this caste-ridden world in which to be female is bad enough – to be a female servant is barely human. (cf. Itzin 1972: 32)

Ultimately, Weldon was left feeling as if she was removed from the production of *Upstairs Downstairs* on the grounds that her writing was too radical and her politics were in conflict with the direction of the series.

Whilst there is little room in this chapter to examine the competing authorial voices within *Upstairs Downstairs*, and, to a certain extent, this project has been undertaken by others (see Itzin 1972; Thornton 1993), this initial moment of conflict is worthy of note in relation to the following analysis.

An analysis of the first two seasons of *Upstairs Downstairs* in particular (the Edwardian seasons) shows the series 'worrying at' issues relating to women and equality. In line with Newcomb and Hirsch's notion of television drama as cultural forum, we might see *Upstairs Downstairs* connecting the issues facing women at the turn of the century and in the early 1970s by raising a set of key questions about women's position in society. The episodic narrative of the long-form serial drama allowed for repeated discussion of issues relating directly to the women's liberation movement: indeed, twenty-three of the first twenty-six episodes of *Upstairs Downstairs* focused directly on the issue of women's role in the public sphere, encompassing topics within individual episodes such as women's education and employment, changing expectations of marriage, domestic life, and divorce, women as desiring and sexual beings and the associated issues of women's health and abortion. Several episodes in both series also dealt directly with the issue of feminism through the representation of the Fabian Society and later the Suffragette movement. These foci continued over the next three series but to a lesser extent, a change that is well documented in Edith P. Thornton's (1993: 27) analysis of the series' shift 'from a female centred, comedic, ensemble piece to a male centred character study with novelistic pretensions', a shift that, she argues, was partly necessitated by its sale to the US.

As well as looking broadly at the kinds of issues covered by individual episodes, we can also follow characters' story arcs throughout the series to chart attitudes towards feminism and feminist issues. In *Upstairs Downstairs*, characters are treated emblematically, in that they represent certain positions and ideas in relation to the women's movement, with nearly all of the central female characters oscillating between positions of liberation and recuperation, whereby they are brought 'back into line' and 'reminded of their place' in society. For example, the wayward maid, Sarah (Pauline Collins), who has 'ideas above her station' and who is never happy in service in the house, starts out as a wilful, worldly, mobile woman who is constantly returned to the home until she acquiesces and becomes a domestic woman (see for example the episodes 'A Voice From the Past' and 'Guest of Honour'). Whilst the narrative moves her toward containment (as her character leaves the series she has been 'tamed' by the family, servants, and eventually her husband), she initially provides moments in which women's independence, sexual freedom and domestic work are explored: in short, she raises feminist questions. Similarly, the story arc of Elizabeth (Nicola Pagett), the daughter of the house, is also one of oscillation between gender rebellion and conformity, and there is a certain mirroring between Sarah and Elizabeth (their physical similarity, the echoes in their story arcs), which suggests that their problems are problems faced by *women*, not *a woman*.

Returning to the idea of expressive studio space, the following analysis offers a specific example of the ways in which *Upstairs Downstairs* 'worried at' the discursive contexts of the women's liberation movement, arguing that the programme raised specific questions about women's role in the public sphere (or their exclusion from it) through the expressive use of studio-based *mise en scène*. This analysis centres on Lady Marjorie (Rachel Gurney), the female head of the household. Whilst being positioned as a conservative figure who polices the unruly women of the household (including the servants and her own daughter), Lady Marjorie's dialogue from the outset tells a different story, expressing her frustration at being confined in her home. Whilst other characters express their frustrations with femininity more vociferously, Lady Marjorie's malaise is more subtly, though no less definitely, expressed. In contrast to her husband, a Conservative member of Parliament, Lady Marjorie continually articulates her frustration at being excluded from the public sphere, unable to act outside of her domicile, and it is this yearning and frustration that underscores her character. Whilst we might also understand Lady Marjorie as a powerful social actor who regulates the activities and behaviour of those around her and takes control from within the domestic space, this character's continual frustration at the displacement of this power runs throughout the first two seasons of *Upstairs Downstairs*. Reading Lady Marjorie through her actions and dialogue we can only understand her as anti-feminist, acting against other women's rebellion; however, if we read her *spatially*, analysing Rachel Gurney's performance in the context of the studio setting, this character tells a different story.

The seventh episode of *Upstairs Downstairs,* 'Magic Casements' (written by John Hawkesworth and directed by Joan Kemp Welch), offers us a case study of this connection between setting and character. This episode focuses on Lady Marjorie's extra-marital affair with Captain Charles Hammond (David Kernan), an army friend of her son who is stationed on the Indian border, and explores the frustrations of married life and her yearning to be free to participate in the outside world. Hammond's position as a soldier stationed on the 'edge of the Empire' further emphasizes the restricted nature of Lady Marjorie's own social world, and the episode rests on her struggle, and eventual failure, to escape the confines of her own home. The title, 'Magic Casements', refers to a line in Keats' 'Ode to a Nightingale', and relates to Lady Marjorie's dreams of a romantic life beyond her domestic space, only to be found through a magic casement. An analysis of three short scenes in this episode will delineate the ways in which her performance in the context of the studio setting is mobilized to explore these narrative concerns.

In the opening shots of the episode, Lady Marjorie's position in the house, compared to that of her husband, is delineated by their respective introductions: whilst Richard Bellamy strides in through the front door, returning from Parliament, Lady Marjorie is encased behind her desk. Here her position behind a heavy piece of furniture, and the sense of control and stasis expressed in her performance within a confined studio space, articulates her sense of frustration; in the scene, she acts as a pivot around which her husband and the camera move. Lady Marjorie's costuming also serves to emphasize a sense of enclosure in this moment, with its Edwardian high collar and heavy corsetry all suggesting a sense of containment. However, in the scene that follows her first 'date' with Captain Hammond, Lady Marjorie's domestic space is transformed.

On her date with Captain Hammond, Lady Marjorie expresses her frustration at being confined to the home in no uncertain terms, sighing,

> What a dull time I've had compared to you ... all my life I've been protected, cosseted, wrapped in a cocoon of fondness ... [I enjoy it] most of the time, until I meet someone like you and I feel rather cross and jealous ... because you have a real life, exciting and worthwhile, which I can never enjoy

During their date at the opera, she listens wistfully to Captain Hammond describe the scenery on the frontier of the British Empire, and, in the following scene, her dressing room is transformed to express this yearning. In this moment, costume and props (which are only seen in this episode) are employed to visually articulate her desire, both for Captain Hammond and for an exotic space beyond the domestic. Her costume (a kimono) and a silk screen elaborately painted with a Himalayan mountain scene, which comes into shot as Lady Marjorie deliberately moves in front of it, are both coded as 'foreign', representing that exotic outside to which she has no access. In front of the screen, she stretches and sighs, resting her arms behind her head as if basking in the sun; the screen therefore operates as a 'magic casement' in this scene, and eloquently expresses this character's interior state, even whilst we are also made aware this is a view of the outside world that must remain only a view, a representation, held at a distance. The room at the beginning of her romance thus speaks of this woman's frustrated desire for access to the world, as well as her longing for sexual freedom and romance.

However, once their affair has been brought to an end we are once again reminded that Lady Marjorie is positioned in a room with no view. At the end of the affair/episode, when Lady Marjorie has been persuaded to stay at home and be a good wife and a good mother (and has successfully persuaded her husband to vote against his will in Parliament), we see her standing forlornly at her drawing room window, looking out of the window. This view has an added frisson within the studio set of course, as a view to nowhere; once again, we are reminded that, as a woman, she may only participate indirectly in the world beyond her window (by persuading her husband to vote), rather than entering into the public sphere herself.

At the end of the episode, a sense of despair and yearning is left in place, with a cut away to Lady Marjorie's face in close-up revealing her sadness as her husband and son discuss her ex-lover in the background. As her husband comes to the window to join her, she looks past him, up and out towards the window, without covering the look of disappointment on her face. A final shot from the doorway of the room reveals the butler closing the door on the room, smiling as he looks at the back of his master and mistress standing together. Whilst we might understand this final shot as restorative, in which domestic equilibrium has been attained once more, affirmed by the butler's self-satisfied smile, we must remember that the viewer has seen the other side of this shot and retains a memory of Lady Marjorie's pained expression. Furthermore, the closure of the door on the image of Lady Marjorie being 'consoled' by her husband can simultaneously be read as a figurative act of closure whereby feminine resistance is laid to rest, or as a further expression of her position of entrapment as she is 'shut into' her home. At this moment, which could be read as a recuperative ending in which the woman in question learns and accepts her (restricted) place in the world, there is a certain conflict between the *mise en scène* of the drama, which expresses her desirous longing and the frustrations of her position in society, and, on the other hand, the dialogue, which speaks of her acquiescence to what is expected of her as a 'wife and mother'. In episodes like 'Magic Casements' then, *Upstairs Downstairs* can be seen to visually 'worry at' important social issues relating to contemporary debates about women's rights and freedom, even whilst the narrative and dialogue of many of the key characters in the series openly reject feminism or an overtly feminist narrative. In line with Newcomb and Hirsch's notion of cultural forum and the idea that 'the raising of questions is as important as the answering of them within the television text', this reading would suggest that the constantly recuperative endings of *Upstairs Downstairs*' serial narrative are less significant than the issues raised throughout each episode.

This preoccupation with the discursive contexts of the women's liberation movement is not confined to *Upstairs Downstairs*; it is also a key narrative preoccupation for other studio dramas of the period (for example, ATV's *Edward the Seventh* opens with Queen Victoria (Annette Crosbie) worrying about her work/life balance, and the balance of gendered power in the public and private spheres). However, it is in the complex interweaving of women's stories and problems in the long-running narrative of *Upstairs Downstairs* that these issues are most obviously present. To conclude, then, whilst radical feminist positions are belittled in the series, the wider text implicitly speaks of women's frustrations within an enclosed domestic space, made plain by the home/

studio parallel. Whereas Douglas and Wollaeger (1982: 210) argue that 'the structure of space in social harmony programmes like *Upstairs Downstairs* presents an unproblematic structural fit between the spatial and social order', we need only to look at the frisson built up around the representation of inside and outside in the series, or at the figure of the woman at the window in a room without a view, to see a more complex, nuanced use of studio space.

Acknowledgements

I gratefully acknowledge the support of the Arts and Humanities Research Board which funded the research project 'Cultures of British Television Drama, 1960–82' at the University of Reading. This article is one of the outcomes of the research.

Bibliography

Annan, Lord (Chair) (1977) *Report of the Committee on the Future of Broadcasting* [1974], Cmd 6753. London: HMSO.

Anon. (1972a) When the king came to dinner, *TV Times*, 16 November.

Anon. (1972b) Jean Marsh, *TV Times*, 20 January.

Barr, C., Hillier, J. and Perkins, V.F. (1975) The Making of *Upstairs Downstairs*: a television series, *Movie*, 21, Autumn: 46–63.

Brunsdon, C. (1997) *Screen Tastes: Soap Opera to Satellite Dishes*. London and New York: Routledge.

Caughie, J. (2000) *Television Drama: Realism, Modernism and British Culture*. Oxford: Oxford University Press.

Cooke, L. (2003) *British Television Drama: A History*. London: British Film Institute.

Dobbin, J. (1970) Biba, *Ideal Home*, 99(3), March: 92–3.

Douglas, M. and Wollaeger, K. (1982) Towards a typography of the viewing public, in R. Hoggart and J. Morgan (eds) *The Future of Broadcasting*. London: Macmillan.

Ellis, J. (2000) *Seeing Things: Television in the Age of Uncertainty*. London: I B Tauris.

Giddings, R. and Selby, K. (2001) *The Classic Serial on Television and Radio*. Basingstoke and New York: Palgrave.

Higson, A. (1993) Re-presenting the national past: nostalgia and pastiche in the heritage film, in L. Friedman (ed.) *Fires Were Started: British Cinema and Thatcherism*. Minneapolis: University of Minnesota Press.

Higson, A. (ed.) (1996) *Dissolving Views: Key Writings On British Cinema*. London: Cassell.

Itzin, C. (1972) *Upstairs Downstairs*: London Weekend Drama Series, *Theatre Quarterly*, 6, April–June: 26–38.
Knowles, S. (1971) The fourth Mrs Osborne believes marriage is here to stay, *TV Times*, 11 March.
Lee, S. (1971a) My marvellous marriage, *TV Times*, 28 January.
Lee, S. (1971b) Together – and making marriage work in separate houses, *TV Times*, 25 March.
London Weekend Television. (1975) *Mrs Bridges'* Upstairs Downstairs *Cookbook*. London: Macmillan.
McArthur, C. (1978) *Television and History*. London: British Film Institute.
Messenger-Davies, M. (2003) Salvaging television's past: what guarantees survival? A discussion of the fates of two 1970s classic serials, *The Secret Garden* and *Clayhanger*. Paper presented to the Reconsidering the Canon: Popular Television Drama in the 1960s and 70s symposium, University of Reading, 19 September.
Nelson, R. (2001) Costume Drama, in G. Creeber (ed.) *The Television Genre Book*. London: British Film Institute.
Newcomb, H. and Hirsch, P. (1987) Television as a cultural forum, in H. Newcomb (ed.) *Television: The Critical View*, 4th edn. Oxford: Oxford University Press.
Newman, F. (1971) Working hard at being a woman, *TV Times*, 4 February.
Parkinson, N. (1971) Princess Anne in her own right, *Vogue*, 128(11), September: 65–70.
Potter, J. (1990) *Independent Television in Britain: Volume 4, Companies and Programmes, 1968–80*. London: Macmillan.
Thornton, E.P. (1993) On the Landing: High Art, Low Art, and *Upstairs Downstairs*, *Camera Obscura*, 31, Spring: 26–47.
Vahimagi, T. (1996) *British Television*, 2nd edn. Oxford: Oxford University Press.
Williams, R. (1989) Drama in a dramatised society, in A. O'Connor (ed.) *Raymond Williams on Television: Selected Writings*. London: Routledge.

Notes

1 ITV's studio-based costume dramas of this period include *Jennie, Lady Randolph Churchill* (Thames, 1974), *Edward the Seventh* (ATV, 1975), and *Lillie* (LWT, 1978), alongside BBC-produced studio-based costume drama such as *I Claudius* (BBC2, 1976) and *The Duchess of Duke Street* (BBC1, 1976–7).
2 There are a few exceptions to this critical absence: Giddings and Selby's (2001) study of the classic serial does include some discussion of

studio-based adaptations made in this period, though their account is mainly BBC-centric.

3 Film, on the other hand, could be viewed repeatedly using Steenbeck editing tables and 16/35 mm projectors and analyser-projectors.

4 A paper delivered by Máire Messenger-Davies at the University of Reading's symposium, 'Reconsidering the canon: popular television drama in the 1960s and 70s' (September 2003), discussed the vital importance of the survival of, and access to, television programmes for historical study of television and the formation of a television canon. It is hoped that the analysis offered in this chapter goes some way towards proving Professor Messenger-Davies' point.

5 School and holiday photographs from the late 1970s and early 80s show that I was bought period costume to wear 'on special occasions' by my parents. My family also had 'Victorian' portrait photographs taken on holiday, in a studio that specializes in period portraits in Whitby, trading on the 'golden era' of the town's Victorian past. The studio is still open to tourists in 2005.

6 Examples include 'My marvellous marriage' (Lee 1971a), an interview with Elizabeth Sellars extolling the virtues of marriage, 'Working hard at being a woman' (Newman 1971), an interview with Diana Coupland about the 'war of the sexes' and finding a work/life balance, 'The fourth Mrs. Osborne believes marriage is here to stay' (Knowles, 1971), an interview with Jill Bennet, John Osborne's wife, about her enthusiasm for marriage, and 'Together and making their marriage work in separate houses' (Lee 1971b), interviewing Clive Swift about his marriage to Margaret Drabble and what it is like to be married to 'an intelligent, independent woman'.

9 REAL PEOPLE WITH REAL PROBLEMS? PUBLIC SERVICE BROADCASTING, COMMERCIALISM AND *TRISHA*

Sherryl Wilson

'Remember: here on *Trisha* we get real, with real people and real problems.' The injunction comes from Trisha Goddard at the end of her eponymous television talk show broadcast on 16 August 2004, warning potential participants and viewers that what we have just witnessed is serious and constitutes actuality. The caution is offered when DNA results reveal that Tom, not Gary, is the father of Amanda's baby. The shock of an uncertainty being made certain, and in public, is visible on the guests' faces as they have moments to digest the news that will have long-reaching consequences for all involved. This moment signals the ever-present tension that characterizes *Trisha*: tabloid sensationalism exists in partnership with the authority and authenticity of 'real' experience on which the show is premised. This 'real' is not limited to the guests' own lives but is extended to Goddard whose credentials as a trained counsellor and survivor of a number of traumas, including depression and her sister's suicide, authenticate her performance as commentator on and facilitator of others in difficulty. In turn, this tension produces a particular form of public service broadcasting that will be explored throughout this chapter.[1]

This form of public service broadcasting is increasingly evident across a range of reality television programming, a genre that is rather baggy and difficult to define but which constitutes the context in which television talk shows are situated, and is a product of television's political economy. The popularization and exploitation of individual (usually miserable) experience in the drive for high viewing figures has attracted numerous claims that reality television in general, and talk shows in particular, are evidence of dumbing down, of the emptying out of meaningful content at the expense of cheap sensationalism. However, I will argue that with its emphasis on advice and therapy *Trisha* performs a function that is both a product of, and a response to, an age marked by insecurity and instability. As such, it provides a point of reference through which strategies for dealing with everyday life and its difficulties are developed.

This is not an easy, unproblematic argument however. The strategies offered in *Trisha* provide a template for living that is morally and ideologically loaded with middle-class bourgeois values while the participants themselves are predominately white and working class and appear to be disadvantaged in terms of educational background and financial resources. It is the combination of commercialism and participant demographic that forms the basis for charges of exploitation commonly levelled at programmes like *Trisha*.

I will attempt here to tease out the complex relationship between commercialism, the excesses of tabloid media, and class and gender because the processes at play within this relationship have a bearing on how we are to understand *Trisha* in the context of ITV. Kevin Glynn (2000) reminds us that tabloidism is marked by sensationalism and a lack of critical distance. In particular, tabloid media incorporate voices that are frequently excluded from 'serious' programming, that the focus is on the bizarre and deviant, and that 'by inserting the abnormal into the space usually occupied by the socially central, the tabloid media invert the values of the "quality press"' (Glynn 2000: 104). As a result, 'Common criticisms of tabloid media find an unholy alliance between commercially interested broadcasters and the prurient interests of audiences' (Glynn 2000: 105).

As a 'commercially interested' broadcaster, ITV needs programmes that produce high viewing figures in order to be attractive to advertisers who want to buy airtime within them. This is in contrast to the BBC, which does not operate under the same commercial pressures (although it does have to maintain high viewing figures in order to justify its licence fee). Talk shows are associated with tabloid culture, which is in turn associated with working-class values and 'trash' culture. These, then, are seen in opposition to middle-class values, and as ITV, rather than BBC. There is, then, a tendency to see bourgeois culture as anti-commercial in that the middle-class discursively asserts itself as opposed to the 'vulgarities' of commercial (working-class) values. However, this is a false dichotomy because the BBC does broadcast shows that can be described as tabloid media. For example in the mid-1990s *The Oprah Winfrey Show* was aired on BBC2 in the late afternoon slot. This indicates that there is an artificial distinction, or at least a distinction that is increasingly blurred, between the kind of public service broadcasting divorced from the vulgarities of commercial pressure and the kinds that are explicitly driven by them. Nonetheless, this type of programming is more closely associated with ITV and the critique of commercial television in relation to 'quality' output reflects this; this has (in part) shaped the debate around talk shows.

The link between class and tabloid media is evident in the current disquiet about commercial television and its apparent role in the degradation of culture (primarily through the rise and rise of reality television). However, Jane Shattuc (1997) reveals that this is not a contemporary phenomenon but places the relationship between class and tabloid media in a historical context. In particular she links the history of television talk shows to that of the tabloid presses when, by the 1880s the editor of the *Sun* (US), Joseph Pulitzer, 'began mixing sensation with commercialism ... much as the daytime talk shows intersperse their dramas with commercials today' (Shattuc 1997: 17).

> [By the] last quarter of the [19th] Century tabloid newspapers were an established component in the cultural and economic class divisions, as are the [television talk] shows. They were cheap, as are the shows ... The tabloids' audience materialized because of the changes in the lower classes, waves of immigrants [in America] and a newly arrived urban working class; the shows are consumed by a growing underclass. (Shattuc 1997: 16)

The connection between tabloidism and (working) class results in charges that it produces cultural contagion. This is particularly evident in the talk show debate that will be discussed below.

To the mix of commercialism and class we also have to add that of gender, not least because *Trisha,* in common with other daytime talk shows, is produced with a young (16–35) female audience demographic in mind. Along with the main subject matter – care of the self – it is the intimate, gossipy mode of address that underpins the 'feminine' quality of the shows and the attendant charges of low-brow culture. Patricia Mellencamp (1990: 155) defines gossip as 'second-hand talk' that is recycled, mediated and consumed; it is a symptom of the shifting border between the private and public domains dissolving the distinction between confession, therapy and information. Linking gossip to class and gender, Mellencamp says:

> Gossip's ... excessive bad taste is a lower class body, frequently a female body, while the upper class body of the news (and its scandals) is sleek, refined, tasteful, discreet, often male. Women as excess, one version of which is affect ... belong in the tabloids – the place of the body and the emotions. Men belong in the legitimate newspapers and magazines – the domain of the intellect and rational thought ... The accepted difference between news and gossip is the difference between women and men. (Mellencamp 1990: 161–2)

Whilst the stories recounted on *Trisha* are not second-hand – they are first person narratives – they typify Mellencamp's classification of gossip and help us understand the processes at play in the show. On the one hand, the guests' narratives signal the dissolution between the public and private, the transgression of boundaries that maintain cultural values of bourgeois society. They also represent the lower-class 'female' body of emotions. On the other hand, traditional cultural values are shored up by the containment of unruliness through the deployment of a therapeutic framework and the dispensation of advice. The threat of degradation is made safe by the insertion of bourgeois values as the prescription for healthy living. For example, Neil ('My ex slept with my sister', tx. 23 August 2004) has drug and alcohol dependency problems leading him to commit crimes for which he is continually in and out of prison. His ex-partner, Amanda, wants Neil to be 'more of a father' to their son. A moral code is offered through diagnosis and prescription that will enable Neil to learn 'how to live in society, be productive'. While other guests are introduced, Neil and Amanda go backstage to work with Jill Cox, a 'relationships expert', returning at the conclusion of the show having reached an agreement over their son. Underpinning this success is Trisha's final advice: Neil must get a job, learn a trade so as to be a positive role model for his son who must learn that going to prison is 'not big and not clever'; his son needs a father he can look up to 'otherwise your lad might be on this show in ten years time'.

It is rather uncomfortable viewing a series of apparently disadvantaged individuals parading their distress for the entertainment of the studio and home audience. However, the processes at work on the show produce a space formed through a complex interplay of commercialism and the rather unbourgeois expression of raw, private experience. These qualities together with its popular address mark *Trisha* as a space in which the difficulties of daily life can be thought through.

Trisha and the television talk show debate

Until Goddard's move to Five late in 2004, *Trisha* was made in Norwich by Anglia Television and broadcast nationally across the ITV network at 9.25 a.m. every weekday morning. Sandwiched between *GMTV* and *This Morning* the show constituted a part of the daytime television landscape that is low on critical prestige but also attracted substantial audience numbers consisting mainly of 16–35-year-old females. *Trisha* consistently maintained high viewing figures for that time of the day; *Broadcast* reports that on 19 March 1999, the show had a 42 per cent share of viewers across the entire output, and, in response to Goddard's move to Five, Paul Revoir and Michael Rosser stated that 'Some ITV insiders' believe Goddard's defection constitutes a huge loss to the company because '*Trisha* is one of the few ITV shows that actually increased viewers year on year.'[2]

The format is owned by Universal but as I have argued elsewhere (Wilson 2003) the personality of the talk show host is a means through which any one programme is differentiated from another. In Goddard's case it is the notion of authenticity that identifies her as significantly different from all other hosts (with the exception of Oprah Winfrey). *Trisha* came to air in 1998 amid a frenzy of press speculation concerning her predecessor, Vanessa Feltz, who hosted a daytime talk show also made by Anglia Television. As a result of her much-publicized argument with ITV over contractual negotiations, Feltz moved to the BBC to present a similar show whilst making room for the introduction of Goddard as her replacement on ITV. Characterized by the press as greedy and arrogant, it was claimed that Feltz had demanded the sum of £3 million in exchange for renewing her contract with Anglia Television. This presented a perfect opportunity for Goddard to be introduced as the antithesis to the noisy, grasping Feltz. Goddard's personal tragedies and counselling training provided the focus of the publicity for the replacement show and combined to underpin claims of authenticity that were presented as markers of both the host and *Trisha* itself. And this notion of her authenticity is important because of two key factors that were at play in 1998. Firstly, this was a moment in time that was marked by a substantial growth in the popularity of television talk shows (broadcast across public and commercial television) provoking an anxiety about the integrity of this form of programming and which is exemplified by the Feltz controversy discussed above. The alarm that arose in response to television talk shows amounted to what can be described as a moral panic, a concept that indicates the process through which 'particular groups in society ... come to be seen as a threat to core values and norms' (Biltereyst 2004: 94).

The second factor was the revelation that some television talk shows employed actors to masquerade as guests. Again, this reflected the *zeitgeist* in which concern over the authenticity of some factual programming more generally was being called into question. For instance, in 1998 Carlton was fined £2 million by the Independent Television Commission for broadcasting its now infamous documentary *The Connection* in 1996, which included scenes that contained actors pretending to be drug traffickers. In the US *Jerry Springer* was alleged to be recruiting bogus guests, and shortly after her move to the BBC Feltz was under attack once more because two producers and a researcher for her programme *The Vanessa Show* were alleged to be recruiting fake guests through entertainment agencies. The BBC online network site published an article on 11 February 1999 describing the alleged *Vanessa* fakes as 'two strippers, who were unrelated, [and] introduced on the show as sisters'. Matthew Bannister, then Chief Executive of BBC Production, is reported to have said 'This is absolutely wrong' while Anne Morrison, head of BBC features, is quoted as saying 'it is very important there is a contract of trust with the viewer.'[3]

The issue of a breach of trust became conflated with the concern over moral degradation. (Why otherwise would the two unrelated women posing as sisters be defined primarily as strippers?) Amongst the concern for trust in media representations and for moral standards the same BBC online article reported that *The Vanessa Show* (BBC1) had been under ratings pressure from its ITV rival *Trisha* before swiftly moving on to citing the Broadcasting Standards Commission's concern over the 'current trend of what it called "victim entertainment" in its last annual report'.[4] The juxtaposition of *Trisha*'s ratings success with anxiety about so-called 'victim entertainment' here, points toward one of the central criticisms made of television talk shows: the exploitation of personal pain for commercial gain. For example, Nicholas Fraser (1999), in an article in *The Guardian* entitled 'The cheap triumph of trash TV', locates the gutter as the place containing the shows in which 'guests revealed their innermost traumas or desires ... [These are] a product of American sensibility ... And talk has changed Americans just as it's beginning to change us.' Referring to the Broadcasting Standards Commission's censuring of *Vanessa* and *Kilroy* for respectively humiliating a guest and for inaccuracy, Fraser (1999: 1–2) claims that this is 'an acknowledgement that Trash TV has finally come to Britain ... Do we want to become Americanised as the result of so much schlock?' Alarm and jingoism aside, Fraser is merely one of many who feared that talk shows evidenced a decline in moral standards in contemporary culture. I will briefly outline this debate in order to contextualize the status of a show such as *Trisha* in the 1990s.[5]

The debate broadly polarizes around two positions. On the one hand, and as already indicated, the genre is seen as both the cause and symptom of the degradation of culture. On the other, talk shows are argued to be a site of empowerment, that they provide a platform from which the marginalized and disempowered can speak. To take the social harm (talk show as degradation of culture) position first: the growth of television talk shows during the 1990s produced alarm on the grounds that they constituted a cultural pollutant. Here, links are made between popular therapy, television and social harm. For example, Teresa Keller exemplifies the argument that the programmes attract the charge of commercial exploitation of the emotionally vulnerable when she says:

> [T]here are unattractive qualities among editions of [*Oprah, Phil, Sally*, and *Geraldo*] ... when they aim for emotional rather than intellectual response. They exploit fear ... Stories are woven around a small part of the truth, often focussing on minute details of sex and sexual dysfunction, of murder, rape, incest and other examples of human disregard for other human life and dignity. (Keller 1993: 204–5)

A much-cited paper by Vicki Abt and Mel Seesholtz (1994) demonstrates an even more extreme antipathy towards television talk shows. Worried about the programmes' attention to the 'fringes of society, to those who break rules' of propriety, they argue that:

> Society is a result, then, of its boundaries, of what it will and won't allow. Shame, guilt, embarrassment are controlling feelings that arise from 'speaking the unspeakable' and from violating cultural taboos ... As we watch, listen and are entertained television is rewriting our cultural scripts, altering our perceptions ... (Abt and Seesholtz 1994: 173)

This position was counterbalanced by a number of scholars who looked at what and how meanings are produced through the programmes. For example Joshua Gamson, focusing on representations of sexualities, concluded that: 'talk shows are, as prime purveyor of public visibility of sex and gender nonconformity, terrific foci for the anxieties and hostilities that a queer presence provokes' (Gamson 1998: 26). The public declaration of sexual status speaks to concerns of taste, inextricably bound with middle-class anxieties over who should populate the public space of talk shows, provoking outrage at moral indecency. This, then, exemplifies Glynn's discussion of tabloid media referred to above. On the other hand, talk shows provide a narrow opening in which 'freaks' talk back 'even if the freak refuses that term' (Gamson 1995: 49). The real point, Gamson argues, is not the shows themselves, but the limits placed on the positions of those speaking.

The idea that the public space of television talk shows privileges the voice of the 'ordinary' person was articulated by Sonia Livingstone and Peter Lunt (1994). Their influential work argued that talk shows mark a shift in the relationship between experts and laity, identifying a *loss* of authority on behalf of the expert as he or she speaks for others, whereas the guest, who speaks for himself or herself represents the voice of the 'authentic'. This formulation raises issues of authenticity and 'truth' that are seen to be constructed through the narration of one's own experiences, the credibility of which is privileged over that of the expert who often has to defend their position.

In fact, *Trisha* exemplifies both aspects of the debate outlined here. Distress and pain *is* exploited for commercial gain while at the same time it is this very process that provides the space in which individuals tell their own stories. Of course there are constraints applied to this: codes of conduct that govern programme output, the time available and the structure of the programmes themselves define and shape the form that the stories take. The guests' narratives are interspersed with commercial breaks that suture their stories into advertisements for supermarkets, hair conditioner, yogurt drinks, children's analgesia, insurance and so on. While this represents a commodification of *Trisha's* subjects, there is a mutual dependency between these and commercial television: the existence of one relies on the existence of the other. Mimi White (1992,

2002) argues that the deployment of therapeutic (and confessional) strategies allows for a direct participation in the production of popular programming. 'They speak in their own voices to help produce the texts of our multiply mediated, information/therapeutic culture. The audience is given the opportunity to speak – as expert, as authority, and as celebrity – even as their voices are channelled and contained to a great extent' (White 1992: 83–4). White's argument is that the audience is already caught up in the therapeutic/confessional mode along with consumer culture made evident through the advertising that intersperses programmes. 'The new therapeutic dynamics of consumer culture embrace a wide range of strategies, encouraging people to manage problems, emotions and fantasies' (White 2002: 313).

What kind of public service broadcasting?

Trisha is a form of public service broadcasting that encompasses commercial, popular television. Much of the vilification of television talk shows, along with most other forms of reality programming, is made on the grounds that they are cheap to produce. And, as Liesbet van Zoonen (2004: 277) states, 'the legacy of the Frankfurt School has ensured a reputation of various popular genres as deeply perverted by commercial interests ... and as numbing and "dumbing" public and individual consciousness ...' However, there is a nascent recognition that reality television is very relevant in the debate concerning public service broadcasting. For example, Laura Ouellette and Susan Murray argue that:

> Reality TV is cheap, common and entertaining – the antithesis of public service television and a threat to well-informed citizenry that it promises to cultivate, according to the conventional wisdom. And yet, a closer look at reality TV forces us to re-think the meaning and cultural politics of public service, democracy, and citizenship in that age of neoliberalism, deregulation, conglomeration, and technological convergence. (Ouellette and Murray 2004: 6)

At a time when, in Britain, the welfare systems are at the point of collapse, and within the increasingly powerful discourse of individualism and personal responsibility, *Trisha* offers a means through which to negotiate personal difficulties made familiar by the consumer/therapeutic culture described by White.

Despite the degree to which information and experience is mediated, it is the heightened sense of the 'real' that produces faith. As Misha Kavka and Amy West (2004: 151) say in a different context, the effect of realness is produced through the 'coincidence of experience' between participants and viewers. Uber-reality emerges in the moments of emotional catharsis that underpin the accounts offered by the guests enabling points of identification even when the specifics of this or that situation may not match. The power of television to produce this kind of faith is increasingly evident in the wide range of forms that reality television takes. For instance, examining lifestyle television Gareth Palmer argues that 'Agreeing to go on television to have some aspect of one's life restyled for public consumption is not ordinary. It is because people now understand television as an *active agent of transformation* ...' (Palmer 2004: 189 emphasis added).

Ascribing television with transformative powers both links with and explains the 'reality effect' that arises from witnessing the experiences of others and helps us to understand *Trisha* as public service television. However, I do not wish to romanticize the transformative or educational power of the show. A report published on behalf of Women's Aid and Refuge looked at a sample of television programmes from 1973 to 2004 where domestic violence was a central issue. It cites *Trisha* as a 'programme [that] pushes the boundaries by focusing on a couple who are currently in an abusive relationship – significantly helping to remove the shame and stigma often associated with domestic violence. Nonetheless, *Trisha's* sensationalist and provocative approach to such a complex issue risks trivialising it ...' (Seymour 2004: 14). It is clear, then, that while the programme does allow for the exploration of private, taboo subject matter, sensationalism circumscribes the degree to which this may be fully useful in a wider political context.

What *Trisha* looks like

The show occupies a 60-minute slot and is divided into four sections; the first, second and third sections each last a minimum of 12 minutes with the first and second together accounting for between 21 and 24 minutes; the fourth section uses what remaining time is available. Love, anger and betrayal[6] provide the key elements through which the stories articulated by the guests cohere and which combine to produce the conditions that form the basis for the participants' narratives while the four-part structure determines the time given to exposition and closure. Although there is a variation to the overall pattern of the programme, generally the first and second sections tend to focus on an opening story whereas the remaining two sections present two different sets of guests and their problems.[7]

Because of the limited time allowed for each section, individual guests are discouraged from supplying back stories so that the narratives articulated by them on the stage represent the situation *as it currently stands* (although, as will be discussed later, Goddard does intervene to supply background details that are relevant to the narrative in order to provide a context in which to understand existing circumstances). What we see and hear, then, is the problem as it is experienced by the participants at the time of their appearance on the show. This gives the initial impression of a tabloidesque rendering of an individual's experience – framed as a problem and/or source of distress – into a series of bite-size fragments. However, one person's testimony alone does not constitute the entire narrative. Rather, significant others are brought in to corroborate or to challenge the initial premise. Either way, a dynamic is produced that simultaneously fills any gaps in the narrative while moving the story forward. The information supplied to the researchers by the guests prior to the show being taped is used by Trisha who chooses which elements on which to draw in order to frame, contextualize and develop what occurs on the stage.[8]

The following is an analysis of an episode broadcast on 8 October 2004 in which I focus on two guests who appear during the first two sections. The selection was made on the grounds that these people typify the participant demographic in that they are economically and socially positioned as working class, and because their story demonstrates a set of dynamics that constitute *Trisha*.

The continuity announcer tells us that before *This Morning* we have 'some shocking revelations. Here's *Trisha*'. The show then opens, as usual, with Goddard giving a piece to camera, in this instance from amongst the studio audience, indicating what is to come. 'Hello I just want to show you a little bit of what is coming up on today's show.' A series of clips from the programme that we are about to see are then shown displaying the participants each of whom appear to be in a state of heightened emotion. After this Goddard says: 'All this and more. Don't miss it.' While the strategy of using the pre-recorded material to indicate what is coming up undercuts the sense of the show being broadcast live, it is one that assists in what *Broadcast* has called the mid-morning 'ratings war zone' (16 April 1999: 14–15), deterring restless viewers from drifting to another channel.

The promise of 'All this and more' precedes the 15 seconds during which we hear the signature tune playing over a series of images of Goddard smiling and encircled by soft shades of yellow, green, purple and orange that mark the beginning of the show. The brevity of the opening sequence allows us to move very quickly onto the first subject of the day. Introducing her first guests Trisha asks 'How true to real life is the movies [sic]?' We are told that 60 year-old Roger wants to marry 30 year-old Caragh who is a prostitute with a drug habit. 'Is Roger heading for a Hollywood wedding [a reference to the film *Pretty Woman*] or is Caragh out for what she can get?' Next we meet Roger whose presence is accompanied by the strapline 'I want to marry a drug addict prostitute'. This, together with the opening introduction, positions both Roger and Caragh as the customary subjects of tabloid television with its focus on scandal and gossip: Roger is either naïve and/or exploiting Caragh who, within the frame of her introduction, is, in turn, likely to be exploiting him.

However, watching the show is a rather dislocating experience: the sensationalism promised by the continuity announcer, the signature colours, Goddard's opening words, the images of people arguing and, most of all, the straplines that underpin the introduction of each guest and that reappear throughout their time on the stage, stand at odds with the ways in which the guests and their stories are handled. As Roger recounts the first time he met Caragh seven years ago he reveals himself to be a rather gentle, kind and possibly lonely man who offered the young woman a lift because it was pouring with rain and she was 'hobbling' on crutches. While Roger tells Trisha in what ways he has taken care of Caragh over the years and that he wants her to come off drugs the strapline says 'Only slept with his prostitute lover 20 times in seven years.' This assertion is not contradicted by Roger's testimony that theirs is a largely non-sexual relationship. However, there is a curious tension produced between the way in which we are positioned to 'read' Roger through the strapline, and the story that emerges through his interview. On the one hand the emphasis on 'prostitute', 'lover' and 'only' '20 times' reduces Roger to a ridiculous failure of masculinity while on the other, and with the story articulated in his own words, we gain insight into the complexities and difficulties that constitute his relationship with Caragh.

This is because of the absence of an element common to many talk shows. Called 'the money shot' by Laura Grindstaff (1997), it is the moment of emotional catharsis signalled by tears/anger/rage that is the aim of television talk show producers. Although there are indeed tears, anger and rage aplenty, Goddard's approach tends to place the emphasis on revealing past histories, which are often sad, to provide a context through which to understand the participant's current dilemma. It is true that, as Jon Dovey says, 'tabloidism is about immediacy, simplicity, black-and-white value systems, human interest stories and triumph over tragedy'. He also correctly adds that 'the talk show offers something like essentialist visions of humanity in which sentiment, self determination and simplistic solutions are prized above complexity' (Dovey 2000: 119). However, I would disagree that (on *Trisha*) these are privileged over 'any sense of the socially situated subject' (Dovey 2000: 19). The time constraints that shape and contain the guests' stories do limit the degree to which the social and cultural formations from which the tales emerge are explored. Nonetheless, Goddard's practice of interpreting current difficulties and of making known additional elements of an individual's background works towards developing a three-dimensionality to the picture.

For instance, the possibility of promoting an easy and sentimental sympathy for Roger is undercut by Goddard's observation that in 'supporting' Caragh through helping her to obtain drugs he might be undermining her attempts at recovery. Although the possibility is raised that Roger is subconsciously complicit in maintaining Caragh's victim status, rendering her dependant on him, there is no time here for development or discussion, although it is raised later by members of the studio audience. We have yet to meet Caragh, but as the commercial break approaches we learn that it is she who contacted the production team asking for help. Goddard reminds Roger (and us) that Caragh 'has had a lot of guts to be here today so you [Roger] need to be really honest'.

On return from the break Caragh recounts her story and we learn that she has been on drug rehabilitation programmes and has had counselling all of which 'doesn't seem to have made any difference'. We also learn that she has been in prison 16 times in the past 10 years; that the longest period inside was one year which was 'the best year' because it enabled her to come off drugs. Asked to tell us what Roger 'doesn't know about Caragh' she says ' Um, lonely. Um, self-hatred.'

Goddard: 'You're not telling me about Caragh.'
Caragh: 'I'm quite a nice person. Quite funny. Intelligent.'

Goddard's use of third person narrative paradoxically shifts the emotional pitch: Caragh becomes very tearful prompting Goddard to join her on the stage and, in holding her hand, fosters an intimacy that matches the content of Caragh's analysis of her relationship with Roger, which includes the declaration that she would not marry him. This scenario fits the tenor of sensationalism set up at the beginning of the show, and which is maintained through the straplines. Caragh's tearful testimony and intimate revelation of her sense of selfhood marks hers as a feminine discourse that exemplifies Mellencamp's formulation of gossip referred to earlier. In addition, the way in which Goddard positions herself in relation to her guests – leaning forward towards them and at an angle that slightly excludes the audience – enhances the sense of (a feminine) intimacy as well as lending gravitas to their testimonies challenging the reductive strapline text.

Certainly, the studio audience's sympathies have been engaged. Picking up on some observations made by Goddard earlier, a young man suggests that while their story is 'not about good or bad people' Caragh has 'picked up' on her 'victim status' which Roger is helping to maintain. Another, older, man – whose 'heart goes out' to them both – observes that theirs is a 'nice relationship' but not one that would suggest marriage. Addressing Caragh he says: 'you need so much help my dear' and 'why not help one another?' This does smack of sentimental and simplistic solution finding, however, I would argue that the testimonies offered by Roger and Caragh enhance understanding of the real struggles that underline the participants' performances.

As in all television talk shows, the studio audience is an important element. On *Trisha* the production team position the studio audience as representatives of the audience at home. Before the taping of the show in which I was among the audience we were told by the floor manager and again, later by Goddard, that offers of common-sense observations and advice for the guests can be a very useful component of the show. 'You know that when you are at home watching, and you say things at the TV? Well we want that from you here.' Limited as it is, this way of validating the audience's own everyday experiences and knowledge of the world underpins the production of the 'real' on which the show is premised.

The interview proceeds with Goddard remaining on the stage during which Caragh's habit of, and reasons for, her habitual self-harm is discussed while Roger's separation from his family and his general aloneness are also acknowledged. The interview comes to a conclusion with Goddard addressing Roger: 'I am talking about self-esteem and self-harm minimization, and you are not trained to do it Roger. And with the best will in the world you are prolonging Caragh's drug use.' Goddard reflects that drug rehabilitation is 'one thing' while 'intensive counselling for a long time is something else'. Here she is reminding us that Caragh had been drug-free for the year that she spent in prison and implying that the real work in coming off drugs involves work on the self over a long period of time. Of course this cannot be represented on the show; what we are offered is an insight into the ways in which these kinds of difficulties impact on individuals and the courses that might be taken in order to begin the process.

What emerges from Roger and Caragh's performance is evidence of the complex interplay between the public and private, gender and class, commercialism and commodification. There is a particular kind of social subjectivity produced through the guests' confessional performances on commercial television. As White argues,

> the difference between the private and the public is effaced in favor of a larger consuming social body where subjectivity can be managed and negotiated through confessional strategies. These programs project individuals and couples as the site where private and public interests commingle, and they invite individual viewers to share in this formation of social subjectivity as a performative, consuming, and consumable therapeutic spectacle. In the process, these reality-based television programmes contribute to a larger process of redefining what it means to be real. (White 2002: 322)

Anxiety and security

The popularity of programmes that work to produce a social subjectivity is linked with the evident appeal of appearing on television to air one's private struggles in order to institute a positive change. Like Caragh, many of the participants on *Trisha* state that their motivation for appearing on the show is to get help; their stories express anxiety concerning relationships with significant others, their drug and/or alcohol dependency, their biological parenthood, their child's drug abuse and so on. Most striking, as stated earlier, is the fact that the participants usually appear on the show as a result of having contacted the production team for help. In addition, and equally noteworthy, is that from the sample of shows I studied, it is clear that the majority of the participants have had prior experience of a range of health care and social services; for whatever reason, these have failed to facilitate the desired changes within the individuals concerned.

So, on *Trisha* we see a series of guests such as Karena ('Do I cancel my wedding?' tx. 18 August 2004) who appears on the show in order to challenge her partner Ben's controlling behaviour; we learn that he has a problem with jealousy and 'is here to get help'. Barbara ('I'm scared of my son', tx. 5 November 2004) appears on the show because she is 'worn out' and 'afraid' of her 15-year-old son recently diagnosed as having an attention deficit disorder. Despite her contact with statuary agencies Barbara's appearance on the show results from a desire to develop some sense of coherence to her life. On being challenged by an audience member over her degree of commitment to her son, she says 'I do love him. I wouldn't be here if I didn't.' In the show cited at the beginning of this chapter Amanda claims that, due to her previous appearance on *Trisha*, she 'realized that I needed to grow up a bit and that I needed to change.' The claim is endorsed by others on the stage.

That the guests see the risk of facing ridicule as the payoff for the possibility of bringing change is evident on a number of occasions. Natalie ('Sisters, stop interfering', tx. 14 October 2004) says of her warring family 'We sound like a *Jerry Springer* family, but we actually do love each other' while Niki ('Stop the accusations', tx. 13 August 2004) insists on her fidelity to her partner claiming that she would not risk 'making a fool' of herself by coming on 'national television' if she was lying.

On more than one occasion, when guests agree to a particular plan of action Goddard reminds them that they are making a commitment in front of millions of people; they can face either triumph or shame depending on their subsequent actions. Testifying in such a public arena clearly has a power to bring about transformation. However, there is more to an appearance on *Trisha* than this. Much of what occurs on *Trisha* can be related to anxiety about self and close others, and which amounts to expressions of fragile selfhood in the post-industrial era. Not only do the discourses of therapy and commodification offer the means of producing a recognizable social subjectivity as White argues, it is also because, in Roger Silverstone's terms (1994) television functions as an object of trust and ontological security. The programme addresses anxiety, both specific and free-floating.

Running through much commentary on contemporary social life is the theme of anxiety. We are seen to be in an age characterized by uncertainty within the ever-changing cultural landscape fostered by the advance of capitalism, the attendant increase of the use of technology, both in the home and in industry, and the apparent collapse of any meaningful metanarrative. Mass consumption, along with the proliferation of images has been linked with the emptying out of the self, producing identities that are fragmented, dislocated, schizophrenic. For example, Zygmunt Bauman argues that the issue of identity is linked with insecurity because 'One thinks of identity whenever one is not sure of where one belongs; that is, one is not sure how to place oneself among the evident variety of behavioural styles and patterns ... "Identity" is a name given to the escape sought from that uncertainty' (Bauman cf Ferguson 1998: 5).

Within this model of contemporary culture, television occupies a paradoxical position: it is simultaneously seen as a primary cause of social fragmentation and the means by which that fragmentation can be addressed. We have already looked at ways in which representations of the 'real' produces a locus of identification for viewers, but Silverstone allows this to be developed further. He discusses television as a means of trust and ontological security within the context of a world that is 'decreasingly reliant on kinship relations and in which locality (neighbourhood, community) no longer has the same significance as the source and support for daily routine ...' (Silverstone 1994: 6). Given that everyday life is ordered as a defence against anxiety and the threat of chaos, the dailiness of television 'has colonised these basic levels of social reality' (Silverstone 1994: 4). Drawing on Anthony Giddens, Silverstone argues that both 'trust and ontological security are the product of an active engagement in the events and patterns and relationships of everyday life'. This active engagement is predicated on cognitive understanding, physical face-to-face communications, affective relationships with people and material objects. These combine to produce a certainty premised on a 'kind of faith' (Silverstone 1994: 5–6). Silverstone (1994: 8) argues that this 'kind of faith' together with television's 'central role' in framing the structure of daily life produces an attachment to the medium which can be understood in terms of what the psychoanalyst D.W. Winnicott calls the transitional object: it acts as a focus for emotions, desires and fantasies. 'I want to suggest that our media, television perhaps pre-eminently, occupy the potential space realised by [the infant's] blankets, teddy bears, and [mothers'] breasts, and function ... as transitional objects' (Silverstone 1994: 13). In other words, television becomes a defence against anxiety. Not only is it a complex communication of sound and images 'with already powerful reality and emotional claims' (Silverstone 1994: 15), it is constant, dependable – it will always be there even when we switch it off. Silverstone argues that television's economies can also be understood as a response to the audiences' deeply felt need for continuity (Silverstone 1994: 16).

In the context of contemporary culture *Trisha* functions as a transitional object offering ontological security through its daily broadcast, 'common sense' approach coupled to a therapeutic address. Of course, 'common sense' is not an unproblematic term in that it is ideologically and culturally loaded, but in terms of public appeal and public service address *Trisha* articulates the familiar and the comforting; it is a buttress against anxiety in its familiarity and through its ability to transmit ways in which specific sets of problems can be managed. Within a narrow frame of reference – 'love, anger and betrayal' – the show presents a particular knowledge of the world and ways in which that world can be negotiated. The episode with Caragh and Roger concludes with Goddard's words 'If you want help with the issues raised on this show phone [number supplied]. A big thank you to all our guests. It takes a lot of courage.' The individuals who contact the programme along with the appeals to future audiences that follows each commercial break – 'Are you married to the laziest man in the world? Or is your wife too masculine? Do you have over protective parents?' – ensure a continuing supply of commercially valuable stories through which the process of therapy and reassurance is maintained.

This does not preclude *Trisha* from the charge of commodifying suffering. However, there are additional elements at play engendering a kind of attachment in the viewers that exceeds the para-social relationship that typifies the dynamic between audiences and screen personae. These factors coexist with the commercialism of independent television producing a text that is contradictory but one that, nonetheless, engenders a degree of trust.

The popularity of television talk shows is in the decline but I would argue that they have left an indelible trace in popular culture that is most evident in the vast range of reality television programmes that have confessional and testimonial address at their core. That *Trisha,* for its duration as an Anglia Television programme, consistently drew large viewing figures is testament to desire in audiences for this kind of popular public service broadcasting.

Acknowledgements

John Redshaw, Deputy Editor for *Trisha,* was very generous with his time for which I am very grateful. I want also to thank Cathy Johnson and Rob Turnock for their helpful comments on earlier drafts and discussions about *Trisha,* and Lesley Welch for bringing my attention to the study of television's representations of domestic violence.

Bibliography

Abt, V. and Seesholtz, M. (1994) The shameless world of Phil, Sally and Oprah: television talk shows and the deconstruction of society, *Journal of Popular Culture,* 28(1): 171–91.

BBC Online Network (1999) 'Vanessa staff suspended over "fake guests"' http://news.bbc.co.uk/1/hi/entertainment/277302.stm, 11 February (accessed 30 July 2004).

Biltereyst, D. (2004) Reality TV, troublesome picture and panics: reappraising the public controversy around reality TV in Europe, in S. Holmes and D. Jermyn (eds) *Understanding Reality Television.* London: Routledge.

Dovey, J. (2000) *Freakshow: First Person Media and Factual Television.* London: Pluto Press.

Ferguson, R. (1998) *Representing 'Race': Ideology, Identity and the Media.* London: Arnold.

Fraser, N. (1999) The cheap triumph of trash TV, *Guardian*, 31 January.

Gamson, J. (1995) Do ask, do tell: frank talk on TV, *The American Prospect*, 23: 44–50.

Gamson, J. (1998) Publicity traps: television talk shows and lesbian, gay, bisexual and transgender visibility, *Sexualities*, 1(1): 11–41.

Glynn, K. (2000) *Tabloid Culture: Trash Taste, Popular Power, and the Transformation of American Television.* Durham: Duke University Press.

Grindstaff, L. (1997) Producing trash, class, and the money shot: a behind the scenes account of daytime TV talk shows' in J. Lull and S. Hinerman (eds) *Media Scandals: Morality and Desire in the Market Place.* Oxford: Polity.

Kavka, M. and West, A. (2004) Temporalities of the real: conceptualising time in reality TV, in S. Holmes and D. Jermyn (eds) *Understanding Reality Television.* London: Routledge.

Keller, T. (1993) Trash TV, *Journal of Popular Culture*, 26(4): 195–206.

Mellencamp, P. (1992) *High Anxiety: Catastrophe, Scandal, Age, and Comedy*. Bloomington: Indiana University Press.

Ouellette, L. and Murray S. (eds) (2004) *Reality TV: Remaking Television Culture.* New York: New York University Press.

Palmer, G. (2004) 'The new you': class and transformation in lifestyle television, in S. Holmes and D. Jermyn (eds) *Understanding Reality Television.* London: Routledge.

Revoir, P. and Rosser, M. (2004) Trisha: why I've switched to Five, *Broadcast*, 5 October.

Seymour, E. (2004) Taboo?: Exploring Television's Representation of Domestic Violence 1973–2004. Bristol: Women's Aid and Refuge.

Shattuc, J. (1997) *The Talking Cure: TV Talk Shows and Women.* New York: Routledge.

Van Zoonen, L. (2004) Popular qualities in public broadcasting, *European Journal of Cultural Studies*, 7(3): 275–82.

Silverstone, R. (1994) *Television and Everyday Life*. London: Routledge.

White, M. (1992) *Tele-Advising: Therapeutic Discourse in American Television*. Chapel Hill: University of North Carolina Press.

White, M. (2002) Television, therapy, and the social subject; or, the TV therapy machine, in J. Friedman (ed.) *Reality Squared: Televisual Discourse on the Real*. New Brunswick: Rutgers University Press.

Wilson, S. (2003) *Oprah, Celebrity and Formations of Self*. Basingstoke: Palgrave.

Notes

1 My analysis is based on programmes broadcast during August through to November 2004.

2 *Broadcast*, 8 October 2004: 5.

3 www.news.bbc.co.uk, 11 February 1999 (accessed 30 July 2004).

4 www.news.bbc.co.uk, 11 February 1999 (accessed 30 July 2004). Although beyond the remit of this chapter, the failure of Feltz's show raises the interesting question about the degree to which this format fits with viewer expectations of BBC programming or whether the show was unpopular for other reasons.

5 See Wilson (2003) for a more detailed analysis of the television talk show debate.

6 This analysis of the shows' dynamic was offered to me by John Redshaw, the show's Deputy Editor.

7 The exception to this in the sample that I analysed is the programme broadcast on 24 August 2004, which looks at what happens to individuals whose tragedies have been the subject of major news stories. In this show each section is filled with a different guest relating the details of the incident before recounting the ways in which their lives have been altered as a result. This show reminds the audience that while 'today's newspapers are tomorrow's fish and chip wrappers' real people live with real consequences of terrible happenstance long after the issue has disappeared from public consciousness.

8 Again, John Redshaw was very helpful in informing me of the ways in which the programme uses the information supplied by guests in advance of the show being taped.

10 WHO WANTS TO BE A FAN OF *WHO WANTS TO BE A MILLIONAIRE*?

Scholarly television criticism, 'popular aesthetics' and academic tastes

Matt Hills

As Glen Creeber (2004: 232) has argued, *Who Wants To Be A Millionaire?* is 'one of the most successful television quiz shows of all time'. Creeber (2004: 232) observes that 'the original British series gained as much as 72 per cent of the television audience when it first aired. Started in 1998, by the end of 2000 it was on air in 35 countries and sold as a format to 45 more.' But while becoming a cornerstone of ITV's prime time scheduling in its early runs, and an example of 'event' television, *Who Wants To Be A Millionaire?* (hereafter *Millionaire*) has also been viewed as an encapsulation of the values of commercial television culture, in both the UK where it originated, and in the US (see Boddy 2001).

In this chapter I will consider how *Millionaire* has been devalued or dismissed in one strand of academic television criticism.[1] *Millionaire* has been taken as a totemic instance of the 'ills' of British commercial television, and so has been attacked by critical scholars for being 'very much a creature of the current trend' towards commercial forces 'eroding public service television' in the UK (Wayne 2000: 216). Supposedly displaying a 'culture of trivial intellect' (Missen 2001: 143) *Millionaire* has, then, been soundly condemned by Marxist media scholars. In such accounts, the question of 'ITV Culture' (that is, singular 'Culture' with a capital C) is displaced via that hoary old binary opposition of 'art' (and public service) versus 'commerce' (and mass-audience-chasing consumerist venality). Whether Mike Wayne (2000) or James Missen (2001) would assent to viewing 'ITV cultures' in the plural as a useful analytical term is something of a moot point. The fact is that both writers critique and dismiss *Millionaire*, and its audiences' pleasures, as implicitly or explicitly *anti*-cultural. The 'culture of trivial intellect' referred to by Missen (2001) is clearly intended to be viewed as improperly 'cultural', and as a denigration of – or a compensation for the absence of – 'authentically' intellectual 'Culture'.

The arguments of Wayne (2000) and Missen (2001) do not represent the only type of academic response to game shows; not all academics have denigrated the game/quiz show for its links to consumerism. However, just such a monolithic tradition has been said to operate outside the academy. Gary Whannel (1990: 104) argues that 'few televisual forms have as low a cultural status as quiz shows. They are regularly derided by middle-class opinion, [and] criticized in government reports.' And in *Television Studies: The Key Concepts*, Bernadette Casey *et al.* (2002: 100) argue that: 'Reflecting the middle-class disdain for . . . game shows, many academics have also been critical of the genre, particularly when identifying the . . . function that it plays in sustaining the values . . . of capitalist society.' Following this point, the critiques of those such as Wayne (2000) and Missen (2001) – which see competitiveness and the acquisition of consumer goods as key aspects of the quiz show and the genre's alleged reinforcing of capitalism – can be located as *one (albeit influential) type* of academic approach to the subject. Here, Marxist academics replay a more general (and frequently class-based) distaste for game shows: 'show[ing] a lofty contempt for the quiz show, radical critical [academic] analysis has been . . . hostile' to the form (Whannel 1992: 180).

Quiz/game shows are devalued by left-wing 'radical' academics on the basis of their supposed vulgarity and because they are assumed to be overly concerned with cash prizes or consumer goods (Tulloch 1976: 111). 'Commercial' game shows are especially attacked for lacking the proper 'Cultural' dimension of 'public service' quizzes whose prizes concern prestige rather than material goods (that is, one 'wins' recognition of one's cultural knowledge). 'Commercial' game shows have also been devalued in comparison with 'public service' quizzes whose questions are legitimated and contextualized within 'specialist subjects' rather than being decontextualized as isolated 'facts' (cf. the BBC's 'intellectual' quiz show *Mastermind*: see Tulloch 1976: 110–11). As Rob Turnock (forthcoming) argues, what historically marked out the earliest 'ITV quiz and game shows from BBC panel games . . . [was] the prizes . . . On ITV, contestants could win actual commodity prizes.' From its inception in 1955, ITV immediately became linked with quiz/game shows as a type of programming, featuring, in its first week of service, *Double Your Money* (1955–68) with a £1000 cash prize, and *Take Your Pick* (1955–68). These two ITV shows 'were the first television quiz games to have cash prizes', being 'central to building . . . a big ITV audience' right from the channel's beginnings (Whannel 1992: 182). By '1957 there were eight quiz shows a week' on the new commercial channel (Whannel 1992: 182), cementing an association of big-prize game shows with 'commercial' television's distinctiveness. It is this historical equation – a cultural construct rather than a 'natural' affinity between game shows and 'commercial' television – which *Millionaire* plays on with its cash prize of £1 million, and which it has been neatly slotted into by Marxist scholars such as Mike Wayne (2000).

However, moving beyond the distaste of Marxist academics, other schools of thought on the game show operate in television studies. For example, in Glen Creeber's (2004) non-Marxist, aesthetic revaluing of *Millionaire*, the show is not automatically lambasted – in advance of textual or audience analysis – for allegedly reinforcing capitalism. And taking an even more positive stance on 'commercial' game shows, John Fiske's (1987) celebratory arguments regarding audience activity can also be applied to *Millionaire*. Fiske (1987: 273) suggests that audiences for quiz shows are especially 'active', and so are not incorporated into consumerist beliefs by virtue of enjoying game shows. Instead, game show fans may imagine themselves participating in these shows, testing themselves against actual participants in a kind of 'self-rating', rather than desiring to win prizes *per se* (Fiske 1987: 274). Of course, audiences may also be 'active' in a more precise manner: 'becoming actively involved in the operation of a programme,' and actualizing 'their involvement by appearing as contestants or members of the studio audience' (Bonner 2003: 95). Frances Bonner terms such audiences a 'community of viewers who ... [make programme] production possible' (Bonner 2003: 95). Against the Marxist/anti-consumerist devaluation of 'commercial' game shows, as in Wayne (2000) and Missen (2001), I will take a stance that borrows from the work of Creeber (2004) and Bonner (2003). This involves transcending the dualism of 'culture' and 'commerce':

> At least in its colloquial form the term 'culture' is associated with meaning and creativity, with works of the imagination and aesthetic practices. 'Commerce', on the other hand, has traditionally been regarded as founded on a 'bottom-line' of profitability, and commercial agents may take delight in ... participating in a vulgar and materialistic, amoral world where human agency is subordinated to the logic of capital. (Jackson *et al.* 2000: 1)

Rather than viewing *Millionaire* as a totemic instance of vulgar consumerism, I will suggest that it makes sense to think of 'popular aesthetics' (Bird 2003) – audience discriminations between 'good' and 'bad' television – as working around, in, and through successful prime-time ITV shows like *Millionaire*. In the next section I will address how work in fan studies has tended to marginalize programmes such as *Millionaire*. I will then go on to consider the 'popular aesthetics' of the show. For if 'England's most successful cultural export in the last 30 years' (*New York Times*, cited in Boddy 2001: 81) has been the Celadorproduced ITV ratings behemoth of *Millionaire*, then we might expect academic attention to have focused more centrally on this.

Academic 'radical criticism' versus television consumption: dismissing *Millionaire*

In *The Uses of Television*, John Hartley points out a curious fact about the origins of scholarly television criticism:

> The textual tradition in TV Studies began when people trained in literary theory ... turned their attention to popular culture. Unfortunately for the cause of television analysis, such training tended to emphasize strong hostility to popular cultural aesthetics ... So whereas many traditions of study in the general area of the arts have presumed some pleasurable investment by the student in the object of study, the textual tradition in television studies set out with the avowed intention of denouncing television and all its works. (Hartley 1999: 66)

Television criticism thus emerged from the assumption that television and its texts were things enjoyed by *other* people: the scholarly 'critic' and the targeted 'consumer' were firmly non-coincident. Alan McKee (2002: 66) has testified to this 'bifurcation' of thought, noting that studies 'of how "we" (intellectuals) consume culture' have emphasized creativity, activity, and expert cultural knowledge, whilst 'studies of how "they" (the working and lower middle classes – the "masses") consume culture' have, until relatively recently, assumed audience passivity and vulnerability to commercial 'messages'. However, this account and worldview have been significantly challenged by television studies from at least the 1980s onward. Rather than separating out the all-seeing academic television critic and the industry-duped consumer, fan studies – from its beginnings in work on soap opera and television science fiction (see Hobson 1982; Jenkins 1992) – has highlighted that '"they" may indeed be "us"' (McKee 2002: 67; see also Barker 1998). Indeed, John Fiske (1987: 280) has remarked that although early scholarly work on soap operas fought to revalue the genre and its fan audiences, there was a marked absence of comparable work occurring at the same time on 'commercial' (rather than the more intellectual and 'Cultural', 'public service') game shows and their audiences. Here, a 'them-and-us' mentality has seemed to remain rather more fixed in place. As Virginia Wright Wexman has argued:

> critics customarily consider themselves disinterested observers ... [although their activities lead] ... to practical valuations of ... texts, [and] one can view current scholarly practices in the light of these valuations. Why are certain ... texts chosen for special attention? (1999: 77; see also Brunsdon 1997: 144–5)

Addressing this question, Wright Wexman (1999: 89) concludes that 'scholars, like others, have ... interests at stake: we are not only critics but also consumers'. Rather than separating out television's academics and its consumers – its scholars and its fans – we can instead suggest that many academic writers on television are hybridized 'scholar-fans' (Hills 2002: 11), whether or not they explicitly adopt this label in their own work. The movement from television criticism as something necessarily detached from television consumption, to a situation where television critics are self-professed consumers and fans, appears to have, positively and progressively, removed the 'us' and 'them' dualism which had structured scholarly engagement with television. This results in a new scenario:

> [T]here has been something of a change in the critical fortunes of the fan. His or her activities have increasingly been seen by ... academics as significant ... in their own right ... It is interesting in this respect that a number of academics, precisely the sort of people who in previous decades would strenuously have objected to being thought of as fans, will now in their writing about various forms of culture ... happily proclaim their own fandom. (Hutchings 2004: 91)

Rather than simply celebrating this sea change, I want to consider its limits. In her recent book *The Audience in Everyday Life*, S. Elizabeth Bird has critiqued television studies' tendency to focus on a limited canon of programmes, and also upon 'canonical' fan audiences:

> there is a tendency to favour programs and genres that may be considered edgy, avant-garde, or attracting a 'cult' audience ... I have rarely heard a [conference] presentation about successful 'middle-of-the-road' offerings – and never from scholars who identified as fans. (Bird 2003: 121)

Alan McKee (2002: 68) has also pointed to the fact that 'although early fan work focused largely on fans of cult programming ... fan responses to television are not confined to fantasy or science fiction genres. There are [for example] fan Internet pages for ... cop shows like *The Bill* ...' But such middle-of-the-road television shows (*The Bill* [1984–] is a long-running ITV drama series) are not attractive to academics aiming to write about this year's modish popular television. Nor may such programmes have their own self-identified 'scholar-fans' – scholars who are also fans of the television shows they study (Hills 2002: 11–15) – with admissions of fandom in the academy typically being restricted to cult successes like *Twin Peaks* (1990–91) and *Buffy the Vampire Slayer* (1997–2003).

This indicates that the recent alignment of television scholars with their 'fan-consumer' identities may be working to reproduce culturally the specific tastes of audience demographics and classes which are over-represented in academia. Although it may be helpful for 'scholar-fans' not to artificially separate themselves from other non-academic audiences, this still leaves television shows that do not resonate with scholarly concerns and fandoms of the 'moment' (or with what's 'in' at any given time in terms of the television industry's self-representations) somewhat out in the cold. Television criticism may, in fact, have moved too closely into line with its writers' television fandoms, as well as with television industry 'buzz' and hype that surrounds certain shows but not others – seeming to make these high profile 'event' shows more interesting to scholars, as well as rendering them more saleable to academic publishers. Christine Geraghty's (2003: 40) recent essay on academics' cultural tastes and television aesthetics offers a timely reminder that 'television studies would ... benefit from academics being more explicit about the evaluative judgements that we inevitably make' (see also Jacobs 2001; Barker 1998: 191 n1).

Given that *Millionaire* was a high profile show – celebrated in media coverage, and newsworthy in its own right when accusations were made that contestants had cheated – why has it not found its way into scholar-fan work? Why has this totemic late-nineties ITV show not been positively canonized, instead turning up as a figure of Marxist academic critique? I want to suggest three answers, relating *Millionaire*'s academic dismissal to issues of genre, 'quality' and 'buzz'.

Firstly, then, there is the matter of genre. As I have already noted, 'commercial' quiz/game shows have frequently been discussed academically as 'placing great emphasis on the dominant norms of a consumerist culture' (Lewis 1984: 44). Being so persistently linked to 'overt consumerist vulgarities' (1984: 43), game shows have been the subject of relatively little positive academic work:

> long periods of critical disdain and indifference [have been] interrupted by infrequent moments of generalized and often hyperbolic critical reaction to the spectacular success of a specific show or format, before the genre recedes again into ... critical obscurity ... [T]he critical literature on TV game shows remains dominated by ... elitist scorn. (Boddy 2001: 79; see also Mittell 2004: 31–2)

By virtue of its genre, format, and discursive positioning as a bad 'commercial' object, *Millionaire* cannot be positively aligned with the Marxist cultural politics prevalent in television studies, and has thus been dismissed out-of-hand as an object unlikely to reward analysis. Its presumed consumerist, avaricious, and grubbily commercial tendencies have seemingly been enough to push it beyond the pale as far as specific academic-Marxist tastes, politics, and interpretations are concerned.

Secondly, there is the matter of how 'quality television' has been constructed in scholarly and industry debate (see Brunsdon 1997). Despite a range of academic work seeking to combine notions of 'quality' with 'popular' credentials (see Jancovich and Lyons 2003), *Millionaire* has not generally been positioned in relation to notions of 'quality television', and its current connotations of cinematic scope/auteurism, generic hybridization/reinvigoration, or challenging representations. Instead, *Millionaire* has generally been dismissed as being solely 'popular' commercial television. In Jancovich and Lyons's edited collection *Quality Popular Television*, only Jennifer Holt's examination of 'prime-time design' refers fleetingly to *Millionaire* (2003: 20). This makes Glen Creeber's (2004) analysis of the show an unusual intervention, because Creeber stresses how the set design, the 'electric blue' colour scheme, and the use of overhead crane shots, all combine to lend *Millionaire* a 'sci-fi inspired ... almost "cinematic" dimension' (2004: 235). Creeber views the programme as a generic 'modernization' which operates in a specific way:

> Perhaps ... the show has simply modernized the [game show] genre, meeting the needs of a contemporary audience who have come to expect the small screen to increasingly replicate the drama and spectacle of the big. Seen in this light, perhaps *Millionaire* is not so much a symbol of British television's sad decline, as proof that ... it can now beat American television at its own game (2004: 235)

Despite the possibility that *Millionaire* could be intertextually contextualized as 'quality popular television' – using the criteria set out by Creeber – notions of quality in recent industry and scholarly definitions have instead tended to be attached to types of US television drama, thus exhibiting both national and generic limitations:

> Clearly, it is not appropriate to apply criteria of authenticity, creativity and innovation in the same way to *Who Wants To Be A Millionaire?* (ITV, 1998–) and *ER* (NBC, 1994–) ... we will not consider a game show ... in the same way as a serial drama, even if they share, on the face of it, dramatic force, narrative dynamics, and creativity. (Jacobs 2001: 430)

Contra Creeber's useful argument, this position seems to devalue discursively the 'commercial' game show in relation to 'artful' television drama. *Millionaire* is also, not coincidently, devalued in relation to *US* television drama. Although appearing to concede that game shows, like 'quality' television drama, can display 'dramatic force' and 'creativity' – using what Charlotte Brunsdon (1997: 134 and 1990: 60) would term a 'traditional aesthetic discourse' – Jason Jacobs nevertheless does not make clear the basis on which 'authenticity, creativity and innovation' cannot be adequately or fully related to *Millionaire*, unlike *ER*. As well as entertainment formats such as the game show being subordinated to television drama as a privileged generic locus of 'quality', commercial television has also frequently lost out in relation to public service television in academic 'quality' debates. Alan McKee (2003: 181) points out how 'many of my colleagues, teaching Media Studies, strongly organize their viewing schedules around public service broadcasting at the expense of commercial programming.' If 'commercial' television is viewed as inherently second-rate or suspect in comparison with the assumed 'quality' of public service television by critics-as-consumers (see also Brunsdon 1997: 144–5), then it may hardly be surprising that connotations of 'quality' have not been significantly attached to ITV shows like *Millionaire*.

Thirdly, where *Millionaire*'s academic devaluation is concerned, there is the matter of industry and scholarly 'buzz' (Seabrook 2000). Quite simply, this went elsewhere: reality television soaked up the 'buzz-factor' academic interest that may have accrued to *Millionaire* (and commercial/ITV culture) at its peak levels of audience interest. It was reality television that became the more 'sexy' route into analysing audience participations/investments, and reality television that became the favoured pathway into debates over intertexts and audience interactivity (see for example, Marshall 2004: 97; Tincknell and Raghuram 2004). In this case, although the commerciality of such shows attracted Frankfurt School-style critique of the type aimed at *Millionaire* (see Andrejevic 2004), such responses were also significantly joined and contested by more populist writing in cultural studies (for example, Foster 2004; Hartley 2004). Commercial television does not, after all, always fail to attract positive scholarly commentary. Rather, certain genres and moments tend to become canonized focal points for debate, meaning that much commercial television, much of the time, goes unanalysed academically, with scholars only semiotically intervening in the ordinary 'flow' of television output when they are prompted to do so by their own tastes and cultural politics, or by controversial flashpoints relating to these interpretive frames. In such a context, television that is aesthetically and morally opposed to scholars' taste cultures – for example, the game show – is either rendered relatively invisible in scholarship (Boddy 2001), or is strongly critiqued. ITV cultures, and commercial television more generally, thus require urgent revisionist attention: books like the one you are reading now can only be a welcome starting point.

Even while arguing for an extended concept of 'popular aesthetics' – how fans value their favoured popular television texts – and highlighting the limits to academic 'taste' and scholar-fandom, it is striking that S. Elizabeth Bird (2003) continues to demarcate one genre of television programming as beyond the pale. There are no prizes for anticipating which it is: the game show. Bird writes: 'I doubt there would be much point in thinking too carefully about the aesthetics of ... [*The Price Is Right* (1956–1965; 1972–)], any more than fans do' (Bird 2003: 144). Assuming that fans of the game show genre do not debate their favoured texts' 'qualities', whereas fans of cult television drama frequently adopt scholarly approaches to debating their show's character and aesthetics, Bird appears to push game shows further from aesthetic criteria linked to notions of quality or audience 'discrimination'. In the following section I want to challenge such assumptions, suggesting that the texts and intertexts of *Millionaire* can be profitably analysed for their 'popular aesthetics'. Rather than condemning *Millionaire* to critical obscurity, and thereby enacting the cultural reproduction of edgy, 'cult' tastes (or 'public service' values) over and above discursively-constructed 'commercial' television cultures, I will go on to examine the popularity *and* the quality of *Millionaire*.

'Popular aesthetics' and participatory commercial culture: discussing *Millionaire*

Despite S. Elizabeth Bird's (2003) rather non-reflexive dismissal of the game show (which recalls Jason Jacobs' (2001) devaluation of *Millionaire* in relation to 'quality' US television drama), I want to reinstate questions of aesthetics here. Bird's notion of 'popular aesthetics' is useful – when not restricted to certain television genres – for emphasizing how non-academic audiences use aesthetic criteria and discourses in their appreciations of popular media texts. Consider, for example, the listing for *Millionaire* at ukgameshows.com, a web site that offers an A–Z of game shows and presents weekly listings of those currently being broadcast, as well as hosting adverts from game show producers seeking contestants. We learn of *Millionaire* that:

> Putting the easy-to-pick-up format and the host aside for one moment, it's clear that some T.L.C. went into the making of the show. In fact, the whole theme of the programme seemed to take the essential classic elements of a quiz but present them using modern metaphors ... The set is one of those 'in the round' numbers. Perhaps not the most original idea in recent times, but it's so nicely constructed (with its suspended Perspex floor with a huge dish-shape underneath ...) you could tell Terrence [sic] Conran would approve. (http://www.ukgameshows.com/index.php/Who_Wants_To_Be_A_Millionaire%3F)

The aesthetics of the show are discussed here in terms similar to Creeber's (2004), with attention being paid to *Millionaire*'s innovative use of 'modernizing' elements and stylings, as well as its visually dominating set-piece of a set. And where Creeber notes the importance of the use of 'varilites' in *Millionaire*, to 'instantly change the atmosphere on the set, [the lighting] gradually getting dimmer as the questions are answered correctly' (2004: 235), ukgameshows.com remarks that:

> The lighting also deserves a passing mention, with the spotlights zooming down on the contestant after each major question

> answered. Even the logo is smartly and wittily executed, mixing the traditional intricate bank note patterns with question marks and pound signs ... [*Millionaire*] even beat some editions of the perennial ITV ratings stalwart, *Coronation Street*. The show deserved these ratings though – it wasn't just any old quiz. (http://www.ukgameshows.com/index.php/Who_Wants_To_Be_A_Millionaire%3F)

The aesthetic discourses drawn on by this web site and television studies scholar (Creeber 2004) thus strongly coincide: *Millionaire* is not denigrated for its vulgar materialism or its crass commercialism in this 'popular aesthetic', but is instead appreciated as an innovative generic text with a sense of aspirational, middle-class style ('Terence Conran would approve'). *Millionaire* is also clearly differentiated from 'just any old quiz' show, with its initially large ratings being viewed as 'deserved'.

This particular web site – which takes 'the UK TV game show' as its point of departure and *raison d'être* – displays the kind of detailed intrageneric discrimination or 'analytical skill' that Nicholas Abercrombie and Brian Longhurst (1998: 142–4) claim is distinctive to 'fans' or 'cultists':

> Consumers tend to use analytical skills in a relatively general manner ... such judgments would tend to revolve around ... relatively untheorized areas of taste ... [where] in consumer mode, we say that we like [a specific television show] ... The fan tends to mobilize analytical skills within the genre or corpus ... The cultist becomes immersed in comparisons within the genre and between shows themselves, and analytical skills become exceptionally developed. (Abercrombie and Longhurst 1998: 145)

In this conceptualization, 'cultists' are akin to more avid, devoted fans. Whilst game show 'consumers', in Abercrombie and Longhurst's terms, may well not draw on any developed aesthetic discourses – stating that they 'just like the programme' – fans and cultists do not fit into this schema, indicating definite limits to Bird's (2003) dismissal of the game show's popular aesthetics. Indeed, a dedicated fan group 'immersed in comparisons' within the game show genre is very much evident through the game show intertexts of ukgameshows.com. The process of detailed intrageneric comparison is formalized through a survey of the top UK game shows. However light-hearted its tone, this survey is nevertheless at pains to distinguish its contributors from the mere 'public' of game-show consumers:

> We wanted to know what the best UK Game Show of all time was. However, we don't give a stuff about the stupid public's opinion. Instead, we questioned the fanatics who subscribe to our Yahoo! Group. The hardcore. The experts. In August 2002, we asked – nay, commanded – them to list their ten favourite UK Game Shows in

> order of merit ... All formats over all time were considered – only programmes that were made abroad and shown in the UK straight from tape are excluded. (http://www.ukgameshows.com/index.php/Good_Game_Guide_1_Top_30_Game_Shows)

And in the results from this survey of game show 'expert, hardcore fanatics', *Millionaire* is very much recognized as 'not just any quiz', coming third in the top ten, (after *The Mole* [2001] and *The Crystal Maze* [1990–1995]), and finishing just one vote above the BBC's *The Weakest Link* (2000–):

> *Millionaire?* ... blitzed EVERYTHING. It had simple rules. Anyone at home could pick up the phone and be in the studio in two days' time to play for one million pounds. Let's just say that again: One. Million. Pounds. The previous highest cash prize was being given by the *The National Lottery Big Ticket* [1998] which offered £100,000 ... Chris Tarrant's catchphrases have entered the public conscious [sic]. It took the rulebook and added a ton of its own rules ... look at its influence on modern day quizzes – they've mostly got metallicy sets, multiple choice questions and gothicy mood music. And most of them have high prizes too. *Millionaire* certainly raised the stakes. (http://www.ukgameshows.com/index.php/Good_Game_Guide_1_Top_30_Game_Shows)

Contrasting *Millionaire* to *The Weakest Link*, ukgameshows.com notes that:

> The Weakest Link on the other hand is very much the anti-game show. *Millionaire* added to the rulebook, *WL* rips it in half and chucks it away. It's got *Millionaire*'s lights and music but that's where the similarities end. First, its pay out (thanks to the licence fee) is far lower – to win the £10,000 on offer the team would need to answer a minimum of 72 questions correctly (out of about 130) and that's without banking. (http://www.ukgameshows.com/index.php/Good_Game_Guide_1_Top_30_Game_Shows)

There is a sense here of public service television being limited in its ability to offer vast cash prizes, although of course this is not a financial restriction, but is rather a cultural one. That is, there is no absolute or financial reason why a licence-fee-funded game show couldn't give away £1 million, but any such act would be likely to attract criticism over its 'irresponsible' use of fee-payers' money. Despite this public service/commercial distinction, where big money prizes are assumed to mark out the commercial culture of *Millionaire* and ITV, ukgameshows.com evidently does not devalue this commerciality *per se*. Rather, it is seen merely as one facet of intrageneric distinction, and one that is subordinated to aesthetic issues such as generic innovation. Having said this, the BBC's neo-game show *The Weakest Link* is depicted as a sort of 'anti-game show', implying that 'straight' game shows are the more 'natural' (that is cultural) territory of commercial television. Survey results are also analysed by UK television channel, indicating that the majority of 'top' game shows belong to commercial television. In fact, as Table 10.1 demonstrates, ITV is best represented in the top 50.

Table 10.1 Results of top 50 by primary channel

Channel	No. of shows in top 50	Points scored[2]
ITV	18	50
Channel 4	12	40
BBC 1	11	19
Channel 5	4	16
BBC 2	4	14
Challenge TV	1	1

Source: http://www.ukgameshows.com/index.php/Good_Game_Guide_1_Top_30_Game_Shows

The predominance of ITV again suggests a powerful link between 'the game show' as a genre and commercial television culture, highlighting why Marxist-indebted television scholars (Wayne 2000) may have taken the game/quiz show as a synecdoche for commercial television and its alleged 'ills'. But ITV's commercial culture is firmly aligned with discourses of generic-aesthetic 'quality' on this web site (that is, a variety of ITV game shows are positioned as 'quality popular television'). Following, and adding to, the rules of the game show and offering substantial monetary prizes are not interpreted as markers of television's decline or of commercialism as a 'bad' object. Instead, they are taken as positive indicators of game show authenticity, 'being true to the genre' (Bird 2003: 131).

Discourses of commercial television are not only subordinated to popular aesthetics at ukgameshows.com, they are also occasionally dematerialized altogether. When the site deals with the decline of *Millionaire*'s ratings we are told the following:

> it [the television programme] got arrogant after its first million win and insisted on being on all the time rather than in two week series that it used to. So, people got bored and whilst it still pulls in the viewers it's only half as popular as it was. (http://www.ukgameshows.com/index.php/Good_Game_Guide_1_Top_30_Game_Shows)

A television studies scholar would be expected to draw upon discourses of commercialism at this point: that is, *Millionaire* was scheduled more frequently on ITV because it had been pulling in high ratings, and so could be used as a lynchpin for scheduling purposes, as well as attracting greater advertising and phone-line revenue. But, by contrast, ukgameshows.com anthropomorphically converts the show into a personality: 'it' became 'arrogant', and 'insisted' on being on all the time. *Millionaire* starts to behave like somebody overstaying his welcome or getting carried away by his own hype/success, and so it pays the price for its 'arrogant', spoilt behaviour. Now, although Marxist critics may want to view such anthropomorphism as simply an 'incorrect' way of viewing the situation, and so as 'lay/folk' theory that should be supplemented by critical media theory, I would suggest that it can also be seen as suggesting one possible limit to attacks on commercial culture or 'ITV culture' (as somehow debased culture). That is, the 'distasteful' commercialism so derided and opposed by certain factions of television scholars may not even discursively feature at key moments within audiences' understandings of genres they aesthetically appreciate/value. Although ukgameshows.com and its contributors are evidently aware of commercial forces, and of debates over 'public service' versus 'commercial' television, they do not *a priori* or consistently pursue economic explanations for the (sub)genres and texts they evaluate, instead moving in and out of discursive framings linked to notions of 'the commercial'. For instance, while *Millionaire*'s large cash prize – in comparison with the likes of the BBC's *National Lottery Big Ticket* – is justified by virtue of *Millionaire* not relying on 'licence fee' money (see above) and hence draws on discourses and concepts of 'commercial' versus 'public service' television, the later discussion of *Millionaire*'s scheduling does not draw on discourses of commercialism. By contrast, this relies on the attribution of psychological characteristics to *Millionaire*, as if it were an 'arrogant' person. In short, I am arguing that values and notions of 'commerciality' – which Marxist scholars use to discursively frame and devalue game shows, partly as a result of the genre's historical role in ITV's emergence – are not always used by popular audiences to discursively frame game shows. Instead, aesthetic, generic, and even anthropomorphic discourses are used to make *Millionaire* meaningful in more positive terms, as well as 'commercial' versus 'public service' distinctions playing a partial role in these audience understandings.

But isn't this state of affairs simply a matter of fans and academics belonging to very different interpretive communities (Hills 2002)? It might be said that by taking the side of 'fan' audiences against Marxist-indebted and political economy scholars, I am guilty of acritical 'cultural populism' (McGuigan 1992). Given the ability of participants in this web site survey to make intrageneric comparisons and to vote for a wide range of UK game shows – and given the structure of ukgameshows.com – it would seem to be significant that this audience *cannot* simply be characterized as fans who 'have a particular investment in a programme' (Pullen 2004: 81). This is not a straightforward 'fan' versus 'academic' debate. *Contra* much work in fan studies (see Hills 2002: xiv), these are not viewers who especially love a single show, such as *Millionaire*. Instead, they are viewers familiar with game shows across television channels: it is the genre and its associated audience activities, not any one programme, which provide a 'corpus' of texts to be pored over and appreciated. Thus, although Kirsten Pullen (2004: 80) suggests that 'the worldwide web has opened up the boundaries of fandom ... designating more television programmes ... as worthy of fan activity', such an observation doesn't seem to fully capture the way in which a host of shows are intertextually contextualized by ukgameshows.com.

Rather than opening up a space for new fandoms, ukgameshows.com appears to blur Abercrombie and Longhurst's (1998) two categories of 'cultist' and 'enthusiast'. These audience identities are distinguished by virtue of the fact that whereas cultists are attached 'to particular programmes and types of programme', enthusiasms are 'based predominantly around activities rather than media ... media use is then likely to be specialized in that it may be based around [material] ... produced by enthusiasts for enthusiasts' (Abercrombie and Longhurst 1998: 139). Abercrombie and Longhurst suggest that devotees of the science fiction television show *Star Trek* are 'cultists', whereas fantasy role-players and war-gamers can be said to represent different generations of 'enthusiasts' (1998: 139).

It is initially unclear to what extent we could 'read off' from the intertexts of ukgameshows.com an audience of 'cultists' dedicated to a specific type of television programme, or a group of 'enthusiasts' dedicated to the hobby or 'enthusiasm' of puzzles/quizzes/games, hence being led to consume – or produce – specific media as a result of this activity-based interest. The fact that ukgameshows.com is a Labyrinth Games site pushes us toward the latter conclusion, Labyrinth being a 'professional puzzle and game consultancy' (http://www.labyrinthgames.com/) which supplies quizzes and puzzles to various newspapers, specialist magazines, and the Reader's Digest, as well as developing television game show formats and publishing a do-it-yourself guide, *How To Devise A Game Show* (Bodycombe 2003). In other words, the encyclopedic and scholarly (even if not professional-academic) interest in television quizzes displayed here can be interpreted as evidence of an enthusiasm rather than as a programme-specific or even genre/medium-specific fandom.

Viewing the intertexts of ukgameshows.com as indicating, or stemming from, a more general interest in puzzles and quizzes beyond the television game show, the disjunction between the site's popular aesthetics and academic dismissals of the commercial culture of *Millionaire* can be seen as more than just fan/academic tensions. Rather, there is an interpretive gap here between professional knowledge workers who view puzzles and quizzes as 'trivial' (Missen 2001) because these do not represent knowledge organized and contextualized into systematic theoretical frameworks, and a group of consumers and producers who instead view puzzles and quizzes – and thus television game shows – as meaningful cultural artefacts. This latter group may not have the boundedness and cohesion of a 'subculture', nor quite the self-representations and cultural identities that we would expect to accompany fan culture, but as a group of 'enthusiasts' they nevertheless appear to value and systematically produce/consume puzzles, quizzes and games. The commercial culture of *Millionaire* thus intersects here with an audience grouping that, whilst aware of 'commercial' versus 'public service' television debates, prioritizes the principles of 'good' gaming and puzzling. And although this 'enthusiast' audience may represent the 'hardcore' and the 'fanatics' of puzzling or quizzing, its detailed engagement with the design and aesthetics of *Millionaire*, among other game shows, demonstrates that academic disparagement of *Millionaire* as 'the endgame' (Wayne 2000: 216) of public service television fails to consider the cultural contexts, and intertexts, within and through which 'ITV cultures' become meaningful for discernible audience fractions, rather than merely being consumed by an undiscriminating 'mass'.

The structure of ukgameshows.com also anticipates and imagines a range of priorities for its users. It promotes the report/manual *How To Devise A Game Show*, interpellating its users as wanting to produce as well as consume game shows. This indicates a sense, common to enthusiasms according to Abercrombie and Longhurst (1998: 150), that 'production has become central' to this audience identity. Enthusiasts make things related to their interests, whether this is via a material or textual type of production. Furthermore, ukgameshows.com's first 'featured' link is 'Be on TV', which at the time of writing (28 February 2005) included 'Contestant calls' for a wide range of quiz/game shows. It should be noted that BBC programmes are, if anything, more in evidence here than those of broadcasters primarily and discursively defined as 'commercial'.

Such intertexts – organized and structured so as to assist audience members to get on game shows – presuppose that appearing on television is a 'natural' or worthy goal in and of itself. Status and prestige is automatically attached to 'media folk'. In Nick Couldry's terms, what is set out in this instance is:

> an opposition between non-media world and media world, between non-media people and media people ... although the hierarchy of value (between 'ordinary person' and 'media person' ...) is *constructed*, the difference of symbolic resources between those outside media institutions and those within them is *real*. (2000: 20)

This difference in symbolic and cultural power is very much recognized by ukgameshows.com. The site's contributors do not seek to challenge the hierarchical value of being a 'media person', but instead desire to cross the ordinary/media boundary in any manner possible, whether this is a fleeting movement within the industry as a contestant, a recurrent series of appearances on game shows, or an interest in devising a game show format. Participation and interaction are therefore crucial tropes in these game show intertexts. However, this is not simply the 'participatory culture' of media fans who seek to rewrite episodes of television dramas, or 'poach' selected meanings from their favoured shows (Jenkins 1992). It is, quite unlike media fans' frequently explicitly anti-commercialist orientations (Hills 2002: 28), a type of participation which appears to be partly premised on commercial and consumerist interests. By desiring to produce game show formats, as well as appear as contestants (see Bonner 2003), this interpellated audience fully recognizes the cultural power that can accrue to 'media' people. Its ethic of participation and interaction would hence seem to be a simultaneously creative/cultural and commercial one, involving desires and efforts to build up cultural and symbolic power alongside financial/commercial 'aspirations'. This is an avowedly *participatory commercial culture*, in which notions and concepts of commerce cannot be wholly or finally separated out from 'enthusiast' or 'fan-like' identities, and in which producing/consuming games is culturally valued by an audience of 'hard core [game show] fanatics'.

It should be noted that this point in no way contradicts my earlier argument that game show 'enthusiasts' move in and out of discourses of commercialism, for what I am terming their 'participatory commercial culture' is never univocally framed as 'commercial'. Rather, it is both participatory and commercial, both 'Cultural'/aesthetic (that is, dealing with an expert knowledge of game shows) and 'commercial' (that is, dealing with the winning of prizes, or the invention of show formats). Specifically Marxist-academic disdain for 'commercial' game shows, and more generally middle-class distaste for the genre's assumed 'crass' commercialism are premised on the idea that commerciality equals audiences brazenly pursuing cash/consumer goods *in opposition to* displaying 'proper' cultural capital. Against such a culture/commerce dualism, the fan-enthusiast audience I've considered here uses its online intertexts to blur together an interest in prize-winning with an interest in TV (sub)genres and their histories, productions, and innovations. Any simplistic binary opposition of 'Culture' versus 'commerce' is hence transcended by this audience fraction. For this audience, the big cash prizes of 'commercial' TV game shows do not simply indicate 'capitalist values': prizes can also be appreciated formally, as part of a genre aesthetic working to maximise dramatic tension. Casey *et al.* (2002: 102) point out that game show audiences 'revel . . . in the distilled drama that is carefully manufactured by the narrative of a quiz show . . . The greater the rewards to be won, the greater this pleasure . . .' Bigger prizes can mean *intensified genre-based drama* for enthusiasts – who tend to appreciate precisely intrageneric differences – rather than indicating consumer greed.

In this chapter I have suggested that although there may not be many scholar-fans of *Who Wants To Be A Millionaire?* this situation is no excuse for consigning such programmes to the obscurity of non-analysis, nor for devaluing them as somehow non-aesthetic/anti-cultural and discursively 'commercial' ITV products. By examining the 'popular aesthetics' evident in one web site's intertexts and appreciations of the television game show, I have argued that 'culture' and 'commerce' cannot be cut apart from one another, and that UK quiz/game enthusiasts actually use similar aesthetic criteria to validate their interests to some television scholars positioned within academic debates on popular television (Creeber 2004). Given that ITV is the best represented UK channel in ukgameshows.com's survey of favoured programmes, rather than viewing the game show as a debased (because it is 'commercial') genre, this survey can be interpreted rather differently outside of scholarly taste cultures, and Marxist cultural politics favouring public service television. Following ukgameshow.com's 'popular aesthetics', we might say that for gaming/quizzing enthusiasts, ITV *does game shows best* in terms of innovating and being 'true to the genre'.

Bibliography

Abercrombie, N. and Longhurst, B. (1998) *Audiences: A Sociological Theory of Performance and Imagination*. London: Sage.

Andrejevic, M. (2004) *Reality TV: The Work of Being Watched*. Lanham, Maryland: Rowman & Littlefield.

Barker, M. (1998) Audiences 'r' us, in R. Dickinson, R. Harindranath and O. Linné (eds) *Approaches to Audiences: A Reader*. London: Arnold.

Bird, S.E. (2003) *The Audience in Everyday Life: Living in a Media World*. New York and London: Routledge.

Boddy, W. (2001) The Quiz Show, and *Who Wants To Be A Millionaire?*, in G. Creeber (ed.) *The Television Genre Book*. London: British Film Institute.

Bodycombe, D.J. (2003) *How To Devise A Game Show*. London: Labyrinth Games.

Bonner, F. (2003) *Ordinary Television*. London: Sage.

Brunsdon, C. (1990) Television: aesthetics and audiences, in P. Mellencamp (ed.) *Logics of Television*. London: British Film Institute.

Brunsdon, C. (1997) *Screen Tastes: Soap Opera to Satellite Dishes*. London and New York: Routledge.

Casey, B., Casey, N., Calvert, B., French, L. and Lewis, J. (2002) *Television Studies: The Key Concepts*. London and New York: Routledge.

Couldry, N. (2000) *The Place of Media Power: Pilgrims and Witnesses of the Media Age*. London and New York: Routledge.

Creeber, G. (2004) *Who Wants To Be A Millionaire?*, in G. Creeber (ed.) *Fifty Key Television Programmes*. London: Arnold.

Fiske, J. (1987) *Television Culture*. London: Methuen.

Foster, D. (2004) 'Jump in the pool': The competitive culture of *Survivor* fan networks, in S. Holmes and D. Jermyn (eds) *Understanding Reality Television*. London and New York: Routledge.

Geraghty, C. (2003) Aesthetics and quality in popular television drama, *International Journal of Cultural Studies*, 6(1): 25–45.

Hartley, J. (1999) *Uses of Television*. London and New York: Routledge.

Hartley, J. (2004) The 'value chain of meaning' and the new economy, *International Journal of Cultural Studies*, 7(2): 129–41.

Hills, M. (2002) *Fan Cultures*. London and New York: Routledge.

Hobson, D. (1982) *Crossroads: The Drama of a Soap Opera*. London: Methuen.

Holt, J. (2003) Vertical vision: deregulation, industrial economy and prime-time design, in M. Jancovich and J. Lyons (eds) *Quality Popular Television*. London: British Film Institute.

Hutchings, P. (2004) *The Horror Film*. Harlow: Pearson Education Limited.

Jackson, P., Lowe, M., Miller, D., and Mort, F. (2000) Introduction: transcending dualisms, in P. Jackson, M. Lowe, D. Miller and F. Mort (eds) *Commercial Cultures: Economies, Practices, Spaces*. Oxford: Berg.

Jacobs, J. (2001) Issues of judgment and value in television studies, *International Journal of Cultural Studies*, 4(4): 427–47.

Jancovich, M. and Lyons, J. (eds) (2003) *Quality Popular Television*. London: British Film Institute.

Jenkins, H. (1992) *Textual Poachers*. New York and London: Routledge.

Lewis, B. (1984) TV Games: People as Performers, in L. Masterman (ed.) *Television Mythologies: Stars, Shows and Signs*. London: Comedia.

Marshall, P.D. (2004) *New Media Cultures*. London: Arnold.

McGuigan, J. (1992) *Cultural Populism*. New York and London: Routledge.

McKee, A. (2002) Fandom, in T. Miller (ed.) *Television Studies*. London: British Film Institute.

McKee, A. (2003) Afterword: What Is Television for? in M. Jancovich and J. Lyons (eds) *Quality Popular Television*. London: British Film Institute.

Missen, J. (2001) Who wants us to be millionaires? The culture of trivial intellect in contemporary game shows, in M. Pomerance and J. Sakeris (eds) *Closely Watched Brains*. Boston: Pearson Education.

Mittell, J. (2004) *Genre and Television: From Cop Shows to Cartoons in American Culture*. New York and London: Routledge.

Moran, A. (1998) *Copycat TV: Globalization, Program Formats and Cultural Identity*. Luton: University of Luton Press.
Pullen, K. (2004) Everybody's gotta love somebody, sometime: online fan community, in D. Gauntlett and R. Horsley (eds) *Web.Studies*, 2nd edn. London: Arnold.
Seabrook, J. (2000) *Nobrow*. London: Methuen.
Tincknell, E. and Raghuram, P. (2004) Big Brother: Reconfiguring the 'active' audience of cultural studies? In S. Holmes and D. Jermyn (eds) *Understanding Reality Television*. New York: Routledge.
Tulloch, J. (1976) Gradgrind's heirs: the quiz and the presentation of 'knowledge' by British television, in G. Whitty and M. Young (eds) *Explorations in the Politics of School Knowledge*. Nafferton: Nafferton Books.
Turnock, R. (forthcoming) *Television and Consumer Culture: Britain and the Transformation of Modernity*. London: I.B. Tauris.
Wayne, M. (2000) *Who Wants To Be A Millionaire?* Contextual analysis and the endgame of public service television, in D. Fleming (ed.) *Formations: A 21st Century Media Studies Textbook*, Manchester: Manchester University Press.
Whannel, G. (1990) Winner Takes All: Competition, in A. Goodwin and G. Whannel (eds) *Understanding Television*. New York and London: Routledge.
Whannel, G. (1992) The price is right but the moments are sticky: Television, quiz and game shows, and popular culture, in D. Strinati and S. Wagg (eds) *Come On Down? Popular Media Culture in Post-War Britain*. New York and London: Routledge.
Wright Wexman, V. (1999) The Critic as Consumer: Film Study in the University, *Vertigo*, and the Film Canon, in B. Henderson and A. Martin (eds) *Film Quarterly: Forty Years – A Selection*. Berkeley: University of California Press

Notes

1 It should be noted that I am not using 'criticism' here to refer to professional 'television critics' or to the journalistic coverage of commercial television.
2 Scoring system: 10/9/8/7/6 points for 1st/2nd/3rd/4th/5th place, 5 points for top 10, 4 points for top 15, 3 points for top 20, 2 points for top 30, 1 point for top 50.

CONCLUSIONS: ITV A HYBRID SUBJECT

Catherine Johnson and Rob Turnock

In its introduction, this book began by outlining the complexity of ITV as an historical object of study, in terms of its shifting institutional and regulatory structure, its wide range of programming (much of which is no longer accessible) and its difficult positioning as a regionally structured, national, commercial, public service broadcaster. The chapters in this book have dealt with these problems in different ways according to the demands of their particular subject and/or approach. To draw a set of overall conclusions from them holds the danger of being unnecessarily reductive. Yet a number of themes do emerge that suggest a possible agenda for future research.

A recurring theme has been the hybrid nature of ITV as a subject of study, most overtly in Jackie Harrison's fascinating account of ITN as a 'hybrid' organization (from which we have borrowed the term). This hybridity has primarily been explored in relation to the apparently paradoxical position of ITV as a commercially funded public service broadcaster. Across a range of ITV histories (from the history of Welsh commercial television, to the history of ITN and *Trisha*) the commercial and public service aims of ITV have been seen to be in potential conflict. The history of ITV is peppered with anxieties about the impact of its commercial funding on its ability to fulfil public service ideals, or of its public service remit on its ability to function as a viable commercial broadcaster. This tension has characterized, and continues to characterize, much of the debate surrounding ITV, frequently returning (in tone if not in word) to the rhetoric of the Pilkington Report's arguments that the aims of a commercial and a public service broadcaster cannot be reconciled.[1] Jonathan Bignell aptly demonstrates the ways in which the tension between commercial and public service has coalesced around accounts of Lew Grade's place in the history of ITV. Grade's perceived role as both patron and publisher, in particular, demonstrates how, in the historiography of ITV, the commercial demands on production have been seen to create a tension between market forces and public service, and between popularity and quality. Meanwhile, Jackie Harrison demonstrates that although ITN has been forced to operate competitively within the market since the deregulation and expansion of broadcasting in the early 1990s, it remains a hybrid organization caught between the (threatened but still present) public service broadcasting requirements on ITV1, and the increasingly commercial demands on ITV as a whole.

Furthermore, a number of the chapters in this book have challenged the dichotomies between commercial and public service broadcasting, popularity and quality. Rod Allen demonstrates the ways in which ITV's PSB requirements, monopoly on advertising, and networking arrangements in the 1970s and 1980s, effectively protected programming from the vagaries of the market, allowing LWT to function simultaneously as a viable commercial *and* public service broadcaster. Jackie Harrison makes a similar argument in relation to the safeguarded financial position of ITN over the 1960s and 1970s, and argues that despite increasing commercial pressure, ITN continues to innovate with its news provision. In relation to talk shows, Sherryl Wilson convincingly argues that public service ideals cannot simply be placed in opposition to commercial demands on production. In doing so, Wilson argues that *Trisha* provides a striking example of programming that, although commercial and commodified, provides an important public service.

The hybridity of ITV as a subject, however, does not simply emerge around its basis as a commercially funded public service broadcaster. It is also a hybrid in structure and ideology, as a regional and national broadcaster. This tension between regional and national demands is again one that recurs across a number of chapters in this book. Johnson and Turnock examine the ways in which the regional ideals of early ITV have been threatened over its history by networking, competition and regulatory *realpolitik*. Jamie Medhurst further complicates this by examining the problems surrounding the attempts in the early 1960s to set up a commercially funded broadcaster that served the particular needs of Wales, by providing Welsh language and Welsh interest programmes. Here, Welsh programming is seen as particularly 'cultural' and hence problematic for a commercial broadcaster. Yet Medhurst refrains from a too-simple equation of understanding the failure of WWN simply in terms of its lack of commercial viability, and places its failure within the larger context of the difficulties of establishing any Welsh cultural activity within social and cultural structures that are imposed from England.

As such, Medhurst's article raises a further important issue in the study of broadcasting more generally and ITV more specifically: the need for a broad understanding of context. Indeed, the chapters by Bignell, Neale and Allen demonstrate the importance of international markets (in particular the US) for the history of ITV companies and programmes. While, as Bignell argues, accusations of Americanization often characterize ITV programmes as both commercial and progressive/aspirational, Allen argues that the US market made it financially possible for LWT (and other ITV franchises) to produce prestigious high-production value programmes that bolstered its claims to public service broadcasting. The importance of the US market in understanding the history of ITV (and British broadcasting more generally) is particularly apparent in Steve Neale's discussion of *The Adventures of Robin Hood*. Neale not only offers a fascinating account of the production of *Robin Hood*, but also demonstrates that ITV's early filmed action-adventure series need to be understood within a transnational context, and one that significantly complicates the very notion of 'ITV' as a singular (and even a British) object of study.

In emphasizing the importance of international factors these articles challenge a more parochial approach to British television studies, and indicate the broader significance of studies of ITV to our understanding of British broadcasting. Indeed, through a study of ITV, a number of these chapters raise issues whose significance extends beyond an understanding of ITV itself. For example, both Allen and Ellis examine the late 1970s and early 1980s as a pivotal period in which the production practices and aesthetics of British television shifted dramatically, which demands further research. Meanwhile Helen Wheatley's article on the LWT series *Upstairs Downstairs* criticizes the general neglect of studio drama from the existing literature on the costume drama, which has favoured filmed series such as Granada's *Brideshead Revisited*. Whereas *Brideshead* stands as an example of the kind of programming often understood as produced 'despite' the commercial structure of ITV, rather than because of it (see Ellis in this volume), studio dramas such as *Upstairs Downstairs* have been largely ignored in histories of British television drama as commercially successful but academically uninteresting. Wheatley compellingly demonstrates that studio dramas such as *Upstairs Downstairs* are worthy of detailed textual analysis in their own right and, furthermore, reveals the significant gendered address in *Upstairs Downstairs*, in its use of detail and appeal to the existing interests in Victorian and Edwardian styles in women's magazines of the 1970s. As such, although there is a stronger emphasis in Wheatley's arguments on the studio, costume drama rather than on *Upstairs Downstairs*' ITV*ness*, it demonstrates the value of reinstating ITV programming (as a source of hitherto neglected programming) into the histories of British television.

In approaching those programmes that have been neglected in television studies, a number of chapters in this book point to the important and vexed issue of value. All three articles in the final section (Wheatley, Wilson, and Hills) point to a gendered and class-based rhetoric in the historical development of television studies, and evidence this as a significant problem in the analysis of the seemingly more 'popular', 'trivial', and 'commercial' of ITV's programming output. Sherryl Wilson's study of the talk show *Trisha* explores the class-based judgements that shape many of the discourses surrounding the value of commercial television. Similarly Matt Hills, in looking beyond programmes to their audiences, argues for a popular aesthetics against the common Marxist position, which sees commercial artefacts as inevitably anti-cultural, again raising the class-based assumptions upon which much of the dismissal of ITV programming takes place. As such, these articles offer a powerful critique of a persistent hierarchy of value that inflects academic debate, and demonstrate that ITV programming challenges the Marxist-based traditions that have tended to shape television studies' textual and audience analysis. This critique suggests the need for new paradigms or discourses to understand fully the nature and significance of much of ITV's cultures, and television more broadly.

Overall, each chapter in this book raises its own questions and issues for further research, whether a re-evaluation of studio drama, or a more detailed understanding of runaway production in British television. As such, as argued above, these histories of ITV raise sets of questions and issues for the history of British broadcasting more generally. However, despite offering a range of methodologies and topics, this book remains a very partial account of 'ITV cultures'. As indicated in the introduction, there remain a wide number of areas of 'ITV cultures' that are not represented in this book, and that are more generally under-represented in academic study. This includes 'everyday' and ordinary television, which, as John Ellis argues, has not only been neglected but is also often missing from the archives, such as light entertainment (touched on in Bignell's chapter), children's television, and advertisements (generally neglected in television studies) amongst other programme forms. It also includes those 'quality' programmes frequently produced by ITV franchises but seen as atypical in terms of its overall output. It is hoped, therefore, that this book will prompt research not only on those areas and issues explored in its chapters but also into those neglected areas of ITV's history. Such research is not simply an isolated academic activity. With the publication of Ofcom's Phase 3 Report (see Johnson and Turnock) and the proposed switchover to multi-channel digital broadcasting in 2012, the future of ITV is currently a significant area of policy debate. With ITV frequently derided, ignored or lamented, a clearer understanding and critical evaluation of its histories is more pressing than ever.

Notes

1 Indeed it could perhaps be argued that while the rhetoric of the marketplace has come to imbue policy discourses on British television since the mid-1980s, much of the discourse in television studies remains closer to the suspicion of commercial culture in general that emerges in the Pilkington Report.

HISTORICAL TIMELINE: THE ITV COMPANIES AND THE BROADCASTING ACTS

1949

21 June: government committee of inquiry established under Lord Beveridge to consider the future of radio and television broadcasting in the UK.

1951

18 January: *The Report of the Committee of Broadcasting, 1949* (Beveridge Report) which rejected idea that broadcasting should operate on a commercial or competitive basis. The report advocated more broadcasting from Scotland, Wales and Northern Ireland but the BBC's monopoly of broadcasting was confirmed.

1954

30 July: Television Act 1954 legislated for the start of a new commercial television service in the UK to be regulated by a new public body, the Independent Television Authority (ITA).
4 August: ITA established.

1955

22 September: the first ITV company, Associated-Rediffusion, began broadcasting at 7.15 p.m. in the London region, with national and international news provided by ITN. Associated-Rediffusion was contracted to serve the London area during weekdays.
24 September: Associated Television (ATV) began transmission in the London area during weekends.

1956

17 February: Associated Television (ATV) began transmission in the Midlands area during weekdays.

18 February: ABC Television began transmission in the Midlands area during weekends.
3 May: Granada Television began transmission in the north of England (covering Lancashire and Yorkshire) during weekdays.
5 May: ABC Television began transmission in the north of England (covering Lancashire and Yorkshire) during weekends.

1957
31 August: Scottish Television began transmission in central Scotland.
13 May: ITV began first regular television broadcasts for schools.

1958
14 January: TWW began transmission in Wales and the west of England.
30 August: Southern Television began transmission in the south of England.

1959
15 January: Tyne Tees Television began transmission in north-east England.
27 October: Anglia Television began transmission in the east of England.
31 October: Ulster Television began transmission in Northern Ireland.

1960
13 July: Committee on Broadcasting appointed, chaired by Sir Harry Pilkington.

1961
29 April: Westward Television began transmission in south-west England.
1 May: start of Television Advertisement Duty.
1 September: Border Television began transmission in the Borders (covering Cumbria and the Scottish borders).
30 September: Grampian Television began transmission in the north of Scotland.

1962
5 June: *Report of the Committee of Broadcasting, 1960* (Pilkington Report) published. Proposals of the Pilkington Committee included the restructuring of commercial television, the allocation of a second television service to the BBC and the start of television broadcasting on 625 lines UHF.
1 September: Channel Television began transmission in the Channel Islands.
14 September: Wales (West and North) (WWN) began transmission in west and north Wales.

1963
31 July: Television Act 1963 passed, legislating for the start of BBC2 on 625 lines UHF.

1964
All ITV contractors reappointed until 1967.
26 January: WWN ceased trading and the franchise was taken over by TWW.
25 March: Television Act 1964 (Consolidating Act) consolidated the Television Act 1954 and the Television Act 1963.
20 April: BBC 2 began transmission on 625 lines UHF.
30 July: television advertisement duty was replaced by an exchequer levy on revenue from advertising.

1967
All ITV contracts were extended until 1968.
1 July: colour television began transmission on BBC2.

1968
ITV franchise rounds.
4 March: Harlech Television (HTV) replaced TWW to serve Wales and the West of England.
29 July: Granada's transmission area was reduced as Yorkshire Television was contracted to serve Yorkshire.
30 July: ABC and Associated-Rediffusion were forced to merge to form Thames Television to take over from Associated-Rediffusion and serve London during weekdays.
30 July: ATV took over ABC's weekend service to serve the Midlands during weekdays and weekends.
30 July: Granada took over ABC's weekend service to serve the north of England during weekdays and weekends.
2 August: London Weekend Television (LWT) took over from ATV to serve London during the weekends.
All other ITV contracts renewed until 1974.

1969
15 November: colour television was extended from BBC2 to BBC1 and ITV on 625-line UHF.

1972
12 June: Sound Broadcasting Act 1972 legislated for the start of commercial radio (Independent Local Radio) in the UK. The ITA was renamed the Independent Broadcasting Authority (IBA) with responsibility for regulation of commercial radio and television.

1973
April: IBA announced a new teletext service, named ORACLE, to transmit textual information to television.
23 May: Independent Broadcasting Authority Act 1973, consolidated the Television Act 1964 and the Sound Broadcasting Act 1972.

1974
All ITV contracts extended to 1976.
10 April: Committee on the Future of Broadcasting appointed, chaired by Lord Annan.
23 May: Independent Broadcasting Authority Act 1974 legislated further changes to the ITV levy.
31 July: Independent Broadcasting Authority Act 1974 extended the life of the IBA from 1976 to 1979.
23 September: the BBC teletext service, CEEFAX, began transmission.

1976
All ITV contracts extended until 1979.

1977
24 March: the *Report of the Committee on the Future of Broadcasting* (Annan Report) was published. The Annan Report proposed greater plurality in British broadcasting, and recommended that a fourth television service should be regulated by a new public body.

1978
31 July: Independent Broadcasting Authority Act 1978 extended the life of the IBA from 1979 to 1981.

1979
All ITV contracts renewed until 1981.
4 April: Independent Broadcasting Authority Act 1979 sanctioned the IBA to undertake the necessary technical work to establish a fourth channel.
10 August–19 October: a strike by the Association of Cinematograph, Television and Allied Technicians (ACTT) against ITV companies blacked out transmission.

1980
13 November: Broadcasting Act 1980 extended life IBA until 1996 and widened its remit to include a fourth channel. The Act also legislated for the new Broadcasting Complaints Commission.
28 December: ITA announced the result of the franchise rounds to commence broadcasting in 1981/82.

1981

1 June: the Broadcasting Complaints Commission began operating.
21 July: the Broadcasters' Audience Research Board (BARB) began, providing audience research for both BBC and ITV and replacing their separate audience measurement services.
12 August: Television South West (TSW) replaced Westward Television to serve south-west England.

1982

1 January: Television South (TVS) replaced Southern Television to serve south and south-east England.
1 January: ATV was restructured as Central Independent Television to serve east and west Midlands.
Contracts to run until 1989. All other ITV contracts renewed until 1989.
1 November: S4C began broadcasting Welsh language programming to Wales.
2 November: Channel 4 began broadcasting to England, Northern Ireland and Scotland. The channel was funded by subscriptions from the ITV companies, who in return sold advertising on the new service. The channel took programmes from the ITV companies and the independent sector, and had a remit to be innovative and appeal to diverse tastes and interests.

1983

17 January: BBC launched the first breakfast programme, *Breakfast Time*.
1 February: *TV-am* began transmission of national breakfast television service for ITV.

1985

27 March: government committee of inquiry on the future financing of the BBC appointed, chaired by Sir Alan Peacock.

1986

1 April: Exchequer levy on ITV changed by the Finance Act 1986.
3 July: *Report of the Committee on Financing the BBC* (Peacock Report) was published. It rejected funding of BBC through advertising, but proposed wide changes to structure of commercial television, including franchise auctions.
December: IBA awarded first direct broadcasting by satellite (DBS) contract to British Satellite Broadcasting (BSB) for three television services. BSB was made up by a consortium of the Granada Group, Anglia Television, the Virgin Group, Amstrad Electronics and Pearson plc.

1987

9 April: the Broadcasting Act 1987 extended the existing ITV contracts until 31 December 1992.

1 June: television broadcasting hours were extended, and Thames Television was the first company to have a regular 24-hour service.
6 August: the IBA announced an agreement to increase the number of ITV programmes commissioned from independent producers.

1988
16 May: the start of the Broadcasting Standards Council established as non-statutory standards watchdog.
11 December: Astra satellite launched, to transmit 16 television channels, including Sky, to British homes with satellite dishes.

1989
5 February: Sky began service from Astra.
27 August: BSB launched Marcopolo satellite.

1990
1 January: ITV exchequer levy changed to mixed levy on domestic profits and advertising revenue.
25 March: BSB began broadcasting on cable.
29 April: BSB began broadcasting from Marcopolo satellite.
1 November: Broadcasting Act 1990, legislated for the Independent Television Commission (ITC) to combine the roles of the IBA and the Cable Authority. The Act included the auction of ITV franchises and privatization of the IBA's transmitters as National Transcommunications Ltd (NTL). The Act also legislated for the start of a new commercial, terrestrial television service, Channel 5, under the regulation of the ITC. Allocation of Channel 5 was to be auctioned using same procedure as ITV licences. Under the Act Channel 4 took over selling of own advertising. As a safety net, if Channel 4's advertising revenue dropped below 14 per cent of the total terrestrial television advertising revenue, the ITV companies would have to make up the difference. If Channel 4 earned more than 14 per cent, additional revenue would be divided between the ITV companies. The Broadcasting Standards Council was made into a *statutory* standards watchdog.
2 November: BSB and Sky announced a merger to form British Sky Broadcasting (BSkyB).

1991
1 January: the ITC officially took over regulation of commercial television from the IBA, and regulation of commercial radio passed to the Radio Authority. During the year the ITC held an auction of regional ITV franchises in a two-stage process. The stages involved a quality threshold and a financial test.
16 October: the ITC announced the results of the franchise renewal/auction. Carlton Television took over from Thames Television (London

weekday), GMTV took over from TV-am (national breakfast-time), Meridian took over from TVS (south and south-east England) and Westcountry Television took over from TSW (south-west England). The remaining 12 regional companies had their licences renewed.
All licences were contracted to operate from 1 January 1993 to 1 January 2003 in the first instance.

1992
Yorkshire Television and Tyne Tees Television merged to form Yorkshire Tyne Tees, although their ITV franchises remained separate.
14 April: ITC announced the launch of competitive tendering for a new Channel 5 licence.
1 December: official start of the ITV Network Centre to commission and schedule programmes.
18 December: the ITC announced that no licence for Channel 5 would be awarded after receiving only one application.
31 December: the final transmission date for ITV companies that lost their regional licences – Thames Television, TSW, TVS and TV-am.

1993
1 January: the new licences came into effect: Carlton Television, GMTV, Meridian and Westcountry.
1 January: Channel 4 took over the selling of its own advertising.
1 January: Teletext Ltd, a private company, took over ORACLE.
June 1993: Thames Television (former ITV licence holder for the London weekday area) was bought by Pearson plc.

1994
January 1: regulation of the ownership of ITV franchises is relaxed making it possible for one company to own two ITV licences outside of the London region. Carlton purchased Central, Meridian (MAI, later United News and Media) purchased Anglia, and Granada took over LWT.

1995
After a second auction for the Channel 5 licence (starting in 1994, and with four applicants), the ITC announced the award to Channel 5 Broadcasting, a consortium with backing from Pearson and MAI.

1996
Carlton took over Westcountry.
24 July: the Broadcasting Act 1996 legislated for the relaxation of ownership rules. The Act also established the Broadcasting Standards Commission, which took over the responsibilities of the Broadcasting Standards Council and the Broadcasting Complaints Commission.

1997
Granada purchased Yorkshire Tyne Tees.
United News and Media (UNM) purchased HTV.
30 March: Channel 5 started broadcasting.

1998
June: ITV companies had the opportunity to renew their licences early on the basis of financial modelling by the ITC to assess how much the licences would cost if put out to competitive tender. Eight companies were granted renewal on new terms for a further 10 years. The companies were Carlton, HTV, Meridian, Tyne Tees, Ulster, Westcountry, Yorkshire and GMTV.
October: BSkyB launched Sky Digital.
November: Carlton and Granada launched ONdigitial, a subscription, terrestrial and digital service.
7 December: ITV2 launched on cable and satellite.

1999
February: end of Channel 4 payments to ITV from advertising revenue as originally required in the Broadcasting Act 1990. Channel 4 made final payment of £66 million.
8 March: ITN's *News at Ten* moved from 10 p.m. scheduling slot.
November: announcement of plans to merge Carlton and UNM.

2000
July: the merger between Carlton and UNM was allowed on the condition that they sell Meridian. This condition was rejected and UNM sold its ITV franchises (Meridian, Anglia and HTV) to Granada. HTV was then sold on to Carlton in order to prevent Granada from infringing the regulations governing ownership of ITV franchises.
1 August: ITN News Channel launched on cable, satellite and digital.

2001
April: the remaining seven companies had their licences renewed (with financial terms) for 10 years.
August: ONdigital is relaunched as ITV Digital. ITV Sports channel also launched.

2002
27 March: ITV Digital goes into administration.
June 2002: ITN News Channel relaunched as ITV News Channel.

2003
17 July: the Communications Act 2003 legislated for the new regulator Ofcom to assume a range of regulatory responsibilities in broadcasting and telecommunications, and removed the regulatory barriers to a single merged ITV.

18 December: the ITC ceased to exist.
29 December: Ofcom replaced ITC, and also inherited the duties of the Broadcasting Standards Commission, Office of Telecommunciations, the Radio Authority, and the Radiocommunications Agency.
During the year consultation with competition watchdog and Department of Trade and Industry resulted in a merger between Carlton and Granada being allowed.

2004
2 February: the merger between Carlton and Granada took place, creating ITV plc, with Scottish Television, Grampian, Ulster and Channel making up the rest of the ITV1 network.
1 November: ITV3 was launched as a digital cable and satellite service.

2005
8 February: Ofcom published the Phase 3 Report of public service broadcasting review, *Competition for Quality*.
22 September: 50th anniversary of the launch of ITV.

ITV programme companies 2005

ITV plc:	
Anglia Television	central and east England
Border Television	border region England and Scotland
Carlton Television	London weekday
Central Television	east and west Midlands
Granada	north England
HTV	Wales and west of England
London Weekend Television	London weekends
Meridian	south and south-east England
Tyne Tees	north-east England
Westcountry	south-west England
Yorkshire	Yorkshire
Scottish Media Group:	
Grampian Television	north of Scotland
Scottish Television	central Scotland
Other regional companies:	
Channel Television	Channel Islands
Ulster Television	Northern Ireland
National franchises:	
ITN	news provision
GMTV	national breakfast
Teletext Ltd.	teletext services

Main sources

Bonner, P. (with Aston, L.) (1998) *Independent Television in Britain, Volume 5, ITV and IBA, 1981–92: The Old Relationship Changes*. London: Macmillan.

Bonner, P. (with Aston, L.) (2003) *Independent Television in Britain, Volume 6, New Developments in Independent Television, 1981–92: Channel 4, TV-am, Cable and Satellite*. London: Palgrave Macmillan.

MacDonald, B. (1994) *Broadcasting in the United Kingdom: A Guide to Information Sources*, 2nd edn. London: Mansell.

MacDonald, B. (2001) Independent Television from ITV to Channel 3, in J. Ballantyne (ed.) *The Researcher's Guide: Film, Television and Related Documentation Collections in the UK*, 6th edn. London: British Universities Film and Video Council.

Ofcom web site, www.ofcom.org.uk.

INDEX

TELEVISION AND SEXUALITY
Regulation and the Politics of Taste

Jane Arthurs
University of the West of England, Bristol, UK.

In recent years there has been a marked increase in both the volume and diversity of sexual imagery and talk on television, condemned by some as a 'rising tide of filth', celebrated by others as a 'liberation' from the regulations of the past. *Television and Sexuality* questions both these responses through an examination of television's multiple channels and genres, and the wide range of sexual information and pleasures they provide.

The book explores the way that sexual citizenship and sexual consumerism have been defined in the digital era to reveal the underlying assumptions held by the television industry about the tastes and sexual identities of its diverse audiences. It draws on the work of key thinkers in cultural and media studies, as well as feminist and queer theory, to interrogate the political and cultural significance of these developments. With topics including the regulation of taste and decency, sex scandals in the news, the biology of sex in science programmes, and gay, lesbian and postfeminist identities in 'quality' drama, this book is key reading for students in cultural and media studies and gender studies.

Contents:
Series editor's foreword – Acknowledgements – Introduction – Sexual citizenship in the digital age – Pornography and the regualtion of taste – Sex scandals – The science of sex – Documenting the sex industry – Gay, Lesbian and Queer sexualities in UK drama – Postfeminist drama in the USA – Conclusion – Glossary – Appendix – Bibliography

208pp 0 335 20975 0 Paperback £16.99 0 335 20976 9 Hardback £55.00